International Political Economy Series

The global political economy is in flux as a series of cumulative crises impacts its organization and governance. The IPE series has tracked its development in both analysis and structure over the last three decades. It has always had a concentration on the global South. Now the South increasingly challenges the North as the centre of development, also reflected in a growing number of submissions and publications on indebted Eurozone economies in Southern Europe. An indispensable resource for scholars and researchers, the series examines a variety of capitalisms and connections by focusing on emerging economies, companies and sectors, debates and policies. It informs diverse policy communities as the established trans-Atlantic North declines and 'the rest', especially the BRICS, rise.

More information about this series at
http://www.palgrave.com/gp/series/13996

Mustafa Kutlay

The Political Economies of Turkey and Greece

Crisis and Change

palgrave
macmillan

Mustafa Kutlay
City University of London
London, UK

International Political Economy Series
ISBN 978-3-030-06517-1 ISBN 978-3-319-92789-3 (eBook)
https://doi.org/10.1007/978-3-319-92789-3

This Palgrave Macmillan imprint is published by the registered company Springer Nature Switzerland AG
The registered company address is: Gewerbestrasse 11, 6330 Cham, Switzerland

Acknowledgment

This book is on the political economy of Turkey and Greece, two pivotal countries located in the Mediterranean region. It aims to offer an analytical framework to account for persistence and change in the turbulent times of Turkish and Greek politics. A comparative analysis on contemporary Turkey and Greece is an exciting but challenging endeavor. The political and economic developments over the last decade have been extraordinary even by the standards of the Turkish and Greek politics.

I owe a debt of gratitude to many scholars, colleagues, and friends, who significantly contributed to the intellectual content of this book. I would like to extend particular thanks to Ziya Öniş, Chris Rumford, M. Fatih Tayfur, Şuhnaz Yılmaz, Caner Bakır, Sadık Ünay, E. Fuat Keyman, Neophytos Loizides, Iosif Kovras, Zühre Aksoy, George Pagoulatos, Dimitri A. Sotiropoulos, and Altay Atlı.

I would like to express my great appreciation to my editors, Christina Brian and Timothy Shaw, for their constant support and encouragement. Also, I would like to thank Clara Heathcock for her guidance and help in the production stages of this book.

I struggle for sufficient words to thank my family for their very strong support. Finally, I wish to thank Muzaffer for her companion. This book would not have been completed without her encouragement.

Contents

List of Figures

List of Tables

CHAPTER 1

Introduction

This book probes into the political dynamics of economic transformations in reactive states. The politics of major reforms is one of the controversial issues in international/comparative political economy literature. There is no clear-cut and agreed-upon template for how successful reforms are initiated and consolidated. State's role in the governance of economic transformations is an even more contested theme.[1] The institutionalist political economy literature, which has made a strong comeback after the global financial crisis vis-à-vis orthodox neoclassical accounts, suggests that "state capacity" is a precondition, not an obstacle for reforming the domestic economic structures.[2] However, states are not standardized commodities whereby their capacity diverges substantially across cases. Two main types

[1] For earlier political economy reviews, see Stephan Haggard and Robert R. Kaufman, ed., *The Politics of Economic Adjustment* (Princeton: Princeton University Press, 1992); Dani Rodrik, "Understanding Economic Policy Reform," *Journal of Economic Literature* XXXIV (1996): 9–41. For a recent review, see Hal Hill, "The Political Economy of Policy Reform: Insights from Southeast Asia," *Asian Development Review* 30, no. 1 (2013): 108–130.

[2] Peter Evans, "The Eclipse of the State? Reflections on Stateness in an Era of Globalization," *World Politics* 50, no. 1 (1997): 62–87. For the importance of "state capacity," see Ha-Joon Chang, *Globalization, Economic Development and the Role of the State* (London and New York: Zed Books, 2004).

M. Kutlay, *The Political Economies of Turkey and Greece*,
International Political Economy Series,
https://doi.org/10.1007/978-3-319-92789-3_1

of states are postulated in the literature with respect to state capacity discussions: "Proactive" and "reactive" states.[3]

Proactive states tend to have the capacity to initiate economic reforms as part and parcel of a comprehensive strategy. Thanks to the institutional complementarities in state-market relations, economic transformations in these states are commenced as a result of prudently crafted and patiently implemented long-term policies.[4] Reactive states, on the other hand, tend to suffer from reform-biased institutional structures that underlie collective action problems toward instigating paradigmatic changes.[5] In these political economies, state remains at the center of the perennial who-gets-what struggle among different interest groups, and its relative strength vis-à-vis other domestic/international centers of power tends to be weak. The reactive state is defined with reference to (a) political systems imbued by intense political polarization and uncontrolled populism, (b) state bureaucracies characterized by very limited "embedded autonomy," and (c) domestic policy coalitions—that is, state's relations with business elite and labor class—permeated by rent seeking and clientelism. The state in these political economies depicts a Janus-faced nature. On the one hand, it frequently intervenes into the functioning of the markets. On the other hand, these interventions tend to be ad hoc, fragmented, and lopsided that arbitrarily favors a narrow circle of privileged coalitions against overall welfare of the society.

In reactive states, institutional structures are set in a way that informs rent-seeking behavior at the agency level. Accordingly, state tends to be captured by special interests and, as a result, turns into an impediment to initiate reforms rather than assuming a steering role. In this setting, institutional arrangements create various mechanisms for state agents to bandwagon the deeply entrenched rent-seeking coalitions. Moreover, these policies are likely to be more exposed to the vagaries of global finance so that international dynamics play a much more pronounced role. The postponement of reform decisions, in turn, paves the way for the accumu-

[3] Linda Weiss, *The Myth of the Powerless State: Governing the Economy in a Global Era* (Cambridge: Polity Press, 1998); Ziya Öniş and Fikret Şenses, "Global Dynamics, Domestic Coalitions and Reactive State: Major Policy Shifts in Post-War Turkish Economic Development," *METU Studies in Development*, no. 34 (2007): 251–286.

[4] Chang, *Globalization, Economic Development and the Role of the State*, Chaps. 2 and 3.

[5] Olson decades ago pointed out that well-organized minority interests are overrepresented and diffuse majority interests are sidelined due to "free rider" problems. Mancur Olson, *The Logic of Collective Action: Public Goods and the Theory of Groups* (Cambridge: Harvard University Press, 1965).

lation of deep-seated economic problems. More often than not, paradigmatic changes are set in motion in the wake of exogenous shocks:

> Reactive states tend to be more fragmented and enjoy a much lower degree of relative autonomy from key domestic constituencies... Hence, [their] ability to overcome sectional conflicts and concentrate their attention on longer-term strategic goals tends to be more limited... [In reactive states] in the absence of crises, the existing coalitions supporting a particular policy regime tend to display considerable resistance to change in spite of the fact that there might be clear signs indicating that the existing policy regime might no longer be viable or sustainable.[6]

Economic crisis, in this context, is a forceful game-changer that may disturb domestic power relations and predominant ideational paradigms underlying intricate relationships between incumbent agents and institutional structures. However, as the literature suggests, not all crises invite major changes.[7] In fact, crises per se fall short of explaining post-crisis variations across cases since crises with a similar magnitude lead to diverging reform outcomes, as the empirical chapters of this book demonstrate. This leads to the main research questions: What are the dynamics of reform cycles in reactive states? When and how economic crises lead to paradigmatic reforms in these political economies?

This book develops a three-stage framework that addresses these questions. The conceptual framework explains why implementing economic reforms are so difficult in reactive states and explores when and how crises alter this recalcitrant path dependence. It offers *crisis narrative approach* as an organizing concept of the conceptual framework. This book concentrates on the political economy of contemporary Turkey and Greece to reveal the causal mechanisms of persistence, crisis, and change in peripheral countries. The rest of this introductory chapter is organized as follows: The second part lays out the logic of case selection. The third part explains methodology and data sources. The final part outlines the organization of chapters.

[6] Öniş and Şenses, "Global Dynamics, Domestic Coalitions and Reactive State," *METU Studies in Development*, 255, 261.

[7] Arjen Boin Allan McConnell and Paul 't Hart, *Governing After Crisis: The Politics of Investigation, Accountability and Learning* (Cambridge: Cambridge University Press, 2008), 5; Jeffrey W. Legro, "The Transformation of Policy Ideas," *American Journal of Political Science* 44, no. 3 (2000): 419–432.

1.1 Why Turkey and Greece?

This book examines Greece and Turkey, which are similar cases concerning state capacity and state-market relations. These two states can be considered as part of the "southern varieties of capitalism." It is astonishingly striking, however, that comparative political economy research on Greece and Turkey is an under-studied area in the literature. This book argues that Greece and Turkey are reactive states due to three main reasons. First, for idiosyncratic historical-sociological reasons, political context is imbued by intense and intentional polarization that hampers consensus-based reform activism while uncontrolled populism tends to lie in wait in both cases. In Greece, for instance, deep-seated patronage politics pursued in a polarized pluralist system penetrated into the state apparatus.[8] A similar historical pattern is also much pronounced in the Turkish case. Turkish political system is frequently defined with reference to polarized pluralism and an under-developed culture of consensus-based policy-making.[9] Second, the economic bureaucracy in both countries remains under heavy influence of patronage politics, which paves the way for weak institutional insulation and coherence. For instance, "embedded autonomy" remained a distant objective in Greek economic bureaucracy.[10] Similarly, weak institutionalization of intra-bureaucratic cooperation and nascent institutional autonomy of economic bureaucracy have dominated Turkish political economy. Third, state's relations with non-state economic stakeholders tend to be inward looking and rent seeking in both cases. Pappas notes that patron-client relations and political patronage are deeply entrenched in Greece to the extent that exclusive distribution of political rents to targeted interest groups have created de facto immunity from the law.[11] In terms of interest intermediation structures, Greece approximates to the

[8] Takis S. Pappas, "Why Greece Failed?" *Journal of Democracy* 24, no. 2 (2013): 31–45. Vassilis Monastiriotis and Andreas Antoniades, "Reform That! Greece's Failing Reform Technology: Beyond 'Vested Interests' and 'Political Exchange,' " in Stathis Kalyvas, George Pagoulatos, and Haris Tsoukas, eds., *From Stagnation to Forced Adjustment: Reforms in Greece, 1974–2010* (London and New York: Hurst Co. and Columbia University Press, 2012), 31–47.

[9] Ersin Kalaycıoğlu, "Turkish Democracy: Patronage versus Governance," *Turkish Studies* 2, no. 1 (2001): 54–70.

[10] Anastassios Chardas, "State Capacity and 'Embeddedness' in the Context of the European Union's Regional Policy: The Case of Greece and the Third Community Support Framework (CSF)," *Southeast European and Black Sea Studies* 12, no. 2 (2012): 221–242.

[11] Pappas, "Why Greece Failed?" *Journal of Democracy*, 37–38.

model of "disjointed corporatism" delineated by state-led, fragmented, and non-institutionalized state-business and state-labor relations.[12] The institutional context of interest intermediation in Turkey also fits into the reactive state category. Institutional economic players in the Turkish context suffer from ubiquitous organizational failures; thereby, their mode of interaction with state tends to remain state dependent, ad hoc, and myopic.[13] Greece and Turkey have a state tradition of frequent intervention in the functioning of the markets; however, the mode of state intervention tends to remain short-term oriented, which informs collective action problems that fortify many different forms of reform inertia.

This brief comparison demonstrates that defining characteristics of state-market relations are similar in both countries. It therefore provides a fertile ground for comparison. The drivers of economic crises and post-crisis reform outcomes in these two cases are also striking. In 2001, Turkey experienced the deepest economic crisis of its modern history due to the culmination of structural problems in the form of a bloated public finance and a bankrupted financial system. The crisis, however, opened up a window of opportunity in the sense that substantial economic reforms were initiated in the immediate aftermath of the crisis. Greece also faced with a profound economic shock in 2009, which is considered as the deepest turmoil in the peacetime history of modern Greece. The crisis, however, turned into a missed opportunity since pro-change coalitions assembled around a reformist narrative could not be generated. As Ladi claims, "major paradigm shift has not taken place. [Instead] the reforms are either cut spending or incremental."[14] The crisis triggered a series of blame games as a result of which Greece is still in the throes of deep political-economic instability seven years after the inception of the crisis.

The comparison of the Turkish and Greek cases poses interesting puzzles in addressing main research questions presented at the outset. Despite weak state capacity in both countries and despite deep economic crises hit two countries, paradigmatic changes were initiated in Turkey, while an opposite trend prevailed in Greece. How did Turkey succeed at breaking down paradigm dependence and why could the crisis not be exploited

[12] Kostas A. Lavdas, *The Europeanization of Greece* (Basingstoke: Macmillan Press, 1997).

[13] Öniş and Şenses, "Global Dynamics, Domestic Coalitions and Reactive State," *METU Studies in Development*.

[14] Stella Ladi, "Austerity Politics and Administrative Reform: The Eurozone Crisis and Its Impact upon Greek Public Administration," *Comparative European Politics* 12, no. 2 (2014): 202.

toward the creation of pro-change coalitions in Greece? From a broader perspective, this book aims to offer a comparative analysis of contemporary Turkish and Greek political economy. In this sense, the post-2011 developments in Turkish politics that gradually paved the way for the deterioration of rule-based state-market relations are also discussed in detail to extrapolate the drivers of institutional regression. It is the premise of this book that both cross-case variations (between Turkey and Greece) and within-case analyses (Turkey and Greece, respectively) enable us to propose bounded generalizations that apply to reactive states.

1.2 Methodology and Data Sources

This book relies on comparative historical analysis. As Mahoney and Rueschemeyer[15] and Bennett and George[16] convincingly suggest, case studies are quite insightful in generating new hypotheses, revealing omitted variables and building new conceptual frameworks. Since this book offers a framework that applies to late-developed reactive states, in-depth comparative analysis is of particular value to assess the single and combinative impacts of different mechanisms at work.

Tarrow argues that comparative case studies are also functional in determining tipping points,[17] which are essential in producing contextualized knowledge on the drivers of paradigm dependence and change in reactive states. To this end, this book explores how crises open up opportunity windows to alter the path-dependent processes. By explaining the mechanisms of crisis and change in Turkey and Greece, it investigates when and how path-dependent structures are amenable to transformation. This book utilizes process tracing to open the black box of crisis-change relationship. According to George and Bennett, process tracing "identifies the intervening processes—the causal chain and causal mechanism—between independent variables and the outcome of the dependent variable."[18] Thus, process tracing enables researchers to assess whether hypothesized outcome occurs in the particular sequence and timing stated by the conceptual framework.

[15] James Mahoney and Dietrich Rueschemeyer, *Comparative Historical Analysis in the Social Sciences* (Cambridge: Cambridge University Press, 2003).

[16] Alexander L. George and Andrew Bennett, *Case Studies and Theory Development in the Social Sciences* (Cambridge: MIT Press, 2005).

[17] Sidney Tarrow, "Bridging the Quantitative-Qualitative Debate in Political Science," *American Political Science Review* 89, no. 2 (1995): 471–474.

[18] George and Bennett, *Case Studies and Theory Development*, 206.

Multiple data sources inform this research. First, this book primarily relies on 29 in-depth semi-structured elite interviews to unravel the views of the main political actors who were directly involved in the design and implementation of the post-crisis reform packages and business elites, labor movement representatives, and bureaucrats that inform the post-crisis reform outcomes, either in a positive or negative way. The interviews also reflect the views of third-party observers and opinion leaders to gain insight about the inner workings of Turkish and Greek politics and economy (see Appendix). Second, this book draws on press statements, op-eds, and speeches of policy-makers, and business and labor unions in Turkey and Greece to map out the crisis narratives of key agents. The documents in question supplement the interview data and field research. Third, official reports and descriptive statistics produced by international organizations are consulted. Finally, this book triangulates the data via thematic review of a sample of newspapers in both countries to double-check the chronology of events and ensure the accuracy of the sequence and timing of developments.

1.3 Organization of Chapters

The chapters of this book are organized according to two interwoven dimensions: historical evolution of events and the stages that form the sequential formation of the conceptual framework.

Chapter 2 discusses the step-by-step construction of the three-stage framework. The crisis narrative approach developed in this chapter is built upon three interrelated literatures, which are state capacity, critical junctures, and policy entrepreneurship.

Chapter 3 discusses the consolidation of a reactive Greek state, which covers 1974–2009. It offers an analysis on the evolution of state capacity with reference to domestic and external factors that directly inform the procrastination of economic reforms in post-authoritarian Greece. Chapter 4 deals with the deepest economic crisis in Greece's recent history. It seeks to explore the drivers as to why Greek crisis was poorly managed and paved the way for the collapse of entire economy. The chapter also discusses the rise of populist parties with particular reference to SYRIZA in the aftermath of the crisis.

Chapter 5 discusses the consolidation of a reactive Turkish state from 1970s to 2001. It discusses the evolution of state capacity in Turkey with reference to domestic and external factors, and reveals the drivers of economic profligacy accumulated over years. Chapter 6 delves into Turkey's 2001 economic crisis. The crisis, which endured deep socio-political and economic costs, was exploited as an opportunity window. Thus, substantial changes took place that pave the way for the emergence of a regulatory state. The chapter also discusses the reversing fortunes of Turkish political economy in the post-2011 period.

Chapter 7 puts the parts of the jigsaw together by offering a comparative analysis. This chapter draws generalizable inferences that are applicable in other contexts. Finally, Chap. 8 concludes the book with a brief discussion on mainstream approaches in the subject field and explains how conceptual framework developed in this book contributes to our understanding on persistence and change in peripheral political economies.

References

Boin, Arjen, Allan McConnell, and Paul 't Hart. *Governing After Crisis: The Politics of Investigation, Accountability and Learning*. Cambridge: Cambridge University Press, 2008.

Chang, Ha-Joon. *Globalization, Economic Development and the Role of the State*. London and New York: Zed Books, 2004.

Chardas, Anastassios. "State Capacity and 'Embeddedness' in the Context of the European Union's Regional Policy: The Case of Greece and the Third Community Support Framework (CSF)." *Southeast European and Black Sea Studies* 12, no. 2 (2012): 221–242.

Evans, Peter. "The Eclipse of the State? Reflections on Stateness in an Era of Globalization". *World Politics* 50, no. 1 (1997): 62–87.

George, Alexander L., and Andrew Bennett. *Case Studies and Theory Development in the Social Sciences*. Cambridge: MIT Press, 2005.

Haggard, Stephan, and Robert R. Kaufman, eds. *The Politics of Economic Adjustment*. Princeton: Princeton University Press, 1992.

Hill, Hal. "The Political Economy of Policy Reform: Insights from Southeast Asia." *Asian Development Review* 30, no. 1 (2013): 108–130.

Kalaycıoğlu, Ersin. "Turkish Democracy: Patronage versus Governance." *Turkish Studies* 2, no. 1 (2001): 54–70.

Ladi, Stella. "Austerity Politics and Administrative Reform: The Eurozone Crisis and Its Impact upon Greek Public Administration." *Comparative European Politics* 12, no. 2 (2014): 184–208.

Lavdas, Kostas. *The Europeanization of Greece*. London: Palgrave Macmillan, 1997.

Legro, Jeffrey W. "The Transformation of Policy Ideas." *American Journal of Political Science* 44, no. 3 (2000): 419–432.

Mahoney, James, and Dietrich Rueschemeyer. *Comparative Historical Analysis in the Social Sciences.* Cambridge: Cambridge University Press, 2003.

Monastiriotis, Vassilis, and Andreas Antoniades. "Reform That! Greece's Failing Reform Technology: Beyond 'Vested Interests' and 'Political Exchange'." In *From Stagnation To Forced Adjustment: Reforms In Greece, 1974–2010*, edited by Stathis Kalyvas, George Pagoulatos, and Haris Tsoukas, 31–47. London and New York: Hurst Co. and Columbia University Press, 2012.

Öniş, Ziya, and Fikret Şenses. Global Dynamics, Domestic Coalitions and Reactive State: Major Policy Shifts in Post-War Turkish Economic Development *METU Studies in Development*, no. 34 (2007): 251–286.

Pappas, Takis S. "Why Greece Failed?" *Journal of Democracy* 24, no. 2 (2013): 31–45.

Rodrik, Dani. "Understanding Economic Policy Reform." *Journal of Economic Literature* XXXIV (1996): 9–41.

Tarrow, Sidney. "Bridging the Quantitative-Qualitative Debate in Political Science." *American Political Science Review* 89, no. 2 (1995): 471–474.

Weiss, Linda. *The Myth of the Powerless State: Governing the Economy in a Global Era*. Cambridge: Polity Press, 1998.

CHAPTER 2

Reforming the Reactive States: A Framework for Analysis

This chapter develops a conceptual framework that explains persistence and change in reactive states. Reform outcomes are the products of complex interplay between agents and institutional structures. Having relied on state capacity, critical junctures, and policy entrepreneurship literatures, this chapter proposes a three-stage framework that tries to capture this intricacy. Accordingly, the first stage of the framework aims to explore how state capacity is deteriorated in a gradual and path-dependent way, and how sub-optimal equilibrium of state-market relations conditions rent-seeking agency behavior. The procrastination of economic reforms in this stage is more likely to pave the way for the accumulation of economic profligacy, which in turn buttresses structural roots of the economic crises.

In the second stage, crisis opens up an opportunity window to initiate change by reshuffling power balances within the system and providing leeway for the emergence of a new paradigm. However, critical junctures are highly uncertain and contentious episodes, which invite massive fluidity. The outcomes in this stage are shaped according to the *crisis narratives* emerged along domestic-external nexus. Accordingly, two main trajectories may unfold in the third stage: If a dominant crisis narrative emerges, collective action problems may be resolved and domestic ownership of reforms may be ensured. However, if multiple and fragmented crisis narratives dominate policy-making agenda, blame games occupy the political

M. Kutlay, *The Political Economies of Turkey and Greece*,
International Political Economy Series,
https://doi.org/10.1007/978-3-319-92789-3_2

landscape. This, in turn, results in muddling through and the eventual restoration of status quo ante.

This chapter delves into different phases and mechanisms of three-stage framework. The rest of this chapter proceeds as follows: The second part offers a critical review and reclassification of "state capacity" literature. Third part lays out the details of the conceptual framework. This part also elaborates on *crisis narratives* approach as an organizing concept. The fourth part summarizes the stages that form the parts of the conceptual framework that is deployed in the empirical chapters.

2.1 Unpacking "State Capacity"

The conceptualization of "state capacity" varies significantly in political science literature. The concept is defined in a wide range to the extent that it suffers from concept-stretching problem in comparative politics.[1] Different approaches deploy a variety of concepts such as "strong states," "weak states," "proactive states," and "reactive states" based on their particular understanding of state capacity. The archipelago of definitions therefore requires a reclassification of the literature to make it operational. This part maps out the literature and reformulates the concept. It argues that an analytical distinction between "stateness" and "state capacity" is necessary to make the term rather applicable for comparative political economy studies.

Stateness: Strong Versus Weak States

One should first clarify what state capacity means within the context of stateness. State building, state failure, conflict, and international relations studies refer to the *stateness* of a state when they refer to state capacity concept. According to this line of research, strong states are the ones that have control over their territory and maintain government authority even at the sparsely populated and mountainous areas within the borders of a country.[2] The territorial control of a state includes its capability to avoid

[1] Sartori eloquently discusses the problem of "concept stretching" in comparative politics. See Giovanni Sartori, "Concept Misformation in Comparative Politics," *American Political Science Review* 64, no. 4 (1970): 1033–1053.

[2] Robert I. Rotberg, *When States Fail: Causes and Consequences* (Princeton: Princeton University Press, 2003), 2–3.

other states and non-state armed groups to claim authority across its borders. Furthermore, strong states are claimed to be resistant to the challenges of their legitimacy over the use of force within its own territory. Thereby, core functions of a state, including security provision to their citizens against domestic and external threats, are also regarded as an indicator of state strength.

Weak states or failed states, on the other hand, exhibit an absence of this capability.[3] State building and state failure literature in comparative politics concentrate on this particular aspect of the issue. Migdal is one of the scholars who problematized and systematically evaluated state capacity/capabilities especially within the context of state building in third world countries. According to Migdal, state capabilities include the capacities to "penetrate society, regulate social relationships, and extract resources."[4] Weak states lack territorial control, fail to avoid other states and non-state armed groups to claim authority over its own territory, and cannot extract resources. According to Acemoğlu,[5] resource extraction remains at the heart of stateness. The states with high capabilities to proffer these functions are defined as strong states, whereas weak states are placed on the polar opposite of the spectrum.[6] Similarly, Fukuyama employs state capacity as the organizing concept in recent state building and state failure literature. According to Fukuyama, "the essence of stateness is enforcement, [which is] the ultimate ability to send someone with a uniform and a gun to force people to comply with the state's laws."[7]

In short, strong states/weak states in comparative politics ought to be placed along a continuum with reference to their capacity, which is comprised of (a) ability to control their territory, (b) capacity to provide core state functions, and (c) legitimacy over domestic and external challengers.

[3] James D. Fearon and David D. Laitin, "Ethnicity, Insurgency, and Civil War," *American Political Science Review* 97, no. 1 (2003): 75, 80, 88; Ann Hironaka, *Neverending Wars: The International Community, Weak States, and the Perpetuation of Civil War* (Cambridge: Harvard University Press, 2005).

[4] Joel S. Migdal, *Strong Societies and Weak States: State-Society Relations and State Capabilities in the Third World* (Princeton: Princeton University Press, 1988), 4–5.

[5] Daron Acemoglu, "Politics and Economics in Weak and Strong States," *Journal of Monetary Economics* 52, no. 7 (2005): 1199–1226.

[6] Fearon and Laitin, "Ethnicity, Insurgency, and Civil War," *American Political Science Review*, 80, 81, 88.

[7] Francis Fukuyama, *State Building: Governance and World Order in the Twenty-first Century* (London: Profile Books, 2005), 7–19.

Therefore, leitmotif of the debate in these fields is the *stateness* of a state. However, state capacity concept in comparative political economy focuses on a particular aspect of the issue, namely state's capability to intervene, steer, and reform domestic economic structures and mobilize new winning coalitions. This suggests that state capacity debate in comparative political economy takes the *stateness of a state* for granted and deals with a sample of states that do not encounter substantial problems in maintaining territorial integrity and supply of core public goods.

State Capacity: Proactive Versus Reactive States

The reactive/proactive state categorization refers to an advanced level of debate in state capacity literature because both "reactive" and "proactive" states meet the basic criteria of stateness. It does not mean that these two research streams have nothing in common. On the contrary, they have interwoven dimensions, yet they refer to analytically distinct categories, which deserve separate analysis. In comparative political economy literature, both reactive and proactive states basically meet the Weberian state template as being the "monopoly of the legitimate use of physical force within a given territory."[8] States in this category can provide core state functions and extract resources from their society while remaining loyal to rule-based institutional frameworks, despite the quality of rule of law and governance diverge across cases.

The historical evolution of state capacity concept in this stream of research can be broken down in two major periods. The first generation is dominated by historical comparative studies of Katzenstein[9] and Krasner.[10] In his forceful critique of third image approaches to international politics, Katzenstein argued that the divergence and variations of foreign economic policies are not derived from the "functional logic of different types of

[8] Max Weber, "Politics as a Vocation," in H. H. Gerth and C. Wright Mills, eds., *From Max Weber: Essays in Sociology* (London: Routledge, 1948), 78.

[9] Peter J. Katzenstein, "International Relations and Domestic Structures: Foreign Economic Policies of Advanced Industrial States," *International Organization* 30, no. 1 (1976): 1–45; Peter J. Katzenstein, ed., *Between Power and Plenty* (London: the University of Wisconsin Press, 1978).

[10] Stephen D. Krasner, *Defending the National Interest: Raw Materials Investment and U.S. Foreign Policy* (Princeton: Princeton University Press, 1978); Stephen Krasner, "US Commercial and Monetary Policy: Unravelling the Paradox of External Strength and Internal Weakness," *International Organization* 31, no. 4 (1977): 635–671.

international effects but the constraints of domestic structures."[11] Third image approaches to international politics posit that the main determinants of politics are ultimately derived not from the human nature—first image—or the internal structure of states—second image—but from the structure of international system.[12] However, Katzenstein claims, not the dynamics of international system, but the nature of state-society relationship and the degree of centralization determine the type of economic policies pursued by nation-states. Strong state/weak society combination—that is, state-centered polity,[13] enables a state to intervene into the organization of economic relations and mobilize economic actors toward state-directed ends. Weak state/strong society combination—that is, society-centered polity, on the other hand, paves the way for hands-off approach of the state toward initiating fiscal, financial, and industrial reforms.[14]

The first generation of state capacity discussions adopts a dualist understanding of state-market relations that formulate the concept in terms of state's coercive power over society. In his second-generation critique, Evans questions unilateral statist approaches by offering an alternative framework.[15] Evans argues that states must combine autonomy with some kind of "embeddedness" with economic interest groups.[16] According to Evans, the underlying analytical logic of state capacity revolves around a competent and meritocratic state bureaucracy that have high-transformative capability in building credibility across the state-private nexus so as to change the preference functions of economic elite toward a reform-oriented outlook. For Evans, "embeddedness" provides networks for states to receive robust feedbacks from private interest groups and to overcome collective action problems, whereas "autonomy" provides isolation for state agents to pursue coherent and long-term-oriented reform

[11] Katzenstein, "International Relations and Domestic Structures," *International Organization*, 15.

[12] Kenneth Waltz, *Man, the State and War: A Theoretical Analysis* (New York: Columbia University Press, 1959).

[13] Katzenstein, *Between Power and Plenty*, 310, 324.

[14] Ibid.

[15] Peter B. Evans, "The State as Problem and Solution: Predation, Embedded Autonomy and Adjustment," in Stephan Haggard and Robert Kaufman, eds., *The Politics of Economic Adjustment: International Constraints, Distributive Politics, and the State* (Princeton: Princeton University Press, 1992); Peter Evans, *Embedded Autonomy: State and Industrial Transformation* (Princeton: Princeton University Press, 1995).

[16] Peter Evans, "Transferable Lessons? Re-Examining the Institutional Prerequisites of East Asian Economic Policies," *The Journal of Development Studies* 34, no. 6 (1998): 66–86.

strategies. An optimum admixture of these two aspects informs the overall capacity of the state:

> A state that was only autonomous would lack both sources of intelligence and the ability to rely on decentralized private implementation. Dense connecting networks without a robust internal structure would leave the state incapable of resolving "collective action" problems of transcending the individual interest of its private counterparts.[17]

Weiss further develops the embedded autonomy concept along the lines of state-market synergy.[18] Weiss convincingly argues that the statist approaches—strong state/weak state portrayal—misconceive state's reform capacity because "state power has been conceptualized in a way that makes it virtually impossible to apply to modern states."[19] Weiss defines state capacity in the economic policy realm as "the ability of policy-making authorities to pursue domestic adjustment strategies *in cooperation with* organized economic interest groups."[20] Therefore, she offers an alternative conceptualization of state capacity, which Weiss calls "governed interdependence" (GI):

> GI refers to a negotiated relationship, in which public and private participants maintain their autonomy, yet which is nevertheless governed by broader goals set and monitored by the state… GI intended to convey a reality in which both state and dominant economic groups are 'strong', i.e. the state is well insulated and industry is highly organized and linked into the policy-making framework via a robust negotiating relationship.[21]

Interdependence is a generic characteristic in all modern states because of the complex nature of state-market relations. What differentiates GI from conventional interdependence is the more institutionally structured and negotiated nature of exchanges between state agents and organized interests toward the implementation of economic reforms. As Weiss argues, "rather than leaving mutual dependence to chance, the state takes a proactive role, drawing business into a negotiating relationship in order to

[17] Evans, *Embedded Autonomy*, 12.
[18] Weiss, *The Myth of the Powerless State.*
[19] Ibid., 27.
[20] Ibid., 5. Emphasis added.
[21] Ibid., 38.

further its projects."[22] However, GI approach rejects top-down management or unilateralism in the regulation of domestic economy. Accordingly, Weiss argues the joint contribution of state bureaucrats and social partners on an equal footing as necessary preconditions of the efficient and timely management of economic reform processes. Contrary to the statist first-generation arguments, which depict a zero-sum relationship between state and market, GI foresees regular and extensive cooperation as the institutional prerequisite of optimal policy change and sustainable reform activism. This means that policy success over the medium- and long-term horizon is determined by state capacity *through* market, not *over* it. In this ideal-typical typology, states are armored to make timely economic decisions and rectify existing policy paradigms, if deemed necessary.

GI concept opens up a productive avenue for understanding the underlying mechanisms of a state's reform capacity by incorporating the crucial role of "dense networks of relations that cross organizational boundaries and the interdependence of state and societal actors."[23] This qualification provides a functional link to policy networks framework. As an integral aspect of state capacity debate, policy networks framework aims to reveal under what conditions and through which interest intermediation structures, states are capable of initiating major policy reforms in collaboration with private actors.[24] Atkinson and Coleman define two main types of policy networks with respect to state capacity: anticipatory and reactive.[25] Accordingly, "what distinguishes an anticipatory approach from a reactive one is the predisposition on the part of the state to intervene in the industrial organization of the sector."[26] Table 2.1 offers a stylized version of the reclassification of literature on state capacity.

There are two major caveats surrounding the use of state capacity literature as an analytic tool for analysis with respect to late-industrialized reactive states. First, dominant approaches to state capacity mainly concentrate either on developmental states or on advanced industrialized countries. Thus, they

[22] Ibid.

[23] Mark Robinson, "Hybrid States: Globalization and the Politics of State Capacity," *Political Studies* 56, no. 3 (2008): 566–583.

[24] For an overview of "policy networks" literature, see Tanja Börzel, "Networks: Reified Metaphor or Governance Panacea?", *Public Administration* 89, no. 1 (2011): 49–63.

[25] Michael M. Atkinson and William D. Coleman, "Strong States and Weak States: Sectoral Policy Networks in Advanced Capitalist Economies," *British Journal of Political Science* 19, no. 1 (1989): 47–67.

[26] Ibid., 61.

Table 2.1 Mapping out the "state capacity": a reclassification of the literature

	Types of states	*Assessment criteria*
"Stateness"	Weak states Strong states	• Control over territory • Capacity to provide core functions • Internal/external legitimacy
"State capacity"	Reactive states Proactive states	• Political context • State bureaucracy • Mode of the relationship between state and domestic policy communities

Source: Author's compilation

eschew the mechanisms of paradigmatic economic policy shifts in late developers. For instance, policy networks framework has limited portability into the late-industrialized reactive states due to qualitative differences in terms of the organization of domestic political setting, state bureaucracy, and domestic policy communities in the latter category (see Fig. 2.1). In these three respects, late-industrialized reactive states tend to suffer from weak state capacity in a categorically different way vis-à-vis advanced political economies.[27] In these polities, state remains at the center of perennial who-gets-what struggle among different interest groups and state's relative strength vis-à-vis other power centers—both internal and external forces—tend to be weak, which is partially conditioned by their developmentalist timing.

First, the political context in reactive states tends to be intensely polarized and conflict-prone due to the historically contingent configurations of state-society relations, which impedes consensus-based governance surrounded by an immature institutional environment. Political polarization, more often than not, underlies uncontrolled populism and patronage politics, which in turn inform gradual erosion of the economic discipline for the sake of short-term electoral purposes.

Second, political patronage and pervasive clientelism are inclined to permeate into state bureaucracy as the latter is generally conceived as an arena to be captured by competing interest groups. Hence, bureaucracy remains fragmented and dependent on arbitrary protection of individual political elites that squanders both bureaucratic "autonomy" and "embed-

[27] Ziya Öniş, and Fikret Şenses, "Global Dynamics, Domestic Coalitions and Reactive State," *METU Studies in Development*, 251–286.

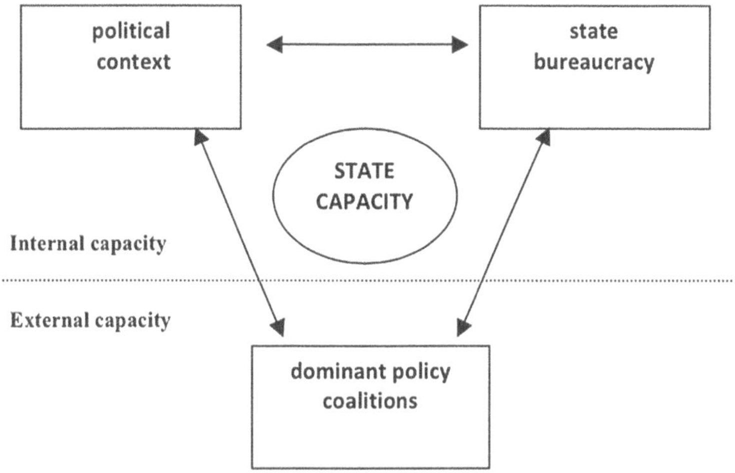

Fig. 2.1 Three pillars of state capacity

dedness." Not surprisingly, as a result, state bureaucracy cannot substantially contribute to the effective formulation and governance of economic reforms in a coordinated way along with the executive authority and non-state interest groups.

Third, rampant rent-seeking and perverse incentives rather than a rule-based institutionalized relationship usually imbue the mode of relationship between state and dominant policy coalitions. The personalistic exchange relations and patronage-motivated interest intermediation structures, again, give ample way to the collective action and credibility of commitment problems. Furthermore, external actors and international organizations play a much more decisive role in reactive states than current approaches acknowledge. Therefore, this book proposes to extend our gaze beyond domestic-oriented and sector-specific analysis to account for persistence and change in reactive states.

The following parts of the book offer a three-stage conceptual framework that incorporates complex interactions among state agents, external actors, and domestic coalitions to account for time and context-dependent dynamics of reform cycles. However, before that, a clarification on conceptual vocabulary is necessary in terms of the epistemological presuppositions of this book.

2.2 Conceptual Vocabulary

The three-stage conceptual framework offered in this book relies on analytic eclecticism. Sil and Katzenstein define any approach "eclectic" that seeks to "extricate, translate, and selectively integrate analytic elements—concepts, logics, mechanisms, and interpretations—of theories or narratives that have been developed within separate paradigms but that address related aspects of substantive problems that have both scholarly and practical significance."[28] Analytic eclecticism fundamentally relies on Hirschman's insightful observation that paradigm-bound research, because of its exclusive emphasis on certain variables, may ignore a "variety of [other] forces at work," which usually paves the way for "a particularly high degree of error."[29] Along these lines, the premise of analytic eclecticism is to overcome the enduring blind spots in paradigm-bound scholarship by addressing complex causal mechanisms at work leading to important policy outcomes:

> Analytic eclecticism generates complex causal stories that forgo parsimony in order to capture the interactions among different types of causal mechanisms normally analysed in isolation from each other within separate research traditions.[30]

Analytic eclecticism is an epistemological approach that "guard against the risks of excessive reliance on single paradigm and the simplifying assumptions that come with it."[31] Sil and Katzenstein highlight three distinguishing features of analytic eclecticism: "its pragmatist ethos [that potentially speak to concrete issues of policy and practice], its open-ended approach to identifying problems, and their complex interactions in diverse contexts."[32] Furthermore, it draws attention to the way in which institutional structures influence agent's capabilities, constraints, and opportunities.[33] Thus, ana-

[28] Rudra Sil and Peter Katzenstein, *Beyond Paradigms: Analytic Eclecticism in the Study of World Politics* (New York: Palgrave Macmillan, 2010), 10.

[29] Albert Hirschman, "The Search for Paradigms as a Hindrance to Understanding," *World Politics* 22, no. 3 (1970): 341, 343.

[30] Rudra Sil and Peter Katzenstein, "Analytic Eclecticism in the Study of World Politics: Reconfiguring Problems and Mechanisms Across Research Traditions," *Perspectives on Politics* 8, no. 2 (2010): 412.

[31] Ibid., 414.

[32] Ibid., 412.

[33] Sil and Katzenstein, *Beyond Paradigms*, 21.

lytic eclecticism is particularly insightful for the purposes of this book because dynamics of crisis and change are complex and multidimensional phenomena emanating from the interactions along domestic-international nexus. That being said, however, analytic eclecticism does not intend to create a shopping list of all imaginable causal factors. Its distinctiveness arises from its effort to determine how "elements of different causal stories [concentrating either on agency or institutional structures] might coexist as part of a more complex argument."[34] Following these basic parameters, this book draws on state capacity, critical junctures, and policy entrepreneurship literatures to develop a coherent framework that accounts for the mechanisms of persistence and change in reactive states. A conscious dialogue among these distinct but interrelated literatures enables researchers to adopt holistic perspective on when, why, and how crises pave the way for paradigmatic reforms.

Second, a clarification is also in order regarding the definition of "reform" or "major policy change." The political economy literature suggests that reforms come in many forms and ways.[35] There is also a vast literature on the definition and types of policy reforms.[36] Similar to other forms of states, many economic changes are constantly engineered in late developers as well, especially in the era of global neoliberalism. That being said, not all changes qualify the definition of "reform" denoted in this book. The hastily crafted ad hoc policy changes and window-dressing exercises are frequently put into practice in all states especially during crisis times. In fact, these shallow and incomplete policy changes often lead to further deterioration of economic structures and social fabric. Thus, insubstantial and non-sustainable policy changes are beyond the analytical scope of this study. By way of analogy from Hall, this book identifies three distinct types of reforms.[37] First-order reform refers to minor policy adaptations in which just the settings of government's policy instruments are

[34] Sil and Katzenstein, "Analytic Eclecticism in the Study of World Politics," *Perspectives on Politics*, 414–415.

[35] For recent reviews, see Hill, "The Political Economy of Policy Reform: Insights from Southeast Asia," *Asian Development Review*, 108–130; Dani Rodrik, "When Ideas Trump Interests: Preferences, Worldviews, and Policy Innovations," *Journal of Economic Perspectives* 28, no. 1 (2014): 189–209.

[36] Mariano Tommasia and Andrés Velascoa, "Where Are We in the Political Economy of Reform," *The Journal of Policy Reform* 1, no. 2 (1996): 187–238.

[37] Peter A. Hall, "Policy Paradigms, Social Learning, and the State: The Case of Economic Policymaking in Britain," *Comparative Politics* 25, no. 3 (1993): 275–296.

altered. Second-order reform refers to medium policy adaptations in which the instruments as well as the settings of the instruments are altered. Third-order reform refers to a set of significant changes in policy that alter both the settings of the instruments, the policy instruments themselves and the ultimate goals and ideational paradigm behind the existing policies. This book refers to third-order reforms, while it also frequently uses "substantial and sustainable reforms," "major policy transformations," and "paradigmatic changes" interchangeably to denote the same phenomenon.

Persistence and Change: A Three-Stage Framework

This book assumes that states are still the most appropriate take-off point regarding the governance of economic reforms because setting common goals, steering policy communities, and promoting public-private partnerships are ultimately mediated by the state despite emergence of alternative governance actors. It is in this context that state capacity appears as the single most important factor in understanding domestic reform dynamics. By definition, the initiative to instigate a virtuous cycle of reform activism usually does not emanate from the concerted and consensus-based interactions of non-state coalitions in reactive states. The change-oriented state agents are expected to set the policy agenda, steer incumbent policy communities toward the implementation of paradigmatic reforms in these political economies.[38] However, there appears a paradox here: As stated above, institutional structures are set in a way in reactive states that existing arrangements create various mechanisms for political actors to bandwagon the deeply entrenched rent-seeking coalitions. Political polarization, clientelistic patronage politics, and underdeveloped culture of consensus-based policy-making create an adverse environment for state agents to prioritize their short-term interests at the expense of long-term societal welfare. Stated differently, those who are supposed to reform the system are usually the ones that are captured by and reap the benefits of the existing institutional settings.

The three-stage framework is organized around two central concepts to address this paradox: *timing* and *context*.[39] The first dimension concerns

[38] B. Guy Peters, "Shouldn't Row, Can't Steer: What's a Government to Do?," *Public Policy and Administration* 12, no. 2 (1997): 57.

[39] Paul Pierson and Theda Skocpol, "Historical Institutionalism in Contemporary Political Science," in Ira Katznelson and Helen V. Milner, eds., *Political Science: State of the Discipline* (New York: W.W. Norton, 2002): 693–721.

the timing of paradigmatic changes. As stated in the preceding paragraphs, reform-biased institutional structures are more likely to constrain agency behavior in the normal course of politics in a way that enforcement of economic reforms turns into an arduous task. Also, political context, state bureaucracy, and incumbent policy coalitions tend to favor deleterious rent-seeking policies rather than promoting long-term-oriented strategies. This episode refers to the *first stage* in the conceptual framework, which this book calls "stagnation and inertia." In this stage, much-needed reforms are more likely to be delayed or watered down. The accumulation of structural problems, most of the time, leads to deep-seated economic crises.

The literature suggests that external shocks are important tipping points that are likely to open up opportunity windows to introduce paradigmatic changes.[40] Jolts and crises constitute critical junctures that "make significant structural changes possible because they render politics highly fluid."[41] Critical junctures are "relatively short periods of time during which there is substantially heightened probability that agents' choices will affect the outcome of interest."[42] This definition proffers that crisis junctures constitute a potential turning point that is distinct from the "normal" historical evolution of the "institutional setting of interests."[43] Therefore, it opens up the *second stage*, that is, "uncertainty and crisis narratives phase." In this stage, ultimate reform outcomes are shaped according to the context-specific interactions along the lines of domestic-external nexus. Jessop argues "that a crisis emerges when established patterns of dealing with structural contradictions, their crisis tendencies and dilemmas no longer work as expected and may even aggravate the situation."[44] In this sense, a crisis is a reverberation of the unsustainable nature of prevailing policy paradigms. An economic crisis, in this sense,

[40] Colin Hay, "Crisis and the Structural Transformation of the State: Interrogating the Process of Change," *British Journal of Politics and International Relations* 1, no. 3 (1999): 317–344; Boin, McConnell and 't Hart, *Governing After Crisis*; John Hogan, and Ana Hara, "Country at a Crossroads: An Insight into How an Economic Crisis Led to Dramatic Policy Change," *Risk, Hazards & Crisis in Public Policy* 2, no. 3 (2011): 1–23.

[41] Geoffrey Garrett "The Politics of Structural Change: Swedish Social Democracy and Thatcherism in Comparative Perspective," *Comparative Political Studies* 25, no. 4 (1993): 522.

[42] Giovanni Capoccia and Daniel R. Klemen, "The Study of Junctures: Theory, Narrative, and Counterfactuals in Historical Institutionalism," *World Politics* 59, no. 3 (2007): 348.

[43] Ibid.

[44] Bob Jessop, *The Future of the Capitalist State* (Cambridge: Polity Press, 2002), 92.

proves to be a forceful game-changer in shifting power balances because it delegitimizes existing paradigms and jeopardizes the power base of the profoundly entrenched vested interests attached to these paradigms.

Crises are manifestations of paradigm failures that reverberate ill-functioning aspects of extant state-market relations. Interest-based political economy accounts cogently demonstrate that deep crises are crucial tipping points for the redistribution of power among competing interest coalitions. An economic crisis in domestic politics resembles the functions of a war in international relations. Gilpin suggested long ago that wars are likely to reshuffle the power relations in the interstate system in a rather dramatic way.[45] Similarly, a crisis renders pre-crisis power relations highly fluid at the domestic arena. The interest-based power transformations hypothesis, however, is too crude to explain the dynamics of new coalition formation in the wake of economic shocks. In fact, crises are not as self-evident as they appear at first glance.[46] The mere accumulation of structural contradictions is insufficient in explaining the emergence and consolidation of new paths in the wake of deep economic crises. Not all crises, however, invite substantial changes. Exogenous shocks per se fall short of explaining post-crisis variations across cases because crises with similar magnitude result in diverging post-crisis outcomes, a point that the empirical chapters demonstrate in detail (Chaps. 4 and 6). The current research also underlines "that the exogenous explanations for sudden and dramatic shifts in policies tend to be crude."[47] Yet, as Hogan and Feeney put it, the literature has not paid much ado to determine the causal mechanisms through which crises result in substantial reforms.[48]

This book suggests that critical juncture approaches must be supplemented by a framework that endogenize complex interactions at the domestic-external nexus in the wake of deep crises to open the black box of crisis-change relationship. A crisis must be narrated in particular ways to overcome collective action problems toward crafting new pro-reform coalitions. This leads us to put more emphasis on the role of ideas during

[45] Robert Gilpin, *War and Change in International Politics* (Cambridge: Cambridge University Press, 1981).

[46] Mark Blyth, *Great Transformations: Economic Ideas and Institutional Change in the Twentieth Century* (Cambridge: Cambridge University Press, 2002), 44–45.

[47] Hogan and Feeney, "Crisis and Policy Change," *Risk, Hazards & Crisis in Public Policy*, 2.

[48] Ibid.

critical junctures.[49] Ideational approaches also suggest that crises are more likely to delegitimize existing paradigms. From a Kuhnian perspective, crises may unravel the perception that dominant paradigms are the main reasons of the present problems.[50] According to Legro, policy change occurs at two distinct ideational realms in crisis episodes: ideational collapse and consolidation of new ideas.[51] Although deep crises delegitimize and/or lead to the collapse of dominant policy paradigms, adopting a particular narrative regarding the existing crisis and bearing the ownership of new ideational paradigms is sine qua non.[52] Blyth argues that the root causes and nature of a crisis becomes *something to be explained* rather than *something with which to do the explaining* during post-crisis political tug-of-wars.[53] In times of extreme uncertainty, the particular narrative about "what has gone wrong" and "what is to be done" makes crisis as "explicable, manageable, and indeed, actionable."[54] In this regard, the degree of narrative match between state agents and external actors do constitute necessary aspect of reform processes in reactive states. Therefore, in times of institutional uncertainty, policy entrepreneurs play crucial functional roles in terms of developing a coherent crisis narrative.

Kingdon offers "multiple-streams approach" that places policy entrepreneurs within the context of three kinds of processes: problems, policies, and politics.[55] Accordingly, paradigmatic transformations occur when change agents meticulously couple these three independent streams.[56] A policy entrepreneur, in this context, refers to "an individual who mobilizes ideas, resolves conflicts, and steers their implementation for policy and institutional changes."[57] The performance of change agents to link problems, policies, and politics toward paradigmatic economic reforms is conditioned by interactions with external actors and domestic policy communities. On

[49] Blyth, *Great Transformations*, 35.

[50] Thomas Kuhn, *The Structure of Scientific Revolutions* (Chicago: University of Chicago Press, 1962).

[51] Legro, "The Transformation," *American Journal of Political Science*.

[52] Hay, "Crisis and the Structural Transformation," *British Journal of Politics and International Relations*, 323, 333–338.

[53] Blyth, *Great Transformations*, 9.

[54] Ibid., 10.

[55] Kingdon, *Agendas, Alternatives, and Public Policies* (New York: Longman, 1995), 122.

[56] Ibid., 172–184.

[57] Caner Bakır, "Policy Entrepreneurship and Institutional Change: Multilevel Governance of Central Banking Reform," *Governance: An International Journal of Policy, Administration and Institutions* 22, no. 4 (2009): 572.

the international side, external actors play decisive roles in determining the scope conditions of post-crisis politicking, as massive power asymmetry emerge in the wake of a deep economic crisis in reactive states. The role of external actors can be subsumed into two categories: supply of resources and supply of credibility. First, external actors provide material support to change agents in their contest to frame a coherent narrative at the domestic realm. The availability of financial resources proves crucial to alleviate distributional pressures emanated from post-crisis adjustment measures. The resources in question might be fiscal bailouts and technical expertise, generally attached to strict conditionality. Second, external actors assume a functional role in the supply of credibility of certain reform ideas and tilt the balance in favor of the pro-change coalitions during the early phases of crisis narration struggles. Therefore, a possible match in the *crisis narratives* of policy entrepreneurs and external actors empowers the former in establishing new winning coalitions and generating public ownership of reform prescriptions. Chwieroth underlines this point as follows:

> When the perceived need for credibility is high, such as during an economic crisis, domestic norm entrepreneurs whose prescriptions resonate with the beliefs of relevant external actors will be empowered. In debates with their opponents, these domestic norm entrepreneurs can employ this resonance to present themselves and their policy blueprint as the only way to establish credibility and resolve the crisis.[58]

The mismatch between the crisis narratives of the domestic and external actors, on the other hand, is likely to jeopardize the access to external resources and international credibility. The congruence along domestic-external nexus should be interpreted as a dynamic process. The crisis narrative approach offered here takes the autonomous functions of state agents into consideration in localizing and domesticating the prescriptions of external actors. The instigation of successful changes necessitates active participation and deliberation of external and domestic stakeholders assembled around a dominant crisis narrative. Though the constraining role of external actors and power asymmetries are too crucial to be neglected, narrative matching is rarely a one-way imposition process.

[58] Jeffrey M. Chwieroth, "How Do Crises Lead to Change? Liberalizing Capital Controls in the Early Years of New Order Indonesia," *World Politics* 62, no. 3 (2010): 496–527.

Finally, the balance sheet of reform outcomes is drawn by institutional structures in which change agents are embedded. Domestic institutional structures, that is, domestic political context, state bureaucracy, and dominant policy coalitions are the primary factors that inform reform outcomes. The ability of policy entrepreneurs or change agents to penetrate into domestic communities and create new winning coalitions is equally important for proper implementation of reform prescriptions. Based on these complex interactions, in the ***third stage*** of the three-stage framework, domestic policy communities are likely to redefine their interests and bandwagon the newly emerging winning coalitions when a dominant narrative is articulated and communicated at the agency level. On the other hand, when fragmented and incoherent narratives dominate policy-making agenda, domestic coalition is likely to reject the idea of change and align toward status quo ante. In this case, domestic ownership problems are most likely to precipitously amplify, which in turn lead to the policy failure regardless of the depth of the economic shock.

2.3 Conclusion: Putting the Jigsaw Together

This chapter offered a three-stage framework that explores political economy dynamics of persistence and change in prevalent economic paradigms in reactive states. This part offers a stylized summary of subsequent stages to sum up the main argument (also see Fig. 2.2).

Stage 1: Stagnation and Inertia

In the first stage, that is, phase of stagnation and inertia, reform attempts are more likely to fail due to the path-dependent interactions along the lines of domestic-external nexus, which inform state's internal and external capacity. The weak state capacity to impose robust discipline often leads to a bloated fiscal and financial regime in reactive states. Furthermore, in the absence of strong state capacity, this sub-set of states is more likely to integrate into globalization processes in a way that further inform moral hazard problems. In this perverse equilibrium, agency behavior is more likely to align toward status quo and potential pro-change agents are likely to fail in their attempts to generate ownership of their reformist agenda. The accumulation of structural problems, more often than not, paves the wave for deep-seated economic turmoil.

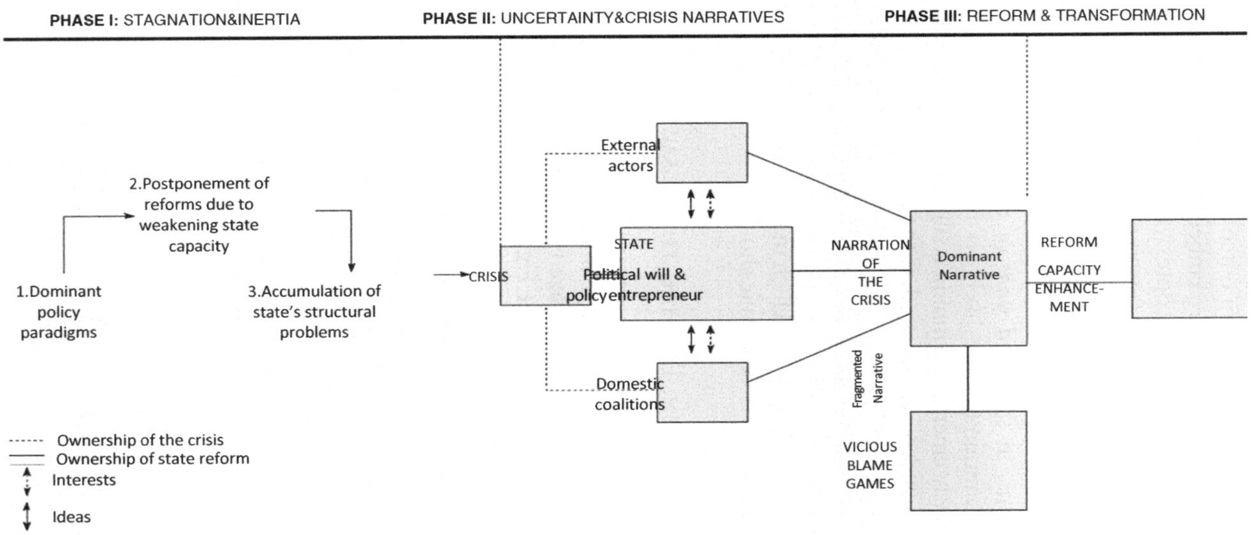

Fig. 2.2 Reform dynamics in reactive states: a three-stage framework

Stage 2: Uncertainty and Crisis Narratives

Economic crisis as a particular form of critical junctures tends to open an opportunity space to introduce new paradigms since exogenous shocks lead to the weakening of reform-resistant domestic institutional arrangements and the ideational paradigms embedded therein. Thus a deep crisis may invite the second stage in three-stage framework, that is, phase of uncertainty and crisis narratives. In crisis episodes, the existence of reform-oriented state agents, possibly policy entrepreneurs, play instrumental role to couple problems, policies, and politics so as to develop a coherent narrative about the root causes of the crisis and the most efficient way to get out of it. Their performance, however, is conditioned by two factors. First, a dominant crisis narrative must be adopted in cooperation with predominant external actors, which are involved in the formulation and implementation of post-crisis reform policies. A high degree of narrative match between state agents and external actors is more likely to facilitate a virtuous cycle of reform activism. Second, the mediating function of domestic institutional structures is crucial in terms of developing ownership of the crisis and the reform agenda. If the agency-level crisis narratives diverge substantially and reform recipes are unilaterally imposed, pro-status quo forces are likely to weather the storm.

Stage 3: Reform and Transformation

Based on the complex interaction of state agents, external actors, and domestic policy coalitions, two ideal-typical policy paths may arise in the third stage. First trajectory is the *emergence of a dominant narrative*, which helps overcome the collective action problems and transform prevailing economic paradigms. The narrative match between state agents and external actors, and the creation of new winning coalitions constitute the basic prerequisites to instigate a new reformist agenda. Second trajectory is the emergence of *multiple crisis narratives*, which emanates due to state agents' failure in framing coherent crisis narrative and matching it with those of external actors. Multiple crisis narratives in the wake of crisis create enormous policy fragmentation and provide leeway for pro-status quo forces to reproduce their privileged positions. This, in turn, triggers a cycle of multi-level blame games and muddling through. Not surprisingly, as a result, the crisis cannot be exploited as an opportunity to alter pre-crisis institutional arrangements if this scenario prevails. The following empirical chapters shall apply three-stage framework to the Turkish and Greek cases.

References

Acemoglu, Daron. "Politics and Economics in Weak and Strong States." *Journal of Monetary Economics* 52, no. 7 (2005): 1199–1226.

Atkinson, Michael M., and William D. Coleman. "Strong States and Weak States: Sectoral Policy Networks in Advanced Capitalist Economies." *British Journal of Political Science* 19, no. 1 (1989): 47–67.

Bakır, Caner. "Policy Entrepreneurship and Institutional Change: Multilevel Governance of Central Banking Reform." *Governance: An International Journal of Policy, Administration and Institutions* 22, no. 4 (2009): 571–598.

Blyth, Mark. *Great Transformations: Economic Ideas and Institutional Change in the Twentieth Century.* Cambridge: Cambridge University Press, 2002.

Boin, Arjen, Allan McConnell, and Paul 't Hart. *Governing After Crisis: The Politics of Investigation, Accountability and Learning.* Cambridge: Cambridge University Press, 2008.

Börzel, Tanja. "Networks: Reified Metaphor or Governance Panacea?" *Public Administration* 89, no. 1 (2011): 49–63.

Capoccia, Giovanni, and Daniel R. Klemen. "The Study of Junctures: Theory, Narrative, and Counterfactuals in Historical Institutionalism." *World Politics* 59, no. 3 (2007): 341–369.

Chwieroth, Jeffrey M. "How Do Crises Lead to Change? Liberalizing Capital Controls in the Early Years of New Order Indonesia." *World Politics* 62, no. 3 (2010): 496–527.

Evans, Peter. "The State as Problem and Solution: Predation, Embedded Autonomy and Adjustment." In *The Politics of Economic Adjustment: International Constraints, Distributive Politics, and the State*, edited by Stephan Haggard, and Robert Kaufman, 139–171. Princeton: Princeton University Press, 1992.

Evans, Peter. "Transferable Lessons? Re-Examining the Institutional Prerequisites of East Asian Economic Policies." *The Journal of Development Studies* 34, no. 6 (1998): 66–86.

Evans, Peter. *Embedded Autonomy: State and Industrial Transformation.* Princeton: Princeton University Press, 1995.

Fearon, James D., and David D. Laitin. "Ethnicity, Insurgency, and Civil War." *American Political Science Review* 97, no. 1 (2003): 75–90.

Fukuyama, Francis. *State Building: Governance and World Order in the 21st Century.* London: Profile Books, 2005.

Garrett, Geoffrey. "The Politics of Structural Change: Swedish Social Democracy and Thatcherism in Comparative Perspective." *Comparative Political Studies* 25, no. 4 (1993): 521–547.

Gilpin, Robert. *War and Change in International Politics.* Cambridge: Cambridge University Press, 1981.

Hall, Peter A. "Policy Paradigms, Social Learning, and the State: The Case of Economic Policymaking in Britain." *Comparative Politics* 25, no. 3 (1993): 275–296.

Hay, Colin. "Crisis and the Structural Transformation of the State: Interrogating the Process of Change." *British Journal of Politics and International Relations* 1, no. 3 (1999): 317–344.

Hill, Hal. "The Political Economy of Policy Reform: Insights from Southeast Asia." *Asian Development Review* 30, no. 1 (2013): 108–130.

Hironaka, Ann. *Neverending Wars: The International Community, Weak States, and the Perpetuation of Civil War*. Cambridge: Harvard University Press, 2005.

Hirschman, Albert. "The Search for Paradigms as a Hindrance to Understanding." *World Politics* 22, no. 3 (1970): 329–343.

Hogan, John, and Ana Hara. "Country at a Crossroads: An Insight into How an Economic Crisis Led to Dramatic Policy Change." *Risk, Hazards & Crisis in Public Policy* 2, no. 3 (2011): 1–23.

Hogan, John, and Sharon Feeney. "Crisis and Policy Change: The Role of the Political Entrepreneur." *Risk, Hazards & Crisis in Public Policy* 3, no. 2 (2012): 1–16.

Jessop, Bob. *The Future of the Capitalist State*. Cambridge: Polity Press, 2002.

Katzenstein, Peter J. "International Relations and Domestic Structures: Foreign Economic Policies of Advanced Industrial States." *International Organization* 30, no. 1 (1976): 1–45.

Katzenstein, Peter J., ed. *Between Power and Plenty*. London: the University of Wisconsin Press, 1978.

Kingdon, John W. *Agendas, Alternatives, and Public Policies*. New York: Longman, 1995.

Krasner, Stephen D. *Defending the National Interest: Raw Materials Investment and U.S. Foreign Policy*. Princeton: Princeton University Press, 1978.

Krasner, Stephen. "US Commercial and Monetary Policy: Unravelling the Paradox of External Strength and Internal Weakness." *International Organization* 31, no. 4 (1977): 635–671.

Kuhn, Thomas. *The Structure of Scientific Revolutions*. Chicago: University of Chicago Press, 1962.

Migdal, Joel S. *Strong Societies and Weak States: State-Society Relations and State Capabilities in the Third World*. Princeton: Princeton University Press, 1988.

Öniş, Ziya, and Fikret Şenses. "Global Dynamics, Domestic Coalitions and Reactive State: Major Policy Shifts in Post-War Turkish Economic Development." *METU Studies in Development*, no. 34 (2007): 251–286.

Peters, B. Guy. "Shouldn't Row, Can't Steer: What's a Government to Do?" *Public Policy and Administration* 12, no. 2 (1997): 51–61.

Pierson, Paul, and Theda Skocpol. "Historical Institutionalism in Contemporary Political Science." In *Political Science: State of the Discipline*, edited by Ira Katznelson, and Helen V. Milner, 693–721. New York: W.W. Norton, 2002.

Robinson, Mark. "Hybrid States: Globalization and the Politics of State Capacity." *Political Studies* 56, no. 3 (2008): 566–583.

Rodrik, Dani. "When Ideas Trump Interests: Preferences, Worldviews, and Policy Innovations." *Journal of Economic Perspectives* 28, no. 1 (2014): 189–209.

Rotberg, Robert I. *When States Fail: Causes and Consequences.* Princeton: Princeton University Press, 2003.

Sartori, Giovanni. "Concept Misformation in Comparative Politics." *American Political Science Review* 64, no. 4 (1970): 1033–1053.

Sil, Rudra, and Peter Katzenstein. "Analytic Eclecticism in the Study of World Politics: Reconfiguring Problems and Mechanisms across Research Traditions." *Perspectives on Politics* 8, no. 2 (2010a): 411–431.

Sil, Rudra, and Peter Katzenstein. *Beyond Paradigms: Analytic Eclecticism in the Study of World Politics.* New York: Palgrave Macmillan, 2010b.

Tommasia, Mariano, and Andrés Velascoa. "Where are we in the Political Economy of Reform." *The Journal of Policy Reform* 1, no. 2 (1996): 187–238.

Waltz, Kenneth. *Man, the State and War: A Theoretical Analysis.* New York: Columbia University Press, 1959.

Weber, Max. "Politics as a Vocation." In *From Max Weber: Essays in Sociology*, edited by H.H. Gerth, and C. Wright Mills. 78. London: Routledge, 1948.

Weiss, Linda. *The Myth of the Powerless State: Governing the Economy in a Global Era.* Cambridge: Polity Press, 1998.

CHAPTER 3

Political Economy of Turkey (1980–2001)

This chapter deals with the institutionalization of a reactive Turkish state in a neoliberal setting between 1980 and 2001. Turkey pursued state-led import-substituted industrialization (ISI) during 1960–1980, following a balance of payments crisis in late 1950s and a coup d'état in May 1960. Accordingly, state heavily involved in the organization of the industrial production, closely governed trade and foreign exchange regimes, and controlled the resource allocation mechanisms through an active planning bureaucracy under the auspices of the State Planning Organization (SPO). In the financial realm, state-led developmental policies were supplemented by repressive measures such as ceilings on deposit and lending rates, credit rationing and subsidized credits to priority sectors through state banks, overwhelming taxation of financial transactions, entry and exit barriers to foreign banks, and the frequent use of the Central Bank as the ultimate creditor of the public finance. Despite certain achievements in terms of rapid industrialization and rather respected growth rates, the ISI regime was subject to high degrees of rent seeking since the governments' arbitrary discretion over the instruments of economic policies increased gradually. State-led regime paved the way for an inflationary bias and non-transparent exchange relationships between the state and well-entrenched interest groups thanks to the generously dispersed but loosely monitored subsidies, randomly imposed quotas, tariffs, and import licenses. In this period, state resources were increasingly diverted to

M. Kutlay, *The Political Economies of Turkey and Greece*,
International Political Economy Series,
https://doi.org/10.1007/978-3-319-92789-3_3

directly unproductive activities, which in turn paved the way for export pessimism toward the end of 1970s. Thus, Turkey mired into a severe economic and political regime crisis in 1980 with the accumulation of state's fiscal imbalances, balance of payment deficits, and external debt.

The governance paradigm that guided the Turkish political economy passed through sea change thanks to the major liberalization reforms following 1980. The initial reform activism, however, was gradually replaced by stagnation and inertia during 1990s. Turkish political economy is characterized by political instability and economic fragility in the wake of twenty-first century. In fact, during the period in question, Turkey's state capacity gradually deteriorated in a way that exacerbated the political economy problems. Thus, Turkey's integration into neoliberal globalization reflects the common patterns depicted by reactive states. This chapter discusses how institutional structures underlying state capacity were set out in a path-dependent way along domestic-international nexus, and how they, in turn, conditioned rent-seeking agency behavior during the internationalization of the Turkish economy. First part explains the political economy of the emergence of a reactive Turkish state in a neoliberal setting during 1980–1994. The second part discusses the 1994 economic crisis and explores why it did not lead to a paradigm chance in mainstream economic policies. The third part deciphers the consolidation of reactive Turkish state by concentrating on 1994–2001 period, which ended with the most devastating crisis in contemporary Turkey. The final part concludes the chapter.

3.1 Emergence of a Reactive State (1980–1994)

The year 1980 posed a critical juncture in Turkish political economy. The ISI regime came to an end with a major crisis and an alternative path emerged in state-market relations. Turkey adopted a new economic paradigm stamped by neoliberal-oriented January 24, 1980 decisions. The reform program was radical and far-reaching in the sense that it incorporated both short-term fiscal stabilization measures and long-term structural reforms. The crisis was a genuine exogenous shock that delegitimized prevailing policy paradigms and eroded the material power of the dominant policy coalitions flourished during the ISI regime. The strong external anchors also informed the direction of change in Turkey. The program, which was underwritten by the "cross-conditionality" of the IMF-World Bank double anchor, tipped the material and ideational balance decisively in favor of the free market model. Turkey received five consecutive loans from the World Bank to implement the reform program. IMF also involved in with a three-year stand-by agreement in June 1980. The amount and duration of the IMF-World Bank support, which Taylor dubbed as "a long leash," was unmatched in the credit history of these institutions.[1]

There were various aspects of the program, but two of them stand out. First, major trade liberalization took place in the post-1980 period. The average tariffs and non-tariff barriers were reduced considerably so that anti-export bias was removed. State also actively offered export subsidies and other forms of investment incentives to promote an export-oriented growth model. Second, all market prices, capital account, and financial transactions liberalized in a step-by-step fashion. The leitmotif of the liberalization reforms was to reduce the role of the state in the economy, which was expected to eliminate rent-seeking opportunities at the disposal of the state and the connected interest groups. Thus, post-1980 was conceived as an opportunity window to craft reform-oriented institutional setting to impose a disciplined economic regime. In retrospect, however, it became apparent that new policy path produced adverse incentives that underlined the gradual eradication of state capacity.

Domestic Political Context

The neoliberal reforms were coupled with radical political transformations in the post-1980. The military coup that took place on September 12, 1980, reshuffled the political arena, depoliticized social life, and rendered the civil society docile. The military monopolized the political arena during 1980–1983 as it banned all political parties and their leaders along with civil society organizations; thereby, liberalization reforms were implemented under intense suppression over distributional coalitions. Kenan Evren, the chief of the general staff who headed the military coup and became Turkey's seventh president in the aftermath, later admitted that "if 24 January decisions were not followed by 12 September military coup, I have no doubt that the reform program would have resulted in fiasco."[2] Following the restoration of multiparty democracy in 1983, therefore, the

[1] Lance Taylor, "The Turkish Experience: Summary and Comparative Notes," in Tosun Arıcanlı and Dani Rodrik, *The Political Economy of Turkey: Debt, Adjustment, and Sustainability* (London: Macmillan, 1990), 269.

[2] Milliyet Gazetesi, "12 Eylül Olmasaydı, 24 Ocak Kararları Fiyasko ile Sonuçlanırdı," January 7, 1991.

pendulum had swung in the opposite direction and populism made a strong call back in domestic political scene to capture the support of the hitherto excluded distributional coalitions. In this new institutional setting, similar to Greece, domestic political context in Turkey depicted major tenets of conflictual tendencies imbued by "strong legacy of populism [with an] overriding faith in charismatic leadership and a personalistic mode of governance characterized by a weak civil society."[3]

Turkey's post-1980 political context can be bracketed under two major episodes. The first episode refers to the "Özal decade" that covered the period from early 1980s up to 1989. Turgut Özal, a former undersecretary of the SPO, emerged as the key state agent in the design and implementation of the post-crisis liberalization reforms. Özal continued to play a key role after September 12, 1980, as deputy prime minister in charge of economic affairs in the interim military government. With the restoration of the multiparty democracy in late 1983, as the charismatic leader of the newly founded Motherland Party—ANAP in Turkish acronym, Özal reappeared as a key figure again, this time with a before-the-scenes role. He succeeded to outperform his political rivals in the first pseudo-democratic elections following the military coup and formed a single party government with a landslide electoral victory on November 6, 1983. Özal was a capable reformist state agent with strong leadership capabilities. Since he spent his lifetime at the highest echelons of the state bureaucracy, private sector, and acquired more experience at the World Bank, he established good connections with international and domestic policy communities. At the domestic realm, Özal enjoyed widespread legitimacy in the eyes of different segments of Turkish society. His hybrid ideology, which he called "four strands," combined elements of liberalism, political conservatism with Islamist connotations, welfarism and nationalism helped him transcend the traditional center-periphery divide in Turkish politics to a certain extent. In addition, Özal had a clear-cut economic reform program, the core elements of which were the elimination of all price controls, liberalization of trade and foreign direct investment, privatization of state economic enterprises, and restructuration of the banking system. It is fair to argue that during his time in the World Bank, Özal internalized the neoliberal model rising in the Anglo-Saxon world and strongly convinced that Turkey's deep-seated economic problems can only be resolved through a market-oriented paradigm.

[3] Ziya Öniş, *State and Market: The Political Economy of Turkey in a Comparative Perspective* (İstanbul: Boğaziçi University Press, 1998), 514.

The Özal government demonstrated strong commitment to its target-oriented reform program until mid-1980s. In the aftermath, alas, state's fiscal discipline waned mainly due to the distributional pressures emanated from the structural adjustment policies and emergent populist cycle. The principal losers of the January 24, 1980 decisions were fixed-wage earners, civil servants, and farmers. Since adjustment program was implemented under severe authoritarian conditions, the military government coercively suppressed the aforementioned distributive concerns. Thus, in a post-democratic setting, ANAP government faced with two conflicting rationalities and an apparent paradox: how to create broad-based support coalitions in a democratic polity and promote adjustment policies, simultaneously? Özal's response to this dilemma was to opt for a highly uncoordinated policy mix of expansionary fiscal policies, discretionary use of resources at the disposal of the state, and wink at corruption to form ad hoc electoral coalitions, what Waterbury called "coalition maintenance through state patronage."[4] Accordingly, this expansionary logic informed gradual detachment from institution-based procedures in the management of economy. Özal, in order to implement economic decisions in a swift way, recurrently inclined to sidestep the bureaucratic and legal procedures, which planted the seeds of uncontrolled populism in the years to come. Accordingly, cabinet degrees rather than acts of parliament constituted the essence of economic policy-making. Many of the key economic decisions regarding privatizations, state economic enterprises, trade and financial liberalization were taken within narrow inner circles instead of consultation with relevant bureaucracy and private interest groups (see below).

The fiscal spending decisions were also conducted along the same logic, mostly starting from mid-1980s onward. In this regard, the frequent use of extra-budgetary funds (EBFs) constitutes a novel fiscal policy related innovation.[5] Özal preferred to spend state's fiscal resources in a flexible manner, as it was the case in the creation of sizeable EBFs such as Mass Housing and Public Transportation Funds. EBFs proved to be useful instruments to disburse state's fiscal resources in a rather discretionary fashion beyond the purview of the Parliament. The number of EBFs ranged from 96 to 134 with total assets estimated to be around 3.5

[4] John Waterbury, "Export-Led Growth and the Center-Right Coalition in Turkey," *Comparative Politics* 24, no. 2 (1992): 133.

[5] Oğuz Oyan, "An Overall Evaluation of the Causes of the Use of Special Funds in Turkey and Their Place in the Economy," *Yapı Kredi Economic Review* 1, no. 4 (1987): 96.

to $5.7 billion in 1988. Their share in the budget gradually expanded and reached to a quarter of the total budget revenues in 1989.[6] The discretionary spending of the EBFs underpinned patronage politics in the economy with deteriorating impacts on the fiscal discipline of the state. Similarly, Özal's lukewarm approach to economic crimes, such as fictitious exports, as well as his tendency to wink at bribery and corruption, once again, reincarnated rent-seeking agency behavior, yet this time via different means.

One of the striking manifestations of the rampant populism was growing informal economy, which resulted in state's inability to implement an efficient and fair taxation system to improve its revenue base. Similar to Papandreou case in Greece, state's unwillingness, and to some extent, incapacity to extract resources from wealthier segments of society limited its taxation capacity. Thus, in the post-liberalization period, state's tax base could not be improved: The tax revenue over GNP declined from 16.8 percent in 1980 to 15 percent in 1989.[7] It is rather paradoxical that Özal's initial reform activism invited subsequent deterioration of state capacity; thereby, put Turkish political economy into a reform-biased path during 1990s. Informed by perverse practices of the previous decade, underpinned by destabilizing impacts of neoliberal globalization, and permeated by increasingly instable and polarized political context, the 1990s turned into a lost decade for the Turkish political economy.

The second phase of Turkish political context in the post-1980, therefore, refers to a string of "weak coalition governments" that covered the period from 1991 to 2002. In 1989, Özal had himself elected to the presidency. Despite the fact that Özal continued to manage ANAP behind the scenes through a loyal caretaker prime minister, Yıldırım Akbulut, the political competition exponentially intensified with the return of once banned veteran political figures. In September 1987 referendum, just over 50 percent of the citizens had voted in favor of lifting bans on more than 200 politicians imposed by military regime. These included two former prime ministers, Süleyman Demirel and Bülent Ecevit, and leading nationalist politician, Alparslan Türkeş. In an increasingly competitive political environment, the general elections in October 1991 brought a new era of

[6] Dani Rodrik, "Premature Liberalization, Incomplete Stabilization: The Özal Decade in Turkey," *NBER Working Paper Series*, working paper no. 3300 (1990): 24.

[7] Ziya Öniş and Steven Webb, *The Political Economy of Policy Reform in Turkey in the 1980s*, World Bank Working Papers, Paper no. 1059 (1992).

weak coalition governments. In this phase, political context in Turkey fits quite well into the category of polarized pluralism. Accordingly, consensus-based policy-making was sidelined, as a result of which political system gradually became dysfunctional. In that sense, Turkish political context resembles the Greek case as increasing polarization dominated the political agenda; the only difference was instable multiparty system in Turkey instead of two-party system established in the latter. In this decade, 11 coalition governments were established with an average lifespan of 449 days (see the next section below). The politics was perceived as a zero-sum game divided according to the ethnic and ideological cleavages.

In the first half of the decade, three highly uncoordinated and incoherent coalition governments were formed with an average duration of 479 days. True Path Party (DYP) and Social Democrat Populist Party (SHP) formed three successive coalition governments in the first half of the 1990s. The electoral base of the DYP-SHP coalitions was composed of the main losers of structural adjustment reforms of the previous decade. DYP was representing the center-right tradition in Turkey and its main support base was composed of the farming community, middle classes, and small- and medium-sized enterprises. On the other hand, SHP emerged as the representative of the weakening labor class. Both of these groups were the principal losers of regressive fiscal policies, which were put into implementation as part liberalization reforms: During 1980s, the share of agriculture in national income declined from 24 to 16 percent. Similarly, the share of wages and salaries also decreased from 27 to 14 percent, whereas rents, profits, and interest income jumped from 49 to 70 percent at the turn of the decade.[8]

Both DYP and SHP inclined to pursue high-wage policies to please their respective electorates. The emergent populist cycle that was triggered in the second half of the 1980s turned into a full-fledged neopopulism during DYP-SHP coalitions in the first half of 1990s. Farmers were supported through generous subsidies, labor class was compensated by high-wage increases, and industrial elite was backed by low tax burdens, low input prices provided via state economic enterprises, and clientelistic policy networks. During 1989–1993, just before 1994 economic crisis, the real wages were almost doubled, whereby the mark-up ratios of the industrial elite remained unchanged around 40 percent, which demon-

[8] Rodrik, "Premature Liberalization, Incomplete Stabilization: The Özal Decade in Turkey," *NBER Working Paper Series*, 24.

strates that state turned out to be the major looser of the populist expansion cycle.[9] In the first half of 1990s, the logic of short-lived coalition governments thus hampered coherent supply and consistent implementation of even the basic economic policies, let alone fostering state capacity to effectively reform domestic economy in line with the changing global dynamics.

In summary, the discretionary policy-making in the 1980s and collective action problems associated with weak coalition governments in the first half of 1990s as well as the contradictory logic of the DYP-SHP coalitions led to insurmountable governance problems. Domestic political context also informed the structure of state bureaucracy and shaped the main contours of the interaction between the state and domestic policy communities. Along these lines, next section will discuss the transformation of state's bureaucratic capacity during the period in question.

State Bureaucracy

State capacity literature suggests that bureaucracy plays a central role in terms of the production and dissemination of high-quality information so as to overcome collective action problems not only within state mechanisms but also between state actors and domestic policy communities toward the implementation of sustainable reforms. However, the existence of an insulated but highly coordinated and meritocratic core economic bureaucracy deemed a distant objective in the Turkish case. In the post-1980 period, state bureaucracy acquired neither "autonomy" nor "embeddedness."

First, the public sector in general and state bureaucracy in particular gradually expanded in the post-liberalization process. In a state-dominated economic structure, "politics was understood and defined as a strategy to build and sustain power by distributing material benefits generated by the state through clientelistic channels."[10] Similar to other reactive states such as Greece, bureaucracy became the battleground for political elite to capture the state and distribute material benefits through patronage networks in Turkey. In retrospect, one of the stated aims of the market-oriented

[9] Erinç Yeldan, *Küreselleşme Sürecinde Türkiye Ekonomisi* (İstanbul: İletişim Yayınları, 2011), 76.

[10] Erinç Yeldan and Ümit Cizre-Sakallıoğlu, "Politics, Society, and Financial Liberalization: Turkey in the 1990s," *Development and Change* 31, no. 2 (2000): 498–499.

reforms was to cure the hemorrhaging public sector through downsizing. The post-1980 developments, however, hollowed out these expectations. As stated in the previous section that restoration of democratic politics aggravated the distributional concerns of the political parties. In this context, state employment provided rewarding opportunities for political elite to satisfy the middle classes as well as to expand their political reach especially at the election episodes. In the early years of post-liberalization period, the number of staff positions in the public sector remained almost stable around 1.2 million. The Özal government pursued austere policies in compliance with ANAP's party program and the recommendations of the IMF and the World Bank. However, during the local election year in 1984, the number of staff rose to 1.29 million by 7.5 percent increase. In the general election year in 1987, the numbers made a big jump again with almost 10 percent increase and hit 1.49 million. Finally, the number of staff positions reached a new plateau with 1.81 million in the wake of 1994 economic crisis, 55 percent higher than the positions in 1980.[11] The state economic enterprises (SEEs) reflect another important dimension that disturbed fiscal discipline. The SEEs continued to be a major source of fiscal instability in the post-liberalization process, despite the frequent articulation of an entirely opposite rhetoric. The contribution of the SEEs to GNP expanded from 11 percent to more than 16 percent at constant prices during 1980s, and no substantial divestiture took place until 1988.[12]

The expansion of the public sector, however, should not be conflated with the increasing impact of the state bureaucracy on economic decision-making processes. Özal targeted the centralization of the economic governance. Therefore, he deliberately excluded traditional state bureaucracy from key decision-making processes. There were historical reasons for Özal to keep economic bureaucracy at arm's length: During the ISI period, economic bureaucracy adopted an inward-looking *étatiste* mindset and enjoyed excessive autonomy vis-à-vis the political elite. The traditional bureaucracy in Turkey was therefore imbued by "pathological bureaucratization" in the words of Heper that favored frequent state

[11] İzak Atiyas, "Uneven Governance and Fiscal Failure: The Adjustment Experience in Turkey," *The World Bank Private Sector Development Department Occasional Paper*, no. 17 (1995): 16–17.

[12] Ziya Öniş, "The Evolution of Privatization in Turkey: The Institutional Context of Public-Enterprise Reform," *International Journal of Middle East Studies* 23, no. 2 (1991): 170.

intervention and procedural maze.[13] Özal's utmost priority was to accelerate the decision-making processes and implement market-oriented reforms in a rather swift way. Accordingly, one of his catchwords was to put an "end to the protectionist and paternalistic state," and obviously, he conceived state bureaucracy as the guardian of this "the paternalistic state."

Özal therefore aimed at reducing the power of economic bureaucracy. He frequently stated that his aim was to circumvent the red tape and vested interests entrenched at the bureaucratic circles. To this end, traditional bureaucratic institutions were increasingly sidelined whereas new institutions were set up under the auspices of the prime ministry. For instance, the power of the Ministry of Finance and the power of the Ministry of Commerce were dramatically curtailed. Instead, an Undersecretariat of Treasury and Foreign Trade was created in the prime minister's office with extensive discretionary rights on state's fiscal decisions. Along the same logic, Department of Foreign Investment, Department of Investment, Export Promotion and Implementation, and Privatization Administration were created. All these new economic institutions were directly responsible to the prime minister and his office. The other key institutions of economic bureaucracy from the previous decades, namely SPO and Central Bank were already at prime minister's disposal so that "Özal came to have direct control over appointments to all top [bureaucratic] executive positions."[14]

The Public Personnel Law was also modified, which enabled the appointment of non-bureaucratic figures to the key posts of state economic bureaucracy. Özal appointed young, well-educated, and outward-oriented figures to the commanding heights of the economic bureaucracy. Most of these people, popularized as "Özal's princess" in the media, were US-educated, high-caliber figures with good connections at the international financial institutions such as the IMF and the World Bank. Özal's aim was to integrate Turkey with the Western economies. Accordingly, he conceived that the dynamism and vision of the newly appointed elite as valuable assets to achieve this goal. Despite new bureaucratic elite injected reform euphoria in the initial phases thanks to the high degree of insula-

[13] Metin Heper, "Negative Bureaucratic Politics in a Modernizing Context: The Turkish Case," *Journal of South Asian and Middle Eastern Studies* 1, no.1 (1977): 80.

[14] Ayşe Öncü and Deniz Gökçe, "Macro-Politics of De-Regulation and Micro-Politics of Banks," in Metin Heper, ed., *Strong State and Economic Interest Groups: The Post-1980 Turkish Experience* (Berlin and New York: Walter de Gruyter, 1991), 104.

tion they enjoyed vis-à-vis the statist bureaucracy and economic interest groups, the top-down and discretionary style of policy-making opened up a slippery slope that associated with a weakening of bureaucratic institutions. The economic bureaucracy lost its corporate identity that rendered core institutions' capacity to control widespread corruption and rent-seeking agency behavior in the private sector.

Turkish state's internal capacity also suffered from extensive policy fragmentation and incoherence, which was mostly emanated from frequent reshuffling of bureaucratic posts in the post-liberalization period. State capacity literature suggests that an organizationally coherent economic bureaucracy facilitates reform activism by undertaking coordinative and communicative roles, enhancing high-quality information flows, fostering trust and credibility of commitments, and reciprocity among societal actors and state elites.[15] The literature also proffers that bureaucratic insulation precedes policy coherence, which means that lack of insulation may easily pave the way for political patronage and arbitrary reshuffling of bureaucratic corps. In the Turkish context, from an historical point of view, economic bureaucracy succeeded to protect its turf and enjoyed a high level of insulation vis-à-vis political and economic elite during the ISI period, partially thanks to the lingering legacy of monist state tradition. However, "autonomy" of the Turkish bureaucracy was not accompanied by "embeddedness." In the post-liberalization period, increasing politicization and fragmentation of state bureaucracy eroded its autonomy while lack of embeddedness prevailed. The over-emphasis on the self-adjustment capacity of the markets and politically motivated appointments put bureaucratic coherence and coordination into serious jeopardy. As a result, the overwhelming majority of the key economic bureaucrats started to come and go with governments, which in turn exacerbated bureaucratic balkanization, policy fragmentation, and incoherence:

> Governments [in Turkey] heavily engaged in unrestrained patronage and nepotism. The resulting arbitrary reshuffling of bureaucrats involved all ranks politicized the bureaucracy and undermined esprit de corps.[16]

[15] Sylvia Maxfield and Ben Ross Schneider, eds., *Business and the State in Developing Countries* (Ithaca: Cornell University Press, 1997), 16–18.

[16] Jesse Biddle and Vedat Milor, "Economic Governance in Turkey: Bureaucratic Capacity, Policy Networks, and Business Associations," in Sylvia Maxfield and Ben Ross Schneider, eds., *Business and the State in Developing Countries* (Ithaca: Cornell University Press, 1997), 286.

In 1984, with Act 3046, ANAP government bypassed the restrictions of Public Personnel Law No 657. With this law, the governments obtained the right to recruit contract-based personnel in key institutions of economic bureaucracy through bypassing the written and oral exams. Following the Act 3046, the conversion of the public service managers to contract status significantly increased. For instance, the number of contract-based administrators was 674 in 1984, which rose to 26,578 in 1986.[17] For instance, the directorate of incentives and implementation, one of the most crucial bureaus of the SPO dealing with state subsidies to private sector, turned into a backyard for patronage-based appointments. Literally, 69 percent of bureaucrats were appointed on contract basis in this department.[18] The data, despite somewhat anecdotal and preliminary, hint that political elite found new ways to permeate into the functioning of the economic bureaucracy. Nevertheless, the worst was yet to come. In the 1990s, weak coalition administrations replaced single party governments of the previous decade. In this new political context, the state bureaucracy turned into a real battlefield of the rival political parties struggling for power in a polarized and populist political setting.

In summary, during 1980s and in the first half of 1990s, all three aspects of state's internal capacity suffered from administrative weaknesses due to the reasons endemic to the reactive states. Thus, economic bureaucracy could not play an active role in the economic decision-making processes.[19] As Boratav, Türel, and Yeldan unearth "decision making and implementation on rent-allocating activities definitely shifted into the prerogative of the political layer of the state structure as the upper bureaucracy was pushed increasingly into a passive position."[20]

Domestic Policy Coalitions

Turkish state's relations with domestic policy communities reflect typical features of "disjointed corporatism." Historically informed analysis suggests that transcendental state tradition, which precipitated ruling from

[17] Waterbury, "Export-Led Growth and the Center-Right Coalition in Turkey," *Comparative Politics*, 138.

[18] Biddle and Milor, "Economic Governance in Turkey: Bureaucratic Capacity, Policy Networks, and Business Associations," 296.

[19] Ibid., 297.

[20] Korkut Boratav, Oktar Türel, and Erinç Yeldan, "Dilemmas of Structural Adjustment and Environmental Policies under Instability: Post-1980 Turkey," *World Development* 24, no. 2 (1996): 378.

above, thwarted the development of civil society and social trust in Turkey. OECD data indicates that along with Greece, Turkey has the lowest levels of general trust, barely higher than Chile.[21] Given the unfavorable historical-institutional background and weak social capital, the bilateral relations between state and major economic interest groups remained state dependent, ad hoc, and lopsided—lacking rule-based and institutionalized reciprocal mechanisms.

In the same vein, peak associations in the labor and business sides fell short of expanding their reach, ensuring the commitment of their members, and overcoming the collective action problems vis-à-vis the state bureaucracy and political elite. Thus, domestic policy communities contributed little to the economic reform processes. Instead, fragmented exchange relationships between state and private interest groups informed rent-seeking patronage politics. There are four main peak associations in Turkey: the Confederation of Turkish Trade Unions (TÜRK-İŞ) and Confederation of Progressive Trade Unions (DİSK) on the labor side, and the Union of Chambers and Commodity Exchanges of Turkey (TOBB) and Turkish Industry and Business Association (TÜSİAD) on the business side.[22]

On the labor side, state played a crucial role in the organization of labor markets. However, state-labor relations in Turkey pose marked contrasts to the corporatist models of advanced Western economies. The weak power capacity of the labor class vis-à-vis the political and business elite also distinguishes the Turkish case from the Greek one. Trade unions in Turkey remained at the margins of the economic policy-making with little opportunity and capacity to influence reform processes noticeably, either in positive or negative ways. During 1960–1980, thanks to the relatively progressive elements of the 1961 Constitution and ensuing labor legislation enacted in 1963, labor unions progressively increased their voice at the political echelons. The tripartite corporatist arrangements, however, could not be crafted during the ISI period. On the contrary, mounting political polarization in the 1970s underpinned the radicalization of the Turkish labor movement. Despite TÜRK-İŞ, the only peak labor organi-

[21] OECD, *Society at a Glance, 2011: OECD Social Indicators* (Paris: OECD Publication Service, 2011).

[22] Independent Industrialists and Businessmen's Association (MÜSİAD in Turkish acronym) should also be taken into consideration as the representative of conservative business elite in Turkey. However, MÜSİAD was established in 1990 and emerged as an important business association in mid-1990s, especially during 2000s with the rise of Justice and Development Party governments. Therefore, I will discuss the role of MÜSİAD in Chap. 4.

zation up to late 1960s, remained state-dependent, new and more autonomous trade unions were established along the lines of ideological cleavages. Accordingly, DİSK, which was founded in 1967, was clearly the most radical one. The vortex of political and social violence that intensified in late 1970s spawned a destructive pattern of conflict and antagonism between the state and labor unions. Parallel to the economic bottlenecks associated with the ISI regime and accompanying political instability, the number of strikes skyrocketed in late 1970s. Accordingly, 39,901 workers joined strikes during 1979, which resulted in a total loss of 2.2 million working days. The announcement of the January 24 decisions struck a nerve with the labor class so much so that 84,432 workers poured into the streets in the first eight months of 1980 with a total loss of 7.7 million working days.

Following the September 12, 1980, intervention, military junta pursued very aggressive suppression policies to enervate the labor movement. All trade organizations, except TÜRK-İŞ, were banned. The 1955 trade union administrators were jailed, strikes were outlawed, and collective bargaining over wages was suspended.[23] Article 51 of the 1982 constitution, which was crafted by interim military regime and the ensuing labor code (Trade Unions Act No. 2821 dated March 5, 1983), institutionalized the peripheral status of labor unions. Accordingly, labor unions were not allowed to form any connections with political parties and their activities were restricted to their own strictly defined sectoral interests. In the absence of institutionalized social dialogue and tripartite corporatist agreements, labor unions were almost entirely excluded from economic policy-making processes in the post-1980 context.

The incoming civil governments did not instill any substantial attempt to empower the legal status of the labor class. Özbudun documented in detail that the legal framework for labor associations remained almost intact despite some marginal improvements achieved after 1987.[24] In the short term, the governments perceived weak labor as an opportunity to engineer real devaluations of the exchange rates and depressed wages to stimulate export-oriented growth model in an era characterized by post-

[23] Yıldırım Koç, "30. Yıl Dönümünde 12 Eylül Darbesi ve İşçi Sınıfı," *Mülkiye Dergisi* 43, no. 268 (2010): 57.

[24] Ergun Özbudun, "The Post-1980 Legal Framework for Interest Group Associations," in Metin Heper, ed., *Strong State and Economic Interest Groups: The Post-1980 Turkish Experience* (Berlin and New York: Walter de Gruyter, 1991), 41–53.

Fordist flexible production structures. In the medium term, however, it paved the way for a precarious legacy with long-lasting adverse impacts on the institutional relations of social dialogue and sustainable reform activism. The differences and similarities with the Greek case are worth noting at this point. In the Greek case, labor extensively politicized and was asymmetrically included into the political processes while labor movement was marginalized and almost completely excluded in the Turkish case. Both Papandreou's social democratic model and Özal's neoliberal paradigm, however, led to similar outcomes in terms of labor's role in reform processes since the mode of inclusion and exclusion paved the way for pervasive populism and fragmentation in the absence of institutionalized deliberation mechanisms that undermined consensus-based reform activism.

State's relations with business elite also reflected lopsided and state-centered equilibrium. State intervention remained the single most important variable that determined the fortunes and misfortunes of the business community in Turkey.[25] In fact, similar to other late industrialized economies, the very creation of capitalist class was state's pet project. From the commencement of the modern Turkish Republic, state assumed a market-making role for the capital holders. Especially during the ISI period, roughly spanned from 1960 to 1980, Turkish state provided lucrative subsidies, legal privileges, import licenses, and arbitrary protection mechanisms to the business elite. Thanks to the buoyant state support, big business expanded its activities: There were very few conglomerates in Turkey before 1963 whereas the number of the newly established ones increased by 19 in the 1960; and by 106 in the second half of 1970s.

The ISI period, however, underpinned the disjointed nature of corporatist state-business relations because over-dependence on state resources lacked regularized forms of consultation and reciprocal deliberation mechanisms. Thus, Buğra labels state-business relations in the pre-1980 period as "market repressive,"[26] which not only limited the role of business elite in the formulation and implementation of reform processes in a concerted and timely manner but also rasped the capacity of the state as it encour-

[25] Ayşe Buğra, *State and Business in Modern Turkey: A Comparative Study* (New York: State University of New York Press, 1994).

[26] Ayşe Buğra, "Political Sources of Uncertainty in Business Life," in Metin Heper, ed., *Strong State and Economic Interest Groups: The Post-1980 Turkish Experience* (Berlin and New York: Walter de Gruyter, 1991), 152.

aged pervasive rent seeking at the agency level. From this viewpoint the critical juncture emerged in 1980 created a new window of opportunity to reverse the past practices in state-business relations. As a matter of fact, Turkish business elite strongly supported Özal government in the initial phases. Ali Koçman, the then president of TÜSİAD, threw full support behind the economic liberalization program to the extent that he even glorified the January 24 decisions as nothing short of "miraculous."[27]

Özal was a former member of TÜSİAD and a top-executive in Sabancı Holding, one of Turkey's largest corporations. Thus, he was well attuned to the priorities of the business elite. In the first Özal government, for instance, 75 percent of the cabinet was composed of politicians who had worked in the private sector in their previous careers.[28] In his 20-seated cabinet, there were 5 economists and 11 engineers with some experience in economics.[29] Özal reflected his business-minded perspective in his foreign policy-making style as well. He did place central importance on economic interdependence with neighboring countries as a practical hand in Turkish foreign policy. Accordingly, Turkish business elite became an integral part of the official state visits Özal paid to foreign countries. The developments in the first half of mid-1980s indicate that burgeoning interaction channels provided new avenues for state-business cooperation and reciprocal deliberation. Despite this enabling background, the institutional basis of state-business relations could not be institutionalized in a way that would contribute to concerted economic policy-making and reform activism. In order to account for the factors that underlie asymmetric and fragmented nature of interest intermediation structures, we should first and foremost concentrate on the organizational characteristics of peak associations.

The first business association in Turkey was established at the behest of the state in 1950. The Union of Chamber and Commodity Exchanges of Turkey (TOBB) assumed a quasi-public role, since membership to TOBB was compulsory for all enterprises in the country. The over-politicization of the union activities in the 1970s and TOBB's exclusive emphasis on the interests of the merchants and small-scale entrepreneurs disentranced the

[27] Milliyet Gazetesi, "Koçman: '24 Ocak Kararları Mucizevi Bir Karardır,'" April 20, 1983.

[28] Yeşim Arat, "Politics and Big Business: Janus-Faced Link to the State," in Metin Heper, ed., *Strong State and Economic Interest Groups: The Post-1980 Turkish Experience* (Berlin and New York: Walter de Gruyter, 1991), 144.

[29] Milliyet Gazetesi, "Mühendisler Hükümeti," December 14, 1983.

big-scale business in the 1970s. Thus, 12 largest industrialists established their own association in 1971, named Turkish Industry and Business Association (TÜSİAD), which became the first voluntary business association in Turkey. TÜSİAD increased its economic and political might over the years. However, inter- and intra-organizational factors crippled its capacity to stand out as an independent power block vis-à-vis the state. First, various circles denounced TÜSİAD for "being a club of the rich" with a narrow membership base. Similarly, it received a lukewarm response from the TOBB. In fact, TOBB perceived itself as the sole legitimate representative of the business class in Turkey and rejected any proposal dispatched from TÜSİAD regarding the improvement of inter-organizational cooperation to overcome collective action problems the side of the capital holders. Second, TÜSİAD suffered from intra-organizational problems that hampered even the compliance of its own members. TÜSİAD members frequently bypassed their own organization and established personnel contracts with political elite to solve their problems.[30]

Inter- and intra-organizational cooperation failures and fragmented interest intermediation structures, therefore, provided ample room for clientelistic exchange relations between state and interest groups. The heterodox elements of the post-1980 economic policies amplified rent-seeking in state-business relations. Two policy instruments were frequently utilized during 1980s. First, investment-incentive regimes, incorporating various elements like exemptions from financial tax and stamp duty, foreign exchange allocation scheme, and favorable credits to business elite were implemented regularly. The incentive regime mostly targeted manufacturing industry to transform production structures and prioritized less developed regions, mostly the eastern parts of the country to overcome lopsided and unequal regional development of Turkish economy. The Turkish incentive regime, however, significantly diverged from the developmental state practices in one crucial aspect. The incentives were mostly delivered inefficiently as incentive contracts routinely violated, incentive schemes frequently changed, and the ratio of reciprocal fulfillment of contract obligations remained extremely low given the absence of an insulated economic bureaucracy capable of screening/monitoring projects, and fragmented nature of peak associations incapable of

[30] Şebnem Gülfidan, *Big Business and the State in Turkey: The Case of TÜSİAD* (İstanbul: Boğaziçi University Press, 1993).

ensuring the compliance of their members.[31] During 1980s, the fiscal costs of incentive supports amounted to 4–5 percent of GNP in annual terms,[32] which, in a path-dependent way, contributed to perverse exchange relationship between state and dominant policy coalitions and the subsequent fiscal crisis of the state in the incoming years.

Second, export-incentive regime was put into implementation in the post-liberalization process. Özal governments placed utmost emphasis on export-promotion strategies to achieve high and rapid economic growth. Export growth was also deemed crucial to mitigate the side effects of distributional conflicts, compensate the depressed domestic demand, and improve Turkey's international creditworthiness. Accordingly, a variety of export-incentive schemes were crafted, including tax rebates, cheap credits, and foreign exchange allocations. Baysan and Blitzer report that state subsidies allocated to manufactured exports amounted to 20 percent of total exports in the first half of 1980s.[33] In fact, state's extensive fiscal support had some initial positive impacts. In the reports of international organizations, the striking increase in Turkey's export performance that helped to overcome the dismal export pessimism of the ISI period was appreciated as the most salient feature of post-liberalization reforms. According to Turkish Statistical Institute, commodity exports increased 15.8 percent annually and reached 10.8 percent of GNP from just 4.2 percent during 1980–1989. Based on a government decree in July 1980 (amended in January 1984) 24 foreign trade companies, all of which except the 2 were affiliates of the Turkish big business, were established. Those qualified for foreign trade companies benefitted from a multitude of incentives in the form of tax rebates, duty free imports, and favorable credits from the state banks. The export-promotion strategies were designed explicitly to replicate the East Asian developmental model. Since the investment and export-promotion strategies were implemented without a proper emphasis on state's monitoring capabilities, however, rent-seeking policy networks among political elites, state banks, and industrial capital were persevered.

[31] Jesse Biddle and Vedat Milor, "Institutional Influences on Economic Policy in Turkey: A Three Industry Comparison," *World Bank Private Sector Development Department*, Occasional Paper no. 3, 1995.

[32] İsmail Arslan, *A Review of Turkish Incentive Systems* (Washington, DC: World Bank Publications, 1993).

[33] Tercan Baysan and Charles Blitzer, "Turkey's Trade Liberalization in the 1980s and Prospects for Its Sustainability" in Tosun Arıcanlı and Dani Rodrik, *The Political Economy of Turkey: Debt, Adjustment, and Sustainability* (London: Macmillan, 1990), 13 and Table 1.2.

In a rather stark contrast to East Asian developmental experiences, arbitrarily designed and poorly implemented incentive and export-promotion schemes led to perverse incentive structures and subsequent fiscal imbalances. It became public with infamous over-invoicing and "fictitious export" incidents that economic governance strategies informed rent-seeking behavior. According to the SPO calculations, "fictitious export" activities composed 15 percent of total exports in the 1980s. Öztürk reports however that SPO estimations prove rather conservative in comparison to other credible accounts, which hover around 30–35 percent.[34]

In summary, all three aspects adversely informed Turkey's state capacity in the post-liberalization juncture. First, political context was imbued by uncontrolled populism and increasing polarization. Second, the state bureaucracy suffered from "embeddedness" and "autonomy," which in turn expanded the reach of discretionary and fragmented economic policy-making. Third, domestic policy communities' mode of relationship with the state resembled disjointed corporatism so that labor unions and business elite could not contribute to the reform processes in a reciprocal and institutionalized manner.

3.2 1994 Economic Crisis: An Opportunity Missed?

The analysis so far suggests that internal and external capacity of the Turkish state remained weak during 1980–1994. However, the picture would remain incomplete if we just focus on the domestic phenomena. In this context, the rise of financial globalization and Turkey's peripheral integration into the liberalization processes played an adverse role, especially during 1990s. The mode of Turkey's exposition to financial globalization exacerbated economic fragilities because it was materialized before the rules of the game, namely robust institutions in charge of fiscal and financial regulation were introduced. In fact, full capital account liberalization in August 1989 was a personnel decision of Özal, which he took despite the contrary advice of economic bureaucracy.[35] The decision, once combined with instable macroeconomic fundamentals, populist political context, inept bureaucracy, and inward-looking state-business relations, a dangerous policy mix and a self-reinforcing vicious cycle were precipitated in the 1990s.

[34] Quoted in Özgür Öztürk, *Türkiye'de Büyük Sermaye Grupları: Finans Kapitalin Oluşumu ve Gelişimi* (İstanbul: SAV Yayınları, 2010), 140.

[35] Hasan Ersel, "The Timing of Capital Account Liberalization: The Turkish Experience," *New Perspectives on Turkey* 15 (1996): 45–64.

The public sector borrowing requirement (PSBR) rose steadily up to 1993 due to expansionary cycle that started in late 1980s. The PSBR reached almost 12 percent of GNP in 1993 up from 3.5 percent in 1986. The budget deficit widened substantially as state's revenue base could not be improved. Accordingly, the budget deficit over GNP, which used to be around 3 percent before 1989 reached at 6.7 percent as of 1993. The public debt also increased to more than 50 percent in 1994. The share of short-term debt over total debt rose from 12 percent in 1989 to more than 28 percent in 1993.[36] In the post-liberalization period, the governments deliberately kept interest rates very high to attract short-term capital for rolling over the public debt. State interest payments over GNP therefore rose from 1.4 percent during 1981–1985 to 7.7 percent in 1994. High interest rates led to the over-valuation of domestic currency, which in turn disturbed current account performance. Thus, current account deficit increased to 3.9 percent of GNP in 1993. Similarly, inflation remained very high around 65 percent partially due to the monetization of public debt.

Turkish economy faced an early test in 1994 due to worsening macroeconomic imbalances in a neoliberal setting. It is interesting to note at this point that Turkey's exposition to the periodic crises was earlier than the Greek case (see Chaps. 5 and 6), despite similar dynamics were at work in both countries. The most plausible explanation of this paradox lies in the broader institutional setting in which these two economies were operating at the time. Since Turkey was not a member of the EU, it was not cushioned against fiscal shocks because it did not enjoy the lucrative EU funds. Furthermore, Turkey heavily suffered from credibility problems and widespread uncertainty given the lack of the EU's shock-absorbing role. As a result, accumulation of the fiscal problems accompanied by an increasingly instable political arena led to an economic crisis in April 1994. In fact, all structural indicators hint that a crisis risk appeared on the horizons in early 1990s. The timing of the crisis, however, was determined by the reactions of international financial agents. In January 1994, two credit rating agencies, first Moody's and then Standard & Poor's, decreased Turkey's ratings. This decision triggered a crisis of confidence resulting in substantial outflows of short-term capital. Hence, the balance of payments crisis triggered

[36] OECD, *Economic Surveys, Turkey: 1994–1995* (Paris: OECD Publication Service, 1995), 1–3.

a rapid depreciation of the exchange rate, which forced the government to implement an IMF-backed stabilization program on April 5, 1994.[37]

The economic crises pose critical junctures to initiate paradigmatic reforms. In retrospect, however, the 1994 economic crisis did not pave the way for Turkey to reverse the vicious cycle that the Turkish economy was entrapped in. On the contrary, as will be elucidated in the following part, post-1994 witnessed further entrenchment of the rent-seeking relations, culminating with a devastating February 2001 crisis. In this sense, an analysis of 1994 crisis provides insights to better explicate the complex relationship between crises and reform outcomes. Why 1994 crisis could not be exploited as an opportunity window to address the fiscal and financial profligacy of the state? How did reform inertia endure in the post-1994 period?

The answer lies at the intersection of complex interactions at the domestic-external nexus. At the agency level, one should concentrate on Tansu Çiller as the main state agent responsible for the management of the economy. Tansu Çiller was an economy professor, who spent years in academia before she was appointed as the minister of state in charge of economic affairs in the DYP-SHP coalition headed by Süleyman Demirel. After President Özal unexpectedly passed away in March 1993, Demirel became the new president. Çiller succeeded him as the leader of the DYP and starting from June 1993, she served as the prime minister for almost three years. Therefore, Çiller was one of the major architects of the economic policies of the DYP-SHP coalition governments. She was also the chief planner and executor of the economic stabilization program after the crisis in 1994. It is interesting to note at this point that Çiller's technocratic and professional background partially resembles Simitis case in Greece. Despite her technical credentials, however, Çiller was not a reformist state agent—or policy entrepreneur—because she did not enjoy necessary legitimacy in the eyes of broader segments of the society and failed to inject adequate confidence to the policy communities during her position in the previous Demirel government. She also had weak interpersonal connections with the financial epistemic communities at the international level. In retrospect, Çiller could not develop a coherent and credible narrative to address the underlying structural problems both in the pre- and post-crisis intervals.

[37] Ziya Öniş and Ahmet Faruk Aysan, "Neoliberal Globalization, the Nation State and the Financial Crises in the Semi-Periphery: A Comparative Analysis," *Third World Quarterly* 21, no. 1 (2000): 129–130.

In the pre-crisis context, starting from the second half of 1993, Çiller made a substantial change in fiscal policies in order to reverse the rising tide of the public debt. Çiller aimed at reducing high interest rates in a rather swift way. In the government program, which was announced in June 1993, the government promised to "reduce real interest rates [as soon as possible] so as to alleviate the debt and interest burden on the public and private sector budgets, which in turn expected to curtail high inflation." The electoral base of the coalition government, mainly small- and medium-sized entrepreneurs were also suffering from exorbitant interest rates and high inflation. The method Çiller pursued, however, was far from being credible and convincing. In the last quarter of 1993, Çiller artificially tried to suppress the interest rates. Accordingly, the government canceled short maturity domestic debt auctions and started to rely on Central Bank resources for the service of the public debt. The idea was to force private financial elite to lend the government over more favorable interest rates. Over the last three months of 1993, Treasury used almost two billion dollars, 30 percent equivalent of Central Bank's foreign exchange reserves. In the first three weeks of 1994, the government used 53 percent of its Central Bank borrowing limit for that year.[38] The hazy messages Çiller sent to the investors, the successive economic policy mistakes, and the decreasing political credibility at the agency level triggered a vicious cycle starting from the beginning of 1994. Private investors showed no interest in government securities and rushed for foreign currency; thereby, the Treasury could not finance its debt up to the end of March, which eventually led to a crisis in April 1994. The Turkish lira depreciated by almost 70 percent and overnight interest rates jumped to 700 percent, an unprecedented level in Turkey's economic history. Inflation also reached three-digit plateau with 106.3 percent for the first time. On top of her economic policy mistakes, Çiller also had to shoulder the previous DYP-SHP government's unfulfilled reform promises under Demirel's leadership. The first DYP-SHP government program, which was announced on November 20, 1991, promised to fix state's fiscal problems and structural imbalances in the economy within 500 days. Thus, Çiller was also perceived as the successor of failed economic policies of the DYP-SHP coalition government.

[38] Fatih Özatay, "The 1994 Currency Crisis in Turkey," *The Journal of Policy Reform* 3, no. 4 (2000): 346–348.

Çiller's policy mistakes in the pre-crisis period, not surprisingly, adversely informed her post-crisis reform performance. In the aftermath of the crisis, the government announced an ambitious reform program, called 5th of April Decisions (5 Nisan Kararları). The program, which Çiller declared as Turkey's "economic war of independence,"[39] was composed of two main components: fiscal consolidation to mitigate public finance deficits and structural reforms to address the sustainability of fiscal balances in the medium term. First, the government adopted front-loaded correction measures to regain the confidence of the financial community. The short-term aim was to achieve primary public sector balance—which was a deficit of some 6.2 percent of GNP in 1993—and reduce PSBR to 6.2 percent of GNP—which was around 12.5 percent of GNP in 1993. To attain these goals, program foresaw immediate price increases in the products of state economic enterprises around 70–100 percent, introduction of a number of one-off tax measures—composing 1.6 percent of GNP, significant reduction in public sector real wages, and reduction of budgetary transfers to state economic enterprises around TL16 trillion.[40] Also, it was declared to dismiss 18,000 public sector workers, to freeze all on-going public investments, and cancel the on-going public procurements.[41] Second, 5th of April Decisions set ambitious aims for structural reforms. These included measures to downsize state economic enterprises in line with a comprehensive liberalization scheme, labor market reforms, and extensive supply and demand side reforms to improve efficiency and equality in the taxation system, restructuring of the bankrupted social security system, and introduction of new competition regulations to cope with the European firms in the post-Customs Union period.[42]

The program achieved some degree of initial success in terms of fiscal consolidation. The PSBR was reduced to 6.5 percent of GNP and budget deficit was curtailed to 4 percent of GNP. Thanks to fiscal consolidation and high economic recovery, the public debt-GNP ratio declined from 58 percent to 48 percent in one year.[43] The reform program also covered certain measures that laid the foundations of a nascent regulatory state in

[39] Milliyet Gazetesi, "İktidarın Son Şansı," April 5, 1994.

[40] OECD, *Economic Surveys, Turkey: 1994–1995* (Paris: OECD Publication Service, 1995), 24–27.

[41] Milliyet Gazetesi, "Ekonomide Sıkıyönetim," April 4, 1994.

[42] OECD, *Economic Surveys, Turkey: 1994–1995*, 34–54.

[43] OECD, *Economic Surveys, Turkey: 1995–1996* (Paris: OECD Publication Service, 1996), 20–22.

the medium term. In 1994, the government enacted a privatization law (law 4046), as a result of which high privatization council, privatization administration, and privatization fund were established. Similarly, initial steps were also taken toward the autonomy of the Central Bank in its relations with the Treasury and other state enterprises. Some partial amendments were introduced in the banking law (law 3182) that targeted the regulation of ill-functioning financial sector. That being said, Çiller government mostly satisfied with short-term-oriented stabilization measures and did not put most of the structural reforms into implementation. The proper realization of the privatization law, for instance, was constantly delayed up until the elections in October 1995. The privatization implementations remained very low around $572 million in 1995, which was barely above the term average during 1991–1995. OECD reports hint that all other important structural reforms highlighted in the program, like tax reform, social security reform, agricultural reforms, and reform of the SEEs shared the same destiny. Thus Çiller's weak commitment to the implementation of reform program created significant ownership problems at the agency level. However, the lack of a reformist agent capable of developing coherent reformist narrative, demonstrating the political will, and overcoming credibility of commitment problems constitutes just one side of the story. One should also concentrate on the enabling/constraining factors that were at work at a crisis juncture to better explicate the relationship between crisis and potential reform outcomes. Accordingly, four aspects are of particular importance.

First factor concerns the depth of the crisis. A deep economic crisis redistributes the power balances within the domestic system and opens up opportunity windows to put a decisive end to the populist policy cycles. It also tends to delegitimize the existing paradigms that shape state-market relations. From these two particular points of view, 1994 crisis was not deep enough to disturb the established patterns and the dominant policy paradigm backing the existing mode of relations. The quick recovery in 1995 and the relatively high, but certainly unsustainable, growth rates in the subsequent years underpinned the sense of complacency. Despite economic output decreased by 6.1 percent and capital outflow reached around $4.2 billion in 1994, growth rates bounced back in the immediate aftermath. Turkish economy registered a swift recovery of 4.8 percent in 1995, 8.5 in 1996, and 8.4 in 1997.[44] It is true that three banks, TYT Bank,

[44] Turkish Statistical Institute, *Statistical Indicators 1923–2011* (Ankara: Turkish Statistical Institute), 754.

Marmarabank, Impexbank declared bankruptcy in the wake of the crisis. However, they were too small to engender systemic risks in the financial sector. Furthermore, public confidence was restored steadily as the government provided full insurance that covered all savings deposits denominated in domestic and foreign currency.[45] In summary, 1994 economic crisis, despite revealed the fragility of the existing fiscal and financial regime, nevertheless, not deep enough to disturb or dismantle the underlying populist cycle.

Second, in the wake of the crisis, domestic political context played a very constraining role. The coalition government was on the knife's sharp edge due to serious corruption allegations. Çiller was under cross fire for hiding the true size of her wealth. It was publicized in the media that Çiller acquired several properties in the US including a villa, shopping mall, hotel, and a flat, which she did not declare previously.[46] Therefore, though indirectly, question marks aroused regarding government's willingness to arrest the deterioration of the fiscal imbalances and misutilization of public funds. The divergence in the preferences of the coalition partners was also inescapably intensified the credibility of commitment problems. The government partners were struggling hard to control state resources in order to broaden their own electoral base. In this regard, the timing of the reform program was telling that reveals the degree of ownership and commitment problems. On January 31, 1994, the then governor of the Central Bank of Republic of Turkey, Bülent Gültekin resigned since, according to him, "Çiller government had not [genuine] political will to effectively implement [necessary] economic reform measures."[47]

Furthermore, the reform package was not a product of consensus reached among coalition members. Murat Karayalçın, the coalition partner, later admitted the high level of non-coordination within the government by saying that he "was not informed by Çiller about the full content of the reform package before the press conference on 5th of April decisions."[48] He, in fact, learned the many details of the program during the press statement. Not surprisingly, therefore, implementation phase was subject to insurmountable collective action and credibility of com-

[45] OECD, *Economic Surveys, Turkey: 1995–1996*, 50.
[46] Milliyet Gazetesi, "Çiller'in ABD'deki Serveti," June 17, 1994.
[47] Milliyet Gazetesi, "Çiller'i Şok Eden İstifa," February 1, 1994.
[48] Mehmet Ali Birand, *Son Darbe 28 Şubat* (İstanbul: Doğan Kitap, 2012).

mitment problems as privatization, tax regulation, and pension reforms were first delayed and then entirely shelved. Whereas the evaluation of whether the reform program was desirable is beyond the scope of this study, one should acknowledge that the leaders of the DYP-SHP coalition government failed to maintain commitment to the very program they crafted in the first instance. The opposition parties also declined to support the reform program. The main opposition party, ANAP categorically rejected the reform measures. ANAP leader, Mesut Yılmaz, criticized the policy mix of the reform program on the ground that it would lead to "social upheavals."[49]

The junior opposition party, the Welfare Party (RP in Turkish acronym) also categorically rejected the stabilization measures. Necmettin Erbakan, the leader of the RP, argued that single-mindedly imposed harsh austerity measures would further "impoverish middle-classes and exacerbate inflationary pressures."[50] Erbakan put emphasis on industrialization and argued that decisions include virtually nothing to achieve this goal. It is therefore apparent that not only the coalition partners but also the opposition parties opted for myopic and polarizing political maneuvers rather than prioritizing consensus-based policy-making. Furthermore, the political context was over-loaded with non-economic problems at the time. Accordingly, the escalation of the military conflicts in the southeastern provinces of the country adversely informed the public agenda and diverted government's attention from the economic reforms. The fight against the PKK (Kurdish Workers Party) exacerbated the already delicate fiscal balances. The military expenditure was officially estimated to be almost around 4.0 percent of GNP in this period. In an increasingly unstable political setting, therefore, urgently needed structural reforms were delayed.

Third, labor unions and business elite also did not play enabling roles regarding the implementation of the economic reform program, albeit for different reasons. The crisis could not be transformed into an opportunity window to initiate major policy changes through the creation of new winning coalitions, not only because of the political leadership and ownership problems but also because of the asymmetric distribution of austerity burdens. In fact, 5th of April 1994 decisions put the onus squarely on the shoulders of labor class and fixed-wage earners. The gov-

[49] Milliyet Gazetesi, "Yılmaz: 'Paket Kötü Bir Kopya,' " April 6, 1994.
[50] Milliyet Gazetesi, "Yılmaz Dinledi, Erbakan Uyardı," April 5, 1994.

ernment accommodated the fiscal disequilibrium by the downward flexibility of the wage labor. In a sense, labor bore the brunt of the adjustment burden almost single-handedly. Concurrently, the manufacturing real wages declined by 30.1 percent in the private sector and 18.1 percent in the public side of the economy.[51] Not surprisingly, as a result, major representatives of the labor unions, that is, DİSK and TÜRK-İŞ, and various sectoral-level unions launched uncoordinated and local-level ad hoc rallies to avert deterioration in the real wages, dismissal of public sector workers, and reverse privatization decisions. TÜRK-İŞ president, Bayram Meral, for instance, dismissed the program: "the government did not consult to TÜRK-İŞ and our recommendations were not taken into consideration. It was designed according to the IMF and the World Bank prescriptions."[52] Despite labor unions in the Turkish context were relatively less powerful than their counterparts in Greece, the disjointed relationships between state and labor created various problems to instigate a coherent reformist paradigm.

Business elite also showed little genuine interest in reforming the fiscal fault lines in the economy. In the first instance, TÜSİAD developed an increasingly skeptical stance toward Çiller government before the crisis due to Çiller's "frequently changing and uncertain economic policies."[53] Big business even considered the reform package as "the last chance of Çiller government" and declared conditional support to the economic program.[54] The reluctant initial support rapidly turned into severe criticisms. TÜSİAD chairman, Halis Komili, argued just one month after the program that "there are two keys to overcome this crisis: flawless implementation [of the program] and trust environment. The government lost both of these keys."[55] As a matter of fact, finance capital did not display genuine will for a paradigm change in state-market relations. Two particular mechanisms were at work that helped big business to shield itself from the negative repercussions of the crisis, which in turn underpinned complacency and reform-biased behavior. First, big conglomerates, once again, veered to export activities because of the currency depreciation and contraction in domestic demand. Yeldan calculates that mark-up ratios of pri-

[51] Erinç Yeldan, "Neoliberal Global Remedies: From Speculative-Led Growth to IMF-Led Crisis in Turkey," *Review of Radical Political Economics* 38, no. 2 (2006): 199.

[52] Milliyet Gazetesi, "Ekonomik Pakete Tepki Yağdı," April 6, 1994.

[53] Milliyet Gazetesi, "TÜSİAD Çiller'e Bir Şans Daha Verdi," February 12, 1994.

[54] Milliyet Gazetesi, "TÜSİAD'tan Hükümete Zorunlu Destek," April 8, 1994.

[55] Milliyet Gazetesi, "TÜSİAD Çiller'e Savaş Açtı," May 5, 1994.

vate capital remained very high around 40 percent during 1989–1993 and reached to a new plateau of 47 percent in 1994.[56] Second, financial and industrial firms continued to exploit rent-seeking opportunities in the aftermath of the crisis. In the pre-crisis period, a significant part of industrial and financial community continued to heavily engage in non-productive activities. In fact, the financial elite implicitly backed reactive state policies in order to secure lucrative profit opportunities extracted from treasury bills that yielded very high rates of returns in real terms. Thus, financial liberalization not only provided perverse incentive structures for political elite to prolong populist cycles but also dramatically altered the way through which state's fiscal profligacy is financed.

In this perverse institutional setting, rather than expanding the tax base, the public deficits were increasingly financed through domestic financial agents, who in turn borrowed from international markets with reasonable interest rates and extended these credits to the state at mind-blowingly high profit margins. Credits extended by commercial banks increased by 8.3 percent annually in the period preceding the crisis. Similarly, the share of foreign liabilities to non-residents over total liabilities sharply increased from 7 percent (1990) to 14.1 percent (1993) of the domestic financial sector.[57] Even the industrial elite took advantage of state's fiscal profligacy not only by extracting poorly regulated subsidies and taking part in public procurement contracts but also by heavily investing in government bonds through affiliated banks. For instance, the share of profits from non-manufacturing activities in total operating profits rose from 15.3 percent (1982) to 54.6 percent (1994) of the largest industrial firms.[58] Therefore, big business was able to shield itself from the side effects of the crisis and ensure profits thorough rentier activities, which explains why they showed no genuine interest in changing established economic paradigm in the aftermath of the 1994 crisis.

Finally, the absence of a strong external anchor also hindered effective formulation and consistent implementation of a credible reform program. The 5th of April decisions were supplemented by a standard IMF stand-by agreement. However, the IMF anchor ceased to exist after a short period as swift economic recovery invited complacency effects. Apart from the lack

[56] Yeldan, *Küreselleşme Sürecinde Türkiye Ekonomisi*, 76.

[57] Özatay, "The 1994 Currency Crisis in Turkey," *The Journal of Policy Reform*, 337–339.

[58] İstanbul Sanayi Odası, *Türkiye'nin 500 Büyük Sanayi Kuruluşu* (İstanbul: İSO Yayınları, 1995), 70.

of political commitment and domestic ownership problems, the reform program was in fact reflecting the main postulates of the Washington consensus that advocated financial liberalization, privatization, and deregulation. However, part of Turkey's fiscal and financial problems was emanated from its integration into financial globalization with weak state capacity, which underestimated the crucial intervening role of the institutional regulatory mechanisms. Thus in the post-1989, state capacity to regulate domestic financial system was significantly jeopardized. Moreover, similar to the EU factor in the Greek case, financial globalization opened up escape avenues for the political elite to postpone economic reform processes because it provided new opportunities to roll-over the state deficits. The economic stability program addressed none of these problems because it was designed according to the dominant ideational paradigm that reflected all weak spots of the Washington consensus. The EU anchor that could offer a set of incentives and conditionality to encourage substantial reforms was also absent in the Turkish context during 1990s. Despite Turkey launched Customs Union with the EU in 1995 that paved the way for the elimination of tariffs and quotas and the promulgation of a regulation law, the Customs Union fell short of fixing the fiscal mismanagement.

3.3 Consolidation of a Reactive State (1995–2001)

The 1994 economic crisis did not invite a new economic regime. None of Turkey's major economic problems were addressed in the wake of the crisis. On the contrary, the post-1994 period witnessed the consolidation of a reactive Turkish state, characterized by recalcitrant reform inertia. The lack of an imaginative leap of statecraft constituted the single most delineating characteristic of the domestic political context. The political plane took a turn for the worse in the second half of 1990s due to acute political polarization, political regime concerns, and serious corruption allegations. In fact, the period in question refers to one of the most instable and polarized episodes in Turkish politics. During 1995–2002, six coalition governments were formed with an average lifespan of 376.3 days. Three of them were minority governments that were backed by other political parties in the parliament, which exposed the governments vulnerable to all kind of political engineering and short-term-oriented tug-of-wars.

The coalition governments were highly fragile and ideologically incommensurable that consensus-based reform activism proved to be beyond the possibility frontier. The coalition governments reflected uneasy political combinations: Islamist and center-right parties (DYP-RP government); center-right and center-left parties (ANAP-DSP-DTP and ANAP-DSP-DYP governments); and center-right, center-left, and ultra-nationalist parties (DSP-MHP-ANAP). Thus, ideological rifts among coalition partners emerged as ubiquitous impediments for a coherent supply and consistent implementation of economic policies. In addition to the intra-governmental collective action problems, two main political cleavages polarized the political agenda during the period in question.

The first one was the intensification of ethnic tensions. The armed conflict between the state security forces and the PKK escalated in the second half of the 1990s with devastating impacts on political, social, and economic life. The annual number of deaths reached 4570 during 1995–1999. In the midst of a severe political regime crisis in 1997, the death toll increased to 8234, an unprecedented number over the history of the conflict.[59] Around 30 percent of the population living in the southeastern provinces was forced to move into the western and southern metropolitan areas. Yükseker reports that more than one million people had migrated from the region, overwhelming majority of which was informally employed in the precarious job market.[60] The massive human mobilization led to acute polarization with devastating impacts on political, social, and economic stability.

Second political cleavage that aggravated political polarization in the post-Cold War context was the revitalization of traditional schism between secular establishment and the rising tide of political Islam. In fact, "the resurgence of Islam has been one of the defining and constitutive elements of the changing nature and formation of Turkish modernity since the 1980s, and this has had a significant impact on Turkish secularism by causing its recent crisis."[61] The ineptitude of mainstream political parties in governing distributional conflicts disenchanted masses, which in turn set a fertile background for the spectacular rise of the RP under the leadership

[59] Milliyet Gazetesi, "26 Yılın Kanlı Bilançosu," June 26, 2010.

[60] Deniz Yükseker, "Neoliberal Restructuring and Social Exclusion in Turkey," in Ziya Öniş and Fikret Şenses, eds., *Turkey and the Global Economy: Neo-liberal Restructuring and Integration in the Post-Crisis Era* (Oxon: Routledge, 2009), 266–267.

[61] E. Fuat Keyman, "Modernity, Secularism and Islam: The Case of Turkey," *Theory, Culture & Society* 24, no. 2 (2007): 223.

of Necmettin Erbakan. RP distinguished itself from the mainstream right- and left-wing political parties by adopting an explicit Islamist agenda. In 1995 general elections, RP increased its share of the national vote to 21.4 percent, which catapulted it into the leading political party in the country. After a series of unsuccessful coalition formation attempts among major parties, RP-DYP coalition emerged as the only alternative under the premiership of Erbakan. RP-DYP government was unmatched in Turkey's political history since for the first time an Islamist party obtained mandate to rule the country. The rise of the RP hit a raw nerve, especially among the circles in the military, which perceived itself as the sole guardian of the secular foundations of the Republic. RP was heavily critical of the traditional notion of secularism that was staunchly advocated by mainstream political and bureaucratic establishment. On the other side of the coin, according to military, the danger was imminent. After almost one year of political tug-of-war, the military finally flexed its muscles by intervening into the political plane on February 28, 1997, for the fourth time since 1946. The "post-modern coup," as the Secretary General of Turkish General Staff then coined the term, initiated a process that precipitated resignation of the RP-DYP coalition government but proved unable to check the rising tide of instant political polarization and instability.

Since the aim of this section is not to enter into a detailed political economy analysis of the rise of Islamist political movements in contemporary Turkey, we should again turn our attention to the way in which political context conditioned interest functions of political and economic agency in mid-1990s. Two strands stand out. First, it created imperatives for weak coalition governments to opt for non-transparent and non-accountable ways of utilizing state largesse to prolong their terms in power. Political parties' lackluster record of democratic accountability and legitimacy markedly weakened state capacity to impose fiscal and financial discipline and steer pro-reform coalitions toward this direction. Second, the rise of identity-dominated zero-sum political outlook legitimized favoritism and non-economic use of state resources along the lines of political "we vs. the rest" divisions, pure and simple. Thus, fierce political competition and conflict-prone policy-making motivated the political elite to capture the state so as to control rent distribution channels.

In summary, due to the imminent fault lines highlighted above, the political structure was not conducive to the formation of "a social pact or a more corporatist formal pact designed to build a consensus around anti-inflationary strategy [and reform-oriented outlook]."[62] Thus, similar to the Greek case, uncontrolled public expenditures turned into the predominant electoral survival strategy that led to a self-defeating debt trap. How did it become possible to sustain this low-level equilibrium?

At the intersection of international and domestic dynamics, one should cast light on the ominous give and take relationships between the state and domestic policy coalitions, since the latter played a conduit role that linked Turkish economy to the financial globalization processes. Turkey's integration into international markets was mediated by bank-based domestic financial system. The banking system became increasingly critical for Turkish political economy in this period. Two major mechanisms linked the state to the dominant policy networks along domestic-global nexus. First, public banks had become the main outlets of state's fiscal profligacy. Given the lack of regulatory state capacity, two largest public banks were totally exposed to the disposal of the governments. Ziraat Bankası, the largest public bank at the time, extended heavily subsidized credits to the farming community whereas Halk Bank served the small- and medium-sized entrepreneurs. As highlighted in OECD reports, credit allocation and entry-exit mechanisms of the banking system was "highly politicized" in this period.[63] State banks, which controlled more than 45 percent of total assets in the sector in 1990 and 35 percent in 1999, operated in line with "bad credits to good friends" principle.[64] The evidence confirms that the rent-seeking coalitions formed among corrupt politicians, state bureaucrats including military elite, and major private financial and industrial groups siphoned-off the state banks so that "duty losses" increased dramatically to 13.3 percent of GNP in 1999 up from 2.2 percent in 1995. In the wake of 2001 economic crisis, the duty losses of the public banks skyrocketed to $25 billion, accounting for 16 percent of GNP.[65]

Second, private banks ceased to play an intermediary role between investors and savers. The financialization of the domestic economy under extremely lax prudential regulations and ever-expanding fiscal profligacy

[62] Ziya Öniş, "Democracy, Populism, and Chronic Inflation in Turkey: The Post Liberalization Experience," *Yapı Kredi Economic Review* 8 (1997): 37.

[63] OECD, *Economic Surveys, Turkey: 2002* (Paris: OECD Publication Service, 2002), 80.

[64] OECD, *Economic Surveys, Turkey: 2001* (Paris: OECD Publication Service, 2001), 17–18.

[65] Fatih Özatay and Güven Sak, "Banking Sector Fragility and Turkey's 2000–01 Financial Crisis," *Brookings Trade Forum* (Washington, DC: Brookings Institution Publications, 2002), Table 2.

had profound effects on the behavior and expectations of private financial agents. The private banks heavily borrowed from the foreign markets with dollar-denominated, mostly short-term, debt instruments and directed these credits to the state sector. Since state turned into an unsinkable customer paying high real interest rates, "an enormous and unsustainable network of some 80 private banks with no connection with the real sector emerged to take advantage of quick returns from public debt."[66] The pace of rupture between the financial and industrial aspects of the economy was striking: During 1990s, the real gross domestic product grew just by 3.4 percent per annum, whereby the real rate of growth in banking assets was more than 13 percent.[67] The misutilization of the existing funds and perverse functioning of the financial system eroded the intermediary function of the banking system: The credits' share in total bank assets declined from 47 percent in 1990 to 32.8 percent in 2000. In the same period, the credit over deposit ratio declined from 84 percent to 51 percent. Similarly, the share of government bills and bonds in total bank deposits increased from 10 to 23 percent during 1990–1999.[68]

Industrial capital had also partaken in the directly unproductive rent-seeking cycle. The business elite demonstrated no genuine interest in reforming the Turkish financial and fiscal system because it captured the lion's share of the rents created by reactive state practices. This reached its zenith in the second half of 1990s. In this period, the widespread corruption allegations linking political parties, state bureaucrats, business elite, and media moguls dominated the headlines of the newspapers. Thus, the state-business relations in the second half of 1990s fully approximated to reform-biased rent-seeking policy networks. Accordingly, fiscal resources were misallocated via "political credits"—to quote a leading Turkish businessman—channeled to the "good friends" in the private sector, non-

[66] Ümit Cizre and Erinç Yeldan, "The Turkish Encounter with Neo-Liberalism: Economics and Politics in the 2000/2001 Crisis," *Review of International Political Economy* 12, no. 3 (2005): 391.

[67] Erol Balkan and Erinç Yeldan, "Peripheral Development under Financial Liberalization: The Turkish Experience," in Neşecan Balkan and Sungur Savran, eds., *The Ravages of Neoliberalism: Economy, Society and Gender in Turkey* (New York: Nova Science Publishers, 2002), 40–43.

[68] Güzin G. Akın, Ahmet F. Aysan, and Levent Yıldıran, "Transformation of the Turkish Financial Sector in the Aftermath of the 2001 Crisis," in Ziya Öniş and Fikret Şenses, eds., *Turkey and the Global Economy: Neo-liberal Restructuring and Integration in the Post-crisis Era* (Oxon: Routledge, 2009), 74.

transparent privatization implementations, and ineffective tax management and public procurement mechanisms.

In addition to the traditional mode of rent extraction mechanisms, financialization tendency also diverted industrial actors' attention from fixed investments to financial arbitrage gains through treasury bills. Since governments opted for foreign capital to finance public deficits, real interest rates remained significantly high during 1990s, which in turn emerged as one of the risk-free income sources for industrial capital. It is no coincidence that almost all large-scale holding companies acquired their own banks in 1990s. Fourteen new banks, which were directly affiliated with industrial conglomerates, were established during 1990s. Financial revenues to net profits before tax ratio increased from 24 percent in 1985 to 219 percent in 1999 of the biggest 500 manufacturing firms in Turkey.[69] At the turn of the century, total internal and external debt stock increased to almost 90 percent of GNP, which was just 47 percent in 1990 and 60 percent in 1995. Uncontrolled populism and ineptitude of weak governments in governing distributional conflicts transformed the state budget into a lucrative rent transfer mechanism. Accordingly, budget deficit increased from 4 percent of GNP to 10.2 percent in 2000, public debt rose to almost 60 percent of GNP, and interest payments over state debt rose steeply to unbearable levels with 16.2 percent of GNP in 2000. The annual interest payments of public debt devoured more than 75 percent of state's total tax revenue. Similarly, PSBR jumped to 15.5 percent in 1999 and then declined to 12.5 percent of GNP.

3.4 Conclusion

This chapter explicated the consolidation of a reactive state in Turkey during 1980–2001. The January 24, 1980 decisions constitute a historical threshold that embarked on sea change in Turkish political economy under the leadership of Turgut Özal. For better or worse, Turkey accomplished major economic transformation from an ISI-led regime to export-oriented neoliberal model. As proposed by reactive state framework, the paradigm change was precipitated after a deep economic crisis. The post-liberalization process, however, was accompanied by gradual deterioration of state capacity. First, political context aligned toward new forms of populism in late 1980s and took a shape of polarized multiparty competition

[69] Yeldan, *Küreselleşme Sürecinde Türkiye Ekonomisi*, 156.

during 1990s, which informed exclusionary policy-making. Similar to the Greek case, state was perceived as an arena to be captured—rather than governed—by competing interest groups. Second, state bureaucracy was sidelined as discretionary decision-making infiltrated into the political context. Third, the path-dependent historical configuration of state-business and state-labor relations informed fragmented and rent-seeking exchange patterns. Thus, economic and political opportunities, which were structured by the state, led to self-reinforcing processes for the entrenchment of clientelistic policy coalitions.

Turkey's integration into vagaries of financial globalization without robust institutional regulatory mechanisms also aggravated fiscal problems. In fact, Ponzi-cum-funding-opportunities enabled policy-makers to postpone necessary reforms so that Turkey faced an early test in 1994. The economic crisis, however, did not invite substantial reforms in Turkish fiscal and financial system. Status quo ante was reproduced because (a) crisis was not deep enough to deteriorate the legitimacy of predominant paradigms and disturb the existing mode of state-market relations, and (b) agency and institutional-level dynamics were unfavorable to initiate any paradigmatic change in the aftermath of the crisis. In his magnum opus, Keynes warns "that speculators may do no harm as bubbles on a steady stream of enterprise. But the position is serious when enterprise becomes the bubble on a whirlpool of speculation. When the capital development of a country becomes a by-product of the activities of a casino, the job is likely to be ill-done."[70] If we draw inspiration from Keynes, in the long history of Turkish economy, the 1990s turned into one of the intervals during which "the job was ill-done." The financialization of Turkish economy and the ineptitude of a string of weak coalition governments during 1990s resulted in the constant procrastination of fiscal and financial reforms. Not surprisingly, as a result, Turkey's "lost decade" terminated with a devastating crisis at the turn of the century.

References

Akın, Güzin G., Ahmet F. Aysan, and Levent Yıldıran. "Transformation of the Turkish Financial Sector in the Aftermath of the 2001 Crisis." In *Turkey and the Global Economy: Neo-liberal Restructuring and Integration in the Post-crisis Era*, edited by Ziya Öniş and Fikret Şenses, 73–100. Oxon: Routledge, 2009.

[70] John Maynard Keynes, *The General Theory of Employment, Interest, and Money* (London: St. Martin's Press, 1960), 159.

Arat, Yeşim. "Politics and Big Business: Janus-Faced Link to the State." In *Strong State and Economic Interest Groups: The Post-1980 Turkish Experience*, edited by Metin Heper, 135–147. Berlin and New York: Walter de Gruyter, 1991.

Arslan, İsmail. *A Review of Turkish Incentive Systems*. Washington D.C.: World Bank Publications, 1993.

Atiyas, İzak. "Uneven Governance and Fiscal Failure: The Adjustment Experience in Turkey." *The World Bank Private Sector Development Department Occasional Paper*, no. 17 (1995).

Balkan, Erol, and Erinç Yeldan. "Peripheral Development under Financial Liberalization: The Turkish Experience." In *The Ravages of Neoliberalism: Economy, Society and Gender in Turkey*, edited by Neşecan Balkan, and Sungur Savran, 39–54. New York: Nova Science Publishers, 2002.

Baysan, Tercan, and Charles Blitzer. "Turkey's Trade Liberalization in the 1980s and Prospects for its Sustainability." In *The Political Economy of Turkey: Debt, Adjustment, and Sustainability*, edited by Tosun Arıcanlı, and Dani Rodrik, 9–36. London: Macmillan, 1990.

Biddle, Jesse, and Vedat Milor. "Economic Governance in Turkey: Bureaucratic Capacity, Policy Networks, and Business Associations." In *Business and the State in Developing Countries*, edited by Sylvia Maxfield, and Ben Ross Schneider, 277–309. Ithaca: Cornell University Press, 1997.

Boratav, Korkut, Oktar Türel, and Erinç Yeldan. "Dilemmas of Structural Adjustment and Environmental Policies under Instability: Post-1980 Turkey." *World Development* 24, no. 2 (1996): 373–393.

Buğra, Ayşe. "Political Sources of Uncertainty in Business Life." In *Strong State and Economic Interest Groups: The Post-1980 Turkish Experience*, edited by Metin Heper, 151–162. Berlin and New York: Walter de Gruyter, 1991.

Buğra, Ayşe. *State and Business in Modern Turkey: A Comparative Study*. New York: State University of New York Press, 1994.

Ersel, Hasan. "The Timing of Capital Account Liberalization: The Turkish Experience." *New Perspectives on Turkey* 15 (1996): 45–64.

Gülfidan, Şebnem. *Big Business and the State in Turkey: The Case of TÜSİAD*. İstanbul: Boğaziçi University Press, 1993.

Heper, Metin. "Negative Bureaucratic Politics in a Modernizing Context: The Turkish Case." *Journal of South Asian and Middle Eastern Studies* 1, no. 1 (1977): 65–84.

İstanbul Sanayi Odası, *Türkiye'nin 500 Büyük Sanayi Kuruluşu* (İstanbul: İSO Yayınları, 1995).

Keyman, E. Fuat. "Modernity, Secularism and Islam: The Case of Turkey." *Theory, Culture & Society* 24, no. 2 (2007): 215–234.

Keynes, John Maynard. *The General Theory of Employment, Interest, and Money*. London: St. Martin's Press, 1960.

Koç, Yıldırım. "30. Yıl Dönümünde 12 Eylül Darbesi ve İşçi Sınıfı." *Mülkiye Dergisi* 43, no. 268 (2010): 43–74.
Maxfield, Sylvia, and Ben Ross Schneider, eds. *Business and the State in Developing Countries.* Ithaca: Cornell University Press, 1997.
Mehmet Ali Birand, *Son Darbe 28 Şubat* (İstanbul: Doğan Kitap, 2012).
Milliyet Gazetesi, "12 Eylül Olmasaydı, 24 Ocak Kararları Fiyasko ile Sonuçlanırdı," January 7, 1991.
Milliyet Gazetesi, "Çiller'i Şok Eden İstifa," February 1, 1994.
Milliyet Gazetesi, "Çiller'in ABD'deki Serveti," June 17, 1994.
Milliyet Gazetesi, "Ekonomide Sıkıyönetim," April 4, 1994.
Milliyet Gazetesi, "Ekonomik Pakete Tepki Yağdı," April 6, 1994.
Milliyet Gazetesi, "İktidarın Son Şansı," April 5, 1994.
Milliyet Gazetesi, "Koçman: '24 Ocak Kararları Mucizevi Bir Karardır,'" April 20, 1983.
Milliyet Gazetesi, "Mühendisler Hükümeti," December 14, 1983.
Milliyet Gazetesi, "TÜSİAD Çiller'e Bir Şans Daha Verdi," February 12, 1994.
Milliyet Gazetesi, "TÜSİAD Çiller'e Savaş Açtı," May 5, 1994.
Milliyet Gazetesi, "TÜSİAD'tan Hükümete Zorunlu Destek," April 8, 1994.
Milliyet Gazetesi, "Yılmaz Dinledi, Erbakan Uyardı," April 5, 1994.
Milliyet Gazetesi, "Yılmaz: 'Paket Kötü Bir Kopya,'" April 6, 1994.
OECD, *Economic Surveys, Turkey: 1995–1996.* Paris: OECD Publication Service, 1996.
OECD. *Economic Surveys, Turkey: 1994–1995.* Paris: OECD Publications Service, 1995.
OECD. *Economic Surveys, Turkey: 2001.* Paris: OECD Publications Service, 2001.
OECD. *Economic Surveys, Turkey: 2002.* Paris: OECD Publications Service, 2002.
OECD. *Society at A Glance, 2011: OECD Social Indicators.* Paris: OECD Publications Service, 2011.
Öncü, Ayşe, and Deniz Gökçe. "Macro-Politics of De-Regulation and Micro-Politics of Banks." In *Strong State and Economic Interest Groups: The Post-1980 Turkish Experience*, edited by Metin Heper, 99–117. Berlin and New York: Walter de Gruyter, 1991.
Öniş, Ziya, and Ahmet Faruk Aysan. "Neoliberal Globalization, the Nation State and the Financial Crises in the Semi-Periphery: A Comparative Analysis." *Third World Quarterly* 21, no. 1 (2000): 119–139.
Öniş, Ziya, and Steven B. Webb. "The Political Economy of Policy Reform in the 1980s." *World Bank Working Papers*, Paper no. 1059, 1992.
Öniş, Ziya. "Democracy, Populism, and Chronic Inflation in Turkey: The Post Liberalization Experience." *Yapı Kredi Economic Review* 8 (1997): 33–50.
Öniş, Ziya. "The Evolution of Privatization in Turkey: The Institutional Context of Public-Enterprise Reform." *International Journal of Middle East Studies* 23, no. 2 (1991): 163–176.

Öniş, Ziya. *State and Market: The Political Economy of Turkey in a Comparative Perspective*, edited by Ziya Öniş, 513–529. İstanbul: Boğaziçi University Press, 1998.

Oyan, Oğuz. "An Overall Evaluation of the Causes of the Use of Special Funds in Turkey and Their Place in the Economy." *Yapı Kredi Economic Review* 1, no. 4 (1987): 83–116.

Özatay, Fatih, and Güven Sak. "Banking Sector Fragility and Turkey's 2000-01 Financial Crisis." *Brookings Trade Forum*. Washington D.C.: Brookings Institution Publications, 2002.

Özatay, Fatih. "The 1994 Currency Crisis in Turkey." *The Journal of Policy Reform* 3, no. 4 (2000): 327–352.

Özbudun, Ergun. "The Post-1980 Legal Framework for Interest Group Associations." In *Strong State and Economic Interest Groups: The Post-1980 Turkish Experience*, edited by Metin Heper, 41–53. Berlin and New York: Walter de Gruyter, 1991, 41–53.

Öztürk, Özgür. *Türkiye'de Büyük Sermaye Grupları: Finans Kapitalin Oluşumu ve Gelişimi*. İstanbul: SAV Yayınları, 2010.

Rodrik, Dani. "Premature Liberalization, Incomplete Stabilization: The Özal Decade in Turkey." *NBER Working Paper Series*, Working Paper no. 3300, 1990.

Taylor, Lance. "The Turkish Experience: Summary and Comparative Notes." In *The Political Economy of Turkey: Debt, Adjustment, and Sustainability*, edited by Tosun Arıcanlı, and Dani Rodrik. London: Macmillan, 1990.

Ümit, Cizre, and Erinç Yeldan. "The Turkish Encounter with Neo-Liberalism: Economics and Politics in the 2000/2001 Crisis." *Review of International Political Economy* 12, no. 3 (2005): 387–408.

Waterbury, John. "Export-Led Growth and the Center-Right Coalition in Turkey." *Comparative Politics* 24, no. 2 (1992): 127–145.

Yeldan, Erinç and Ümit Cizre-Sakallıoğlu. "Politics, Society, and Financial Liberalization: Turkey in the 1990s." *Development and Change* 31, no. 2 (2000): 481–508.

Yeldan, Erinç. "Neoliberal Global Remedies: From Speculative-Led Growth to IMF-Led Crisis in Turkey." *Review of Radical Political Economics* 38, no. 2 (2006): 193–213.

Yeldan, Erinç. *Küreselleşme Sürecinde Türkiye Ekonomisi*. İstanbul: İletişim Yayınları, 2011.

Yükseker, Deniz. "Neoliberal Restructuring and Social Exclusion in Turkey." In *Turkey and the Global Economy: Neo-liberal Restructuring and Integration in the Post-crisis Era*, edited by Ziya Öniş, and Fikret Şenses, 262–280. Oxon: Routledge, 2009.

CHAPTER 4

Turkish Crisis and Aftermath (2001–2016)

This chapter deals with the 2001 crisis and the subsequent transformations in Turkish political economy. The accumulation of fiscal and financial problems during the 1990s left Turkey on the brink of an economic collapse at the turn of the century. The crisis was by far the deepest shock of the contemporary Turkish history and reshuffled domestic power balances. It also delegitimized the prevailing ideational paradigms that had informed state policies for years. However, in the Turkish context, in a stark contrast to Greece, the critical juncture was exploited as an opportunity window as Turkey's economic regime was substantially overhauled. The reforms were nothing short of a silent revolution that corresponded to a fundamental shift in main fiscal paradigm. Therefore, the 2001 crisis paved the way for a new set of policy paradigms in comparison to the pre-crisis period.

This chapter offers time and context-specific explanation of this transformation. The transformation of Turkish politics during the single party governments in the aftermath of the crisis was equally striking. This chapter aims to reveal the dynamics of policy cycles in Turkish political economy during 2001–2016. The second part provides a concise history of the 2001 economic crisis. The third part delves into the domestic and external dynamics that enabled the emergence of a new paradigm. The fourth part deals with the political economy of Turkey in the post-2011 period. The final part concludes the chapter.

M. Kutlay, *The Political Economies of Turkey and Greece*,
International Political Economy Series,
https://doi.org/10.1007/978-3-319-92789-3_4

4.1 2001 Turkish Economic Crisis: A Brief Overview

Turkey experienced the deepest economic crisis while being ruled by a coalition government that was formed on May 28, 1999, incorporating center-left Democratic Left Party (DSP) under the leadership of Bülent Ecevit, Motherland Party (ANAP) under the leadership of Mesut Yılmaz, and Nationalist Movement Party (MHP) under the leadership of Devlet Bahçeli. The government adopted an economic stabilization plan from the early days. In the initial phases, the coalition government was perceived as an opportunity for Turkey since it unified different ideological stances around a reformist agenda. The diverse ideological commitments of the coalition partners, however, turned into important stumbling stones in terms of a consistent and sturdy implementation of the promised reforms. The increasing incoherence among the coalition partners and particularly the resistance of the nationalist MHP to the banking regulations, agricultural reforms, and controversy over privatization of key state organizations, gradually eroded the confidence of investors toward the program starting from mid-2000s.

It shortly became apparent that the stabilization package failed to generate credibility on the part of the market actors. Furthermore, appreciation of the Turkish lira, a swift recovery in domestic demand and surge in energy prices led to an increasing current account deficit. The combination of a series of domestic and external untoward events raised serious questions regarding the sustainability of the exchange rate regime, which left Turkish economy almost entirely vulnerable vis-à-vis the speculative attacks of erratic capital flows. The instability triggered a surge in interest rates and a sharp decline in the price of treasury bills with an increasing demand on short-term liquidity. In this deteriorating environment, the first shock wave hit the economy in November 2000, when a mid-sized private bank holding a large amount of government securities, declared bankruptcy following the rapid deterioration of its capital base. The Central Bank intervened in the markets by selling some $6 billion in addition to the extra credit line opened by the IMF, which temporarily tranquilized and subdued the markets.

The snowball however had continued to roll, as the structural problems were not tackled meticulously due to the timid approach of the government and sub-optimal policy mix and sequencing of the IMF program. The real shock knocked on Turkey's door in February 21, 2001. In a context of diminishing confidence to the political authority, the expectations of the market players turned for the worse after November 2000. This time, the triggering factor that pinpointed the timing of the crisis was political in nature. On February 19, 2001, at an ill-tempered meeting of National Security Council, Prime Minister Bülent Ecevit and President Ahmet Necdet Sezer had a serious dispute. The prime minister stormed out of the meeting. During the press conference, which he arranged immediately after the dispute, Ecevit defined the incident as a big political crisis. The disclosure of the public argument increased the jitters immensely within the markets, which in turn, precipitated a series of events that culminated in the deepest peacetime turmoil in the history of the country.

Gross national product in real terms declined by 9.4 percent; the immediate capital exodus amounted to $7.6 billion; the interest rates jumped to unprecedented levels.[1] This was also the final call to pull the plug of the IMF-sponsored exchange rate-based stabilization program. As the exchange rate was left free to float, domestic currency lost its value by 65.9 percent in total in two months. The massive devaluation in domestic currency also severely jeopardized the balance sheets of financial and non-financial firms due to high levels of open foreign exchange positions they were exposed to. The banks during 1990s borrowed in foreign denominated currencies and directed these funds to Turkish lira denominated funds.[2] Not surprisingly, the accumulation of foreign exchange liabilities left Turkish banks defenseless against currency mismatch problems in the wake of the crisis.[3] In addition to the widespread bankruptcies in the banking sector, which resulted in a massive cost of $47.2 billion, thousands of small- and medium-sized enterprises went out of business during 2001 and 2002. As of the end of 2001, the public sector borrowing requirement

[1] The overnight interest rates had hiked to 2000 percent on February 21, following the public argument between Prime Minister and President, and skyrocketed to more than 4000 percent on February 21.

[2] The government securities were equivalent of 10 percent of total assets of deposit banks in 1990. The figure increased to 23 percent of total assets in 2000. In the same period, the share of loans to the private sector over total assets decreased from 36 percent to 24 percent.

[3] The foreign exchange deposits were composing 58.6 percent of total deposits in Turkish banks in 2000, which was just 25 percent in 1990. The ratio, in itself, demonstrates that "dollarization" became an increasing trend in Turkish economy during 1990s. Following the 2001 economic crisis, the devaluation in the currency severely hit banking sector accustomed to holding balance sheets with large share of domestic currency denominated treasury bills on the asset side, which was mainly financed by foreign currency denominated liabilities.

increased to 15.5 percent; budget deficit skyrocketed to 17.4 percent; and public debt jumped to 97.8 percent of GNP.[4] The distributive consequences of the economic crisis were also significant: almost one million people lost their jobs. The inflation rate rose to 68.5 percent.

4.2 Post-crisis Reform Program: Getting Things Right

The 2001 crisis represents a real turning point in Turkish political economy not only because it was the deepest crisis in the history of the country but also due to the paradigmatic changes that took place during the post-crisis period. In the fiscal and financial realms, substantial reforms were initiated that informed fundamental restructuration of state-market relations. Following the crisis, Turkey prepared a bold and comprehensive reform package entitled *Strengthening the Turkish Economy: Turkey's Transition Program*, the aim of which was declared as to "fundamentally [transform] the functioning of the state."[5] The reform program was attached to strict quantitative and structural conditionality benchmarks in return for the financial and technical assistance. The program offered a three-pronged approach: fiscal consolidation, financial restructuring, and structural reforms to ensure sustainability of the Turkish economy. On the fiscal front, similar to other post-crisis reform programs, the government adopted a set of fiscal consolidation measures.

Second cornerstone of the program was the restructuration of the financial system. As part of *Turkey's Transition Program*, a detailed roadmap entitled *Banking Sector Restructuring and Rehabilitation Program* was released in May 2001 that outlined the "underlying strategy of the BRSA towards establishing a sound banking sector and the action plan for the restructuring of the banking sector."[6] First of all, costly financial restructuration plan was put into practice to recapitalize the two largest state banks (Ziraat and Halkbank).[7] The insolvent private banks were also taken over by Savings Deposit Insurance Fund of

[4] DPT, *Dokuzuncu Kalkınma Planı (2007–2013): Finansal Hizmetler Özel İhtisas Komisyonu Raporu* (Ankara: Devlet Planlama Teşkilatı, 2007), 4.

[5] Undersecretariat of Treasury, *Strengthening the Turkish Economy: Turkey's Transition Program* (Ankara: TCMB, 2001), 34.

[6] BDDK, *Towards a Sound Turkish Banking Sector* (Ankara: BDDK, 2001), 8.

[7] Emlak Bank, the third largest state bank at the time, was closed and assets were transferred to Ziraat Bank.

Turkey (SDIF). As a result, 22 insolvent banks were transferred to SDIF.[8] The SDIF-owned banks were merged, sold, or liquidated after financial streamlining took place. Also, Banking Regulation and Supervision Agency (BRSA), which started its operations in mid-2000 in pursuant to a new banking law of 1999, was granted completely independent operational capacity following the 2001 crisis to adequately supervise the banking sector. Thanks to the substantial amendments in the banking law, all banks were required to fully comply with the BRSA regulations.

The strict prudential regulations adopted in the banking law were put into implementation. Accordingly, an independent governing board, reporting to the Treasury, was appointed in state banks "to apply commercial criteria to operations and pricing policies that ensure profitability."[9] The private banks were also required to restore their capital adequacy ratios and capital deficient banks were forced by BRSA to present capital strengthening plans. All banks were obliged to develop internal prudential mechanisms in addition to strong BRSA-led external supervision. In July 2004, blanket deposit guarantee, which was introduced following the 1994 crisis, was abolished in order to mitigate moral hazard risks. Finally, monetary policy moved toward inflation targeting as the Central Bank of the Republic of Turkey was given "full operational independence in pursuing its primary mandate of maintaining price stability."[10]

The structural fiscal reforms constituted the third pillar of the program. The reforms in this category were claimed to put a clear break with the past habits of state behavior:

> Successful implementation of the structural reforms envisaged in the program will increase the economy's efficiency, thus facilitating sustainable growth with current resources. Structural reforms will also transform fundamentally the functioning of the state. This way, the state will be prevented from returning to the old habits that deteriorate public finances and reduce the efficiency of resource utilization.[11]

[8] This number covers the period between 1997 and 2003. 14 of them were taken over during 2000–2003.

[9] Letter of Intent of the Government of Turkey, May 3, 2001 http://www.imf.org/external/np/loi/2001/tur/02/ (arrived on September 14, 2016).

[10] Ibid., 18.

[11] Undersecretariat of Treasury, *Strengthening the Turkish Economy*, 34.

Similar to the financial reforms, a new regulatory framework was also crafted in the fiscal system. First, a new public borrowing law was promulgated in order to streamline state's fiscal accounts. The new regulations concerning the public borrowing practices brought transparency and clarity to the state borrowing limits, which used to be quite opaque and arbitrary. Keeping the Turkish parliament informed regarding public debt dynamics through quarterly published debt management reports also became legally binding. Second, existing budget law was also amended to make budgetary spending more accountable and tractable.[12] Third, the Turkish parliament promulgated a new public tender/procurement law. Fourth, in pursuant to the stand-by agreement with the IMF, the government also accelerated privatization implementations, primarily in the telecommunication, banking, aviation, sugar, tobacco, steel, and natural gas industries. The Turkish parliament passed 19 vital structural reform laws or regulations, more than half of which were approved in the first four months preceding the economic crisis (see below). In summary, the unified thread of fiscal, financial, and structural reforms were declared as "[to improve] the economic environment through enhanced transparency, better governance, and a strengthened regulatory environment."[13]

The February 2001 crisis points to a new phase in Turkish neoliberalism because, for the first time over years, Turkish policy-makers embarked on a set of substantial reforms that underpinned state capacity. In retrospect, the state succeeded in putting its fiscal house into order so that the budget deficit and public debt were brought under control—to levels consistent with the Maastricht criteria. The financial system was also overhauled significantly so that "banking on government" and "bad credits to good friends" ceased to be policy options for private and public banks.[14] How did it become possible to discipline state's profligate fiscal behavior? Also, how could it become possible to overcome the resistance of rent-seeking policy coalitions? To account for this paradigmatic change, the spotlight should be turned on the agency-level dynamics and institutional structures along domestic-external nexus.

[12] Letter of Intent of the Government of Turkey, May 3, 2001, 9.

[13] Ibid., 5.

[14] Interview with senior official, Capital Markets Board of Turkey, September 11, 2014.

Agency-Level Dynamics: Converging Crisis Narratives

Following the public argument between the prime minister and the president on February 19, 2001, that plunged the economy into a devastating crisis, Prime Minister Bülent Ecevit invited Kemal Derviş, the World Bank's vice-president for poverty reduction and economic management, to handle the economic crisis. The motivation behind the government's appointment was twofold. The first and immediate concern was to extinguish the fire of the markets by ensuring credibility and trust at the top level of economic management. The second and long-term aim was to ensure the assistance of international financial institutions while restructuring the domestic economy.[15] Ecevit's initial intention was to appoint Derviş as the governor of the Central Bank. However, Derviş insisted on a more powerful post since he reckoned that the crisis was too deep to counteract via monetary policy instruments per se.[16]

The government positively responded to his request. As a result, Derviş was appointed as the "minister of state for economic affairs." In his words, Derviş was "offered the position of minister of the treasury, as well as coordinating responsibilities for the Central Bank and Banking Sector Regulation Agency, and the responsibility for negotiations with the IMF and World Banks."[17] From that point onward, Derviş had become the key state agent regarding the management of the economic crisis and coordination of the reform processes.

Derviş was a policy entrepreneur "operat[ing] in different ideational realms as decision maker (e.g., politician and bureaucrat), theorist (e.g., academic and intellectual), and framer (e.g., spin doctor publicizing favourable interpretation of some of the neoliberal ideas), as well as a mediator."[18] First, he was a capable technocratic figure with widespread expertise in theory and practice of economic crises and reform processes. He graduated from the Department of Economics at London School of Economics. He then received a PhD degree in economics from Princeton

[15] Interview with member of the Economic Advisors Committee to Bülent Ecevit, September 10, 2014.

[16] Interview with senior official, Ministry of Economic Affairs, September 11, 2014.

[17] Kemal Derviş, "Returning from the Brink: Turkey's Efforts at Systemic Change and Structural Reform," in Tim Besley and Roberto Zagha, eds., *Development Challenges in the 1990s: Leading Policymakers Speak from Experience* (Oxford: Oxford University Press, 2005), 65.

[18] Caner Bakır, "Policy Entrepreneurship and Institutional Change: Multilevel Governance of Central Banking Reform," *Governance: An International Journal of Policy, Administration and Institutions* 22, no. 4 (2009), 587.

University. Following three-year work experience in two Turkish universities as a professor of economics during 1973–1976, he joined the World Bank, where he spent 24 years until he returned to Turkey in 2001. In addition to his academic credentials and professional expertise, Derviş also gained ample policy-related experience at the World Bank across a range of departments. Second, Derviş had established good connections with international epistemic communities. Derviş, in fact, incarnated mainstream ideas developed in these circles. Third, the time and context were also ripe as he entered into Turkish politics at a critical juncture when the domestic and external trust in established parties and political actors had deteriorated significantly. Derviş, therefore, emerged as an outsider and non-partisan figure.

Following his appointment of significant authority, in a short period, Derviş formed his economic team. Since Derviş appointed his teammates at the end of March, high level of coordination was ensured in the fiscal, monetary, and financial pillars of economic bureaucracy in a very short period, which in turn, helped the development of a coherent and credible crisis narrative. Derviş framed Turkey's economic crisis mainly as a domestic problem, root causes of which emanated from reactive state practices accumulated over the years.[19] Accordingly, he narrated the crisis as an outcome of deleterious policies pursued by rent-seeking vested interests:

> At the heart of Turkey's difficulties was a rent-seeking socioeconomic system where governments had for decades promised and attempted to distribute more resources than they could raise. The private sector encouraged by the political class, spent enormous effort capturing rents in exchange for support to various political groups.[20]

His interpretation is based on a fundamental assumption that Turkey's task was not "one of achieving stabilization or restoring liquidity."[21] According to Derviş and his economic team, what Turkey had to achieve was "a systemic economic change: shifting from a rent-seeking society to a modern, competitive economy with much greater autonomy in the economic sphere, greater separation of politics and markets, greater transparency, and less privilege and therefore a better distribution of income, which would

[19] Interview with senior official, Ministry of Economic Affairs, September 11, 2014.
[20] Derviş, "Returning from the Brink," 66.
[21] Ibid.

also lead to a greater legitimacy of governance and decision-making."[22] Derviş, therefore, prioritized restructuring the financial system and taking irreversible reformist steps regarding the banking sector.[23]

Derviş' initial approach suggests that domestic ownership of the crisis was ensured at the agency level in a consistent way starting from the early stages of the crisis. The major domestic agents responsible for the crisis management openly accepted that the crisis was in fact "made in Turkey" so that fundamental reforms were in order to overcome it. The guiding logic of the reform program was to introduce a "new paradigm in state-market relations that ensures arms-length distance between day-to-day politics and the functioning of the fiscal and financial system."[24] The crisis narrative developed by Derviş and Turkish economic bureaucracy substantially coincided with the perspective of the IMF. This is in fact an expected development due to two main reasons. First, the IMF was a strong advocate of structural reforms in Turkey for quite a long time. For instance, the most important titles of the reform proposals such as privatizations, public borrowing regulations, regulation of the financial sector, and the Central Bank independence were already included in the December 1999 stand-by agreement, but could not be implemented properly. Thus, the IMF welcomed Derviş' approach to the crisis. Stanley Fischer, first deputy managing director of the IMF and the major actor responsible for the management of the crisis on behalf of the Fund, stated this point as follows:

> The Turkish authorities in the negotiations we have been conducting with Minister Derviş and his colleagues have demonstrated their determination to continue on the path of stabilization and reform on which they started at the end of 1999, and to take all the measures, including very tough ones to restructure the banking system and fiscal measures that will ensure a rapid turnaround in the debt situation necessary to restore stability and continue the process of disinflation… Turkey deserves the support of the international community, and it will get it.[25]

[22] Ibid., 66.

[23] Interview with senior official, Ministry of Economic Affairs, September 11, 2014.

[24] Interview with senior official, Central Bank of the Republic of Turkey, September 15, 2014.

[25] Stanley Fischer, "Remarks by Stanley Fischer, First Deputy Managing Director of the IMF, April 25, 2001", 7.

Second, Derviş worked for the World Bank for more than two decades; thereby, he had incorporated the mainstream ideas of the international financial institutions. As a matter of fact, critical accounts of Turkish political economy tend to approach Derviş as the organic representative of the hegemonic capitalist ruling bloc. By doing so, they incline to overlook reformist actors' agency by attributing them an epiphenomenal role, whose actions are preordained by the interests and ideas of international financial institutions. This study tends to diverge from these reductionist interpretations. As suggested, policy entrepreneurs are expected to domesticate international interests and mainstream ideas while transposing them into the domestic field.[26] Nevertheless, by definition, policy entrepreneurs are transnationalized agents that are supposed to have strong linkages with international epistemic communities. From this vantage point, their outlook resonates with international conventional wisdom regarding the fundamentals. This makes narrative matching a more likely outcome at the agency level, which obviously turned out to be the case in Turkey's relations with the IMF under the stewardship of Kemal Derviş. Therefore, the IMF endorsed its confidence from the very beginning:

> We have a great deal of confidence in him [Kemal Derviş] and his team... Derviş is certainly well known, not only in the kind of sort of the IMF/ World Bank sense of the world, but he is someone of international stature... We would be happy to be of assistance in whatever way we can.[27]

Looking from this angle, Derviş adopted a crisis narrative that was fundamentally agreed and backed by the IMF and the World Bank.[28]

That being said, the perspectives of the parties were not entirely overlapping in the initial phases. There were certain points of disagreement especially on the speed and scope of fiscal adjustment. In general, the Turkish side opposed the IMF's insistence on a rapid macroeconomic adjustment and strict austerity measures, since, according to the Turkish team, this move would delegitimize the reform program in the eyes of domestic constituency. Two major points created a fevered environment

[26] Bakır, "Policy Entrepreneurship and Institutional Change," *Governance: An International Journal of Policy, Administration and Institutions*, 591.

[27] IMF, "Transcripts of a Press Briefing by Thomas Dawson, Director of External Relations Department of the IMF, March 12, 2001," 6–7.

[28] Interview with senior official, Ministry of Economic Affairs, September 11, 2014.

between the parties. The first controversy erupted on the inflation rate targets for 2002. Stanley Fischer insisted on a 20 percent inflation rate target for 2002. Derviş and his economic team, however, challenged this idea as they considered the proposed target unattainable and unrealistic. Derviş attributed high importance to macroeconomic targets, because he thought that the credibility of the program might be put in jeopardy in case the program targets were perceived unrealistic.

> Our inflation rate target for 2002 was 40 percent. The IMF insisted on 20 percent. Then, we agreed on the 35 percent inflation target for 2002. The Central Bank governor [Süreyya Serdengeçti] was ordered to negotiate an attainable target. Finally, we succeeded [in both terms]: The IMF accepted our offer and the 2002 inflation realized as 30 percent.[29]

The second important controversy emerged in regard to the increase in the public sector wages. Fischer insisted on freezing the wages of the civil servants in order to comply with fiscal consolidation measures. According to Fischer, an increase in labor wages might pave the way for the deterioration of public finances and the derailment of the entire program.[30] Derviş, on the other hand, opposed Fischer's demands since he thought that freezing public servants' wages might asymmetrically increase domestic audience costs, which in turn might weaken the credibility and support base of the entire program.

Regarding the inflation target, Fischer and the IMF team abandoned their initial ideas and accepted the proposal of Derviş and his negotiation team. The controversy over public wages however proved a more difficult issue. The IMF in the first place resisted any increase in public sector wages. Accordingly, "the entire program come close to the point of collapse" as the Turkish team also refused to change its initial stance.[31] However, it became possible to cut a deal, partially, "thanks to a close personal relationship between Fischer and Derviş."[32] As a result, Turkey secured almost $20 billion of financial assistance within the context of a three-year stand-by agreement (in total, around $30 billion), which in the words of Fischer "demonstrates [IMF's] backing… by providing exceptional financing in its support."[33]

[29] Interview with senior official, Ministry of Economic Affairs, September 11, 2014.

[30] Interview with senior advisor to Kemal Derviş, 26 September 2014.

[31] Interview with senior official, Ministry of Economic Affairs, September 11, 2014.

[32] Interview with senior official, Central Bank of the Republic of Turkey, September 15, 2014.

[33] IMF, "IMF Approves Augmentation of Turkey's Stand-By Credit to US$19 Billion," *Press Release no. 01/23*, May 15, 2001.

4.3 Converging Interests and Ideas

The "Derviş factor," however, needs to be placed into its proper context in order not to exaggerate the role of agency. The qualifications of Derviş do explain only part of the degree of flexibility demonstrated by the IMF toward Turkey and the relatively generous financial assistance it was willing to provide. We need to extend our gaze toward the interests-ideas nexus, to fully grasp the factors that informed the convergence at the domestic-external nexus and facilitated the emergence of a dominant narrative at the agency level in a crisis juncture. Two major interest-related intervening variables increased Turkey's bargaining power in the wake of the crisis.

First, Turkey witnessed the most severe economic crisis in the midst of an IMF-sponsored stabilization program. The exchange rate-based stabilization program was the idea of the IMF staff, which was implemented despite serious objections of the Turkish economic team at the time. Furthermore, IMF did not provide necessary financial support to the introduced substantial structural reforms. The December 1999 stabilization program also failed to offer an appropriate sequencing of reforms.[34] The IMF placed prior emphasis on the elimination of macroeconomic disequilibrium, rather than the restructuration of wobbly financial system. It became apparent that the IMF did not have required information concerning the true depth of fiscal and financial disequilibrium in Turkey. The February 2001 crisis, in this sense, clearly revealed the under-investment of the IMF in terms of acquainting itself with idiosyncratic characteristics of individual economies. The apparent failures of the IMF, in a paradoxical way, turned out to be valuable assets for Turkey as it enlarged its bargaining space. An experienced Turkish bureaucrat, who played major role in negotiations, underscored this point as follows:

> [There was another crucial factor] that strengthened Turkey's bargaining position: One of the reasons that pushed Turkey into a crisis was the exchange rate-based stabilization program. The IMF staunchly advocated this strategy. [From the very beginning] we [the representatives of Turkish negotiation team] argued that this strategy would not work in the Turkish

[34] For a critical account of the IMF's role in Turkey's economic turmoil, see Yılmaz Akyüz and Korkut Boratav, "The Making of the Turkish Financial Crisis," *World Development* 31, no. 9 (2003): 1549–1566.

> context. [After the 2001 crisis] this provided us significant bargaining advantage because we have said this previously. Therefore, the IMF was inclined to accept our suggestions in the post-2001 crisis in comparison to the pre-crisis context... Otherwise, it would not have been possible to receive such a large amount of financial support.[35]

Second, Turkey's geopolitical importance for the US played a considerable role in the post-crisis context. Woods[36] and Oatley and Yackee[37] demonstrate that IMF assistance to emerging markets is not a politically neutral practice since engagement with the IMF provides a conduit of other geopolitical goals for the US over the debtor countries. Turkey's political stability and economic durability appeared as an important concern for the US foreign policy-makers. It was therefore not surprising that just two days after the crisis outbreak, the then US president George W. Bush called Turkish prime minister in order to state "the readiness of the US to support Turkey."[38] As Miller points out, "the US foreign policy interest in maintaining strong relations with Turkey, [provided] the freedom to the IMF to accommodate Derviş's revisions than in other crisis packages."[39] Thus, it is fair to argue in the Turkish case that the foreign policy priorities of the US toward the Middle East and Turkey's geostrategic position as a spearhead in the region proved beneficial for Turkey to receive a considerably larger amount of financial assistance from the IMF. The Fund bailed out Turkey but rejected Argentina's request, a country also experiencing a deep crisis like Turkey but located at the periphery of the US foreign policy interests.[40]

Turkey's geopolitical significance for the US became even more pronounced in the aftermath of the 9/11 terrorist attacks. As the US government prepared to launch military operations in Turkey's neighboring

[35] Interview with senior official, Undersecretary of Treasury, September 10, 2014.

[36] Ngarie Woods, "Understanding Pathways Thorough Financial Crises and the Impact of the IMF: An Introduction," *Global Governance* 12, no. 4 (2006): 379, 384.

[37] Thomas Oatley and Jason Yackee, "American Interests and IMF Lending," *International Politics* 41, no. 3 (2004): 415–429.

[38] Milliyet Gazetesi, "Bush'tan Ecevit'e Telefon," February 24, 2001.

[39] Calum Miller, "Pathways Through Financial Crisis: Turkey," *Global Governance* 12, no. 4 (2006): 458.

[40] For a comparative analysis with reference to diverging geopolitical significance of Turkey and Argentina, inter alia, see Ziya Öniş, "Varieties and Crises of Neoliberal Globalization: Argentina, Turkey and the IMF," *Third World Quarterly* 27, no. 2 (2006): 252.

states, its position in the Western alliance appeared more critical than ever. It is in this context that Turkey applied to the IMF for an extra reserve facility in order to armor itself vis-à-vis the side effects of a reversal in capital flows to Middle Eastern economies and emerging markets. The IMF "immediately promised to open a new credit line of $10 billion."[41] One may claim that Turkey's commitment to the reform program underpinned the credibility of Turkish policy-makers in the eyes of IMF officials. Yet, this would be a grave underestimation to evaluate IMF support in isolation from the concerns of the US government in the post-9/11 security environment. For instance, on December 14, 2001, President Bush personally reiterated his administration's willingness to help Turkey in a meeting with Turkey's ambassador in Washington.[42] In February 2002, the IMF renewed its commitment to Turkey with a revised agreement with new capital. As Woods suggests:

> The permissive support of the IMF reflected both the stake (in terms of advice and resources) the institution had in Turkey's existing arrangements and the significant pressure from the United States, which was concerned about fallout in its relations with a key strategic ally.[43]

The interview findings also confirm that the US closely monitored the implementation of Turkey's restructuration program. The US embassy to Turkey, particularly Ambassador Robert Pierson and deputy chief of mission in Ankara James Jeffrey, frequently met with government representatives. For instance, Jeffrey visited the spokesperson of the government, during the most intense episode of the crisis in order to remind the Turkish government "that the US is responsible to 'control' how the US taxpayers' money [extended to Turkey via the IMF credits] is spent and distributed."[44] One of the top officials of the DSP at the time also stated that the US ambassador frequently visited deputy prime minister, Hüsamettin Özkan, to supervise the progress in reform measures, with a particular interest in the privatization of the energy sector.[45]

[41] Interview with senior official, Ministry of Economic Affairs, September 11, 2014.

[42] Cizre and Yeldan, "The Turkish Encounter with Neo-liberalism," *Review of International Political Economy*, footnote 16.

[43] Woods, "Understanding Pathways Through Financial Crises and the Impact of the IMF," *Global Governance*, 384.

[44] Interview with senior official, MHP, September 4, 2014.

[45] Interview with member of the Economic Advisors Committee to Bülent Ecevit, September 10, 2014.

The preceding debate suggests that the two driving interest-related developments helped Turkey receive relatively timely and large amount of financial assistance. However, these factors do not explain the content and design of the reform program, which bring about the importance of ideas at critical junctures. The major ideational factor that facilitated the emergence of a dominant crisis narrative at the domestic-external nexus was related to the rising economic policy paradigm at the time, namely post-Washington Consensus (PWC). The reform program put a significant emphasis on the regulatory credentials of the Turkish state in the fiscal and financial realms. From this perspective, the reform program went beyond the neoliberal orthodoxy of the Washington Consensus (WC) that increasingly dominated the outlook of the IMF and the World Bank in the post-1980 era. The WC advocated a political economy model revolving around the standard templates of "market liberalization" and "minimal state."[46] The organizing ideational notion of the WC was the unshakable trust placed in the self-adjustment capacity of the markets.[47] Accordingly, it was assumed that "getting prices right… through trade liberalization, privatization, reduced public spending, freeing key relative prices such as interest rates, and lifting exchange controls" would address major problems regarding the proper functioning of the markets.[48] The WC also advocated a minimalist and non-interventionist state. Accordingly, state was perceived as a problem that undermines the proper functioning of the markets, rather than being conceived as a benign agent that facilitates better regulation and more efficient functioning of the markets. Staunchly supported by the hegemonic power centers of international political economy, the basic premises of the WC formed the main policy focus of the IMF and World Bank.

The weak spots and deeply flawed logic of the WC, however, surfaced rather quickly. Two interrelated developments proved crucial in this regard. First, the WC failed to live up to its initial promises. Mounting empirical evidence from Mexico (1994), Asia (1997), Russia (1998), and

[46] For an early account and a set of policy proposals in line with the logic of the WC, see John Williamson, "What Washington Means by Policy Reform?" in John Williamson, ed., *Latin American Adjustment: How Much Has Happened?* (Washington, DC: Institute for International Economics, 1990).

[47] For an in-depth analysis of this badly flawed logic, see Dani Rodrik, *Has Globalization Gone Too Far?* (Washington, DC: Institute of International Economics, 1997).

[48] Ziya Öniş and Fikret Şenses, "Rethinking the Emerging Post-Washington Consensus," *Development and Change* 36, no. 2 (2005): 264.

Argentina (2001) crises, inter alia, clearly demonstrated the flawed intellectual foundations of the WC. These crises also revealed that IMF-sponsored financial liberalization reforms and premature abolition of capital account regimes eventually failed in a variety of cases. As Stiglitz points out, it was understood that "redesigning the regulatory system, not financial liberalization, should be the issue."[49] Second, the "star globalizers" of the post-1980 era were the countries that pursued heterodox policies. As Rodrik puts "globalization's chief beneficiaries are not necessarily those with the most open economic policies."[50] The states known for their heterodox fiscal and financial policies—including active state guidance and intervention—like China, India, and Vietnam protected themselves against the side effects of global financial crises better than the ones pursued orthodox neoliberal dictums.[51] The poor record of the latter increasingly jeopardized the legitimacy and credibility of the Bretton Woods institutions advocating the WC. The spectacular failure of the WC, as a result, laid the groundwork for a kind of self-criticism from within dominant establishment. Accordingly, the concept of conditionality started to be redefined with greater attention being paid to institutional and regulatory reforms rather than single-minded emphasis on austerity measures. The IMF also found itself amidst an identity crisis and faced with severe criticisms not only from external intellectual echelons but also from within circles.[52] It is therefore plausible to argue that this paradigmatic shift also had ramifications on the design and policy mix of Turkey's post-crisis reform program.[53]

In summary, the policy entrepreneurship of Kemal Derviş played its role in sending coherent, credible, and strong signals to the external anchors. However, the "Derviş factor" needs to be placed into a proper context: The combined effects of the interest-based factors that highlighted Turkey's geopolitical advantages and ideational factors that brought important changes in the mind-set of the IMF staff—once com-

[49] Joseph Stiglitz, "More Instruments and Broader Goals: Moving Toward the Post-Washington Consensus," *Revista de Economia Politica* 19, no. 1 (1999): 106.

[50] Dani Rodrik, "How to Save Globalization from Its Cheerleaders," *The Journal of Trade and Diplomacy* 1, no. 2 (2007): 3.

[51] Ibid.

[52] For a lucid analysis see Ben Thirkell-White, *The IMF and the Politics of Financial Globalization: From the Asian Crisis to a New International Financial Architecture* (Basingstoke: Palgrave Macmillan, 2005).

[53] Interview with senior official, Ministry of Economic Affairs, September 11, 2014.

bined with the failure of the December 1999 IMF-imposed program—noticeably enlarged Turkey's bargaining space and facilitated the emergence of a common crisis narrative, relying on the logic of regulatory state.

4.4 Domestic Institutional Structures: Enabling Factors at Work

The domestic institutional structures also facilitated the proper implementation of the reform program in the Turkish context. In fact, the institutional structures and agents mutually contributed to the emergence of a virtuous cycle, as a result of which consensus-based policy-making prevailed. As argued in Chap. 2, new supportive coalitions need to be created along with the dismantlement of the entrenched ones in order to introduce new paradigms. The responses of domestic institutional players and their mode of interactions with reformist state agents and external actors are decisive in this regard. To this end, political context, state bureaucracy, trade unions, and business associations informed Turkey's post-crisis reform performance. The following part discusses the role of institutional players and tries to elucidate how complex interactions informed the emergence and consolidation of new winning coalitions in Turkey.

4.5 Political Context

First, domestic political context aroused as an important factor in Turkey's post-crisis political economy equilibrium. The Turkish political system, more often than not, tended to inform polarized and conflictual mode of governance, which in turn, exacerbated collective action problems toward instigating virtuous reformist cycles (Chap. 3). Thus, similar to other reactive states, political context used to play an adverse role in terms of change. The post-crisis political equilibrium, however, paints a different picture. The crisis empowered the reformist segments of economic bureaucracy relative to political elites. Turkey's preparedness at the bureaucratic level was relatively high in the wake of February 2001 crisis. Thanks to the experiences derived from past economic crises, Turkish economic bureaucracy was aware of the underlying fiscal and financial fragilities. Accordingly, a series of reforms were already in progress for a while to streamline the fiscal and financial system in Turkey.

> Turkish economic bureaucracy had been working on economic fragilities for a long time period. Thus they accumulated significant degree of expertise on what needs to be done. Despite certain political resistance, for instance, Turkey succeeded in establishing BRSA and SDIF before the crisis. More or less, the other vital fiscal and financial reforms were also prepared by economic bureaucracy.[54]

The degree of "preparedness" appeared as a crucial factor in terms of the content and ultimate success of the reform program:

> In fact, technical studies on most of the reform proposals, such as the establishment of BRSA and Central Bank independence law, had already been conducted by economic bureaucracy before the 2001 economic crisis hit the economy. What was required was the political will to put these reform proposals into practice.[55]

The domestic political economy context and international dynamics, however, were not conducive to put these reformist ideas into implementation in a coordinated and determined way. In this sense, Turkey's final economic jolt posed a true critical juncture and leveled the playing field as it exhausted dominant mode of relations and rendered existing institutional arrangements highly fluid. It became apparent that Turkey was in need of deep paradigmatic changes in state-market relations. Thus, the sense of complacency, which used to be defining characteristics of the political modus operandi during 1990s, was replaced by a sense of urgency.[56] Accordingly, broad-based consensus emerged among different segments of society, which seized rare context-specific opportunities for reform-oriented change agents to step smartly through it. As a high-level bureaucrat put it eloquently;

> [In 2001] Turkey experienced the deepest crisis in recent economic history. The crisis created a wave of anxiety and concern among people [different segments of society]. We were also under high pressure from international markets. The overwhelming majority of the population [and interest groups] accepted that structural reforms must be implemented quickly in order to restore economic growth, create new jobs, and mitigate the destructive effects of crisis. It is in this context that we took courageous reformist steps in financial and fiscal areas.[57]

[54] Interview with senior official, Undersecretary of Treasury, September 10, 2014; interview with senior official, Central Bank of the Republic of Turkey, September 16, 2014.

[55] Interview with senior official, Ministry of Economic Affairs, September 11, 2014.

[56] Interview with senior official, Capital Markets Board of Turkey, September 11, 2014.

[57] Interview with senior official, Undersecretary of Treasury, September 10, 2014.

The crisis was a profound exogenous shock for the coalition government in every sense. A wave of panic spread through the coalition partners following the collapse of the banking system and the bankruptcy of state's fiscal accounts. The coalition partners reckoned that stakes were very high because their credibility drastically eroded in the eyes of domestic constituency and international investors.[58] Thus, the depth of the crisis altered the perceptions of political elite as they cognized that they had to bite the bullet and streamline themselves since "there was no alternative but to reform" the public finances and financial system.[59] In other words, "the coalition leaders were on the same page regarding the urgency and necessity of comprehensive structural reforms."[60] It became apparent that "economic catastrophe showed all but the most incorrigibly obtuse that to try and carry on with 'business as usual' would be tantamount to embracing national self-destruction."[61] It is in this context that Derviş was invited to the country as a joint decision of the coalition partners.[62] Thanks to the fragile political equilibrium and because he was considered as the only "exit strategy," the coalition government, in the initial phases, placed unequivocal support behind Derviş. The leader of ANAP and the deputy prime minister at the time, Mesut Yılmaz, stated this point in a lucid manner:

> The political context at the time was not conducive to implement such [reform] program because we were three-partite coalition and would eventually go to elections. All coalition partners had electoral concerns. The implementation of this [ambitious] program was only possible if we made real sacrifices, overcame our immediate interests and put them aside for the future of the country. In order to achieve this, we needed a non-political

[58] The credibility of the entire political system collapsed in the wake of the crisis. The majority of the public was in the opinion that political parties were corrupt and inept. In our interview, the senior official of the MHP, also admitted that the economy was "taken hostage by widespread corruption" at the time.

[59] Interview with senior official, Yapı Kredi Bank, September 28, 2014.

[60] Interview with senior official, Ministry of Economic Affairs, September 11, 2014.

[61] Soli Özel, "Turkey at the Polls: After the Tsunami," *Journal of Democracy* 14, no. 2 (2003): 90.

[62] During my interviews, I was told two different stories about the invitation process. First, some high level technocrats and political elites argued that Stanley Fischer of the IMF advised Prime Minister Ecevit to appoint Kemal Derviş. Second, I was also told that Ecevit did not receive any "advice" from external actors. He decided to call Derviş himself based on their previous connections. Derviş, himself, argued that the second explanation was the true one.

> figure with no political expectations to lead the program. The candidate was also expected to have required experience and expertise to implement the program in a determined and non-compromising way.[63]

The coalition leaders' strong political will opened a large maneuver space for Derviş to couple problems, policies (i.e., solutions), and politics.[64] Thanks to the autonomy and strong mandate provided by the government, Derviş could circumvent tricky political calculations and succeeded to appoint his own economic team, which was desperately absent in Greece (see Chaps. 6 and 7).

4.6 Domestic Policy Coalitions

Second, domestic policy coalitions played crucial role that informed Turkey's reform performance in the post-crisis period. Chapter 3 demonstrated that the domestic coalitions approximated reform-biased rent-seeking networks, which contributed to the procrastination of reform processes and the subsequent fiscal crisis of the state. Thus, the challenge for reformist agents at the domestic level was to steer new winning coalitions to ensure domestic ownership of the change agenda.

Before flying to Turkey, Derviş talked to Guillermo Ortiz, the then finance minister who played a major role in the 1994 Mexican crisis hoping to receive some useful advice. Ortiz advised Derviş to "spend half of his day to inform the public and try to obtain the active support of different interest groups."[65] In retrospect, it seems that Derviş followed this crucial advice as he placed central emphasis to proper dialogue with social partners:

> [Derviş] placed an utmost emphasis on communication [with social partners] and did best to explain the driving logic and necessity of the reform program. [He] regularly informed labour unions, business associations, media, and scholars.[66]

[63] Quoted in Mehmet Ali Birand, *Son Darbe 28 Şubat* (İstanbul: Doğan Kitap, 2012), 336–337.

[64] Interview with senior official of MHP, September 4, 2014; interview with member of the Economic Advisors Committee to Bülent Ecevit, September 10, 2014.

[65] Interview with Kemal Derviş quoted in Işın Çelebi, *Türkiye"nin Dönüşüm Yılları: Yeniden Öğrenme Zamanı* (İstanbul: Alfa, 2012), 372.

[66] Interview with senior official, Ministry of Economic Affairs, September 11, 2014.

The regular communication meetings with social partners yielded concrete results toward creating new pro-reform coalitions. On the business side, TÜSİAD threw unequivocal support behind the IMF-sponsored reform program.[67] In fact, TÜSİAD's policy stance needs to be interpreted within the context of changing power equilibrium in the Turkish finance capital. Turkish business passed through intra-capital bifurcation during the second half of the 1990s.[68] Business elite in Turkey mainly relied on a rentier-oriented capital accumulation model, flourished under the auspices of arbitrary state protection. As Keyman and Koyuncu point out, however, "state tradition [and accompanying state-centred Turkish modernization]… faced a serious legitimacy problem in maintaining its position as the primary context for politics."[69] The exhaustion of prevalent model in state-market relations fully reverberated following the devastating economic havoc in 2001. Accordingly, as a testament to the collapse of reactive policy networks, overwhelming majority of state-dependent firms declared bankruptcy. The natural elimination of otherwise well-entrenched distributional coalitions strengthened the hands of more integrationist and growth-oriented segments of capital holders, which embraced an increasingly critical rhetoric toward state's arbitrary and ambiguous interventions in the functioning of the markets. Represented by TÜSİAD at the institutional level, these firms backed new economic paradigm in the aftermath of the crisis. TÜSİAD president Tuncay Özilhan claimed that the crisis opened up an opportunity space to address Turkey's long-awaited structural economic problems.[70] According to TÜSİAD, "state […] with its inefficient bureaucracy and profligate fiscal policies, constituted Turkey's most important structural economic problem."[71] Thus, the crisis narrative framed at the domestic-external nexus perfectly resonated with TÜSİAD's interests.

[67] Interview with senior advisor to President, TÜSİAD, September 24, 2014; interview with senior advisor to Kemal Derviş September 26, 2014.

[68] Derya Gültekin-Karakaş, *Hem Hasımız* Hem *Hısımız: Türkiye"de Finans Kapitalin Dönüşümü ve Banka Reformu* (İstanbul: İletişim Yayınları, 2009).

[69] E. Fuat Keyman and Berrin Koyuncu, "Globalization, Alternative Modernities, and the Political Economy of Turkey," *Review of International Political Economy* 12, no. 1 (2005): 109.

[70] TÜSİAD, "TÜSİAD Yönetİm Kurulu Başkanı Tuncay ÖzIlhan'ın 5. SİAD Zirvesİ Konuşması," May 9, 2001, 4–5.

[71] Ibid., 5.

> The content of the reform program was significantly overlapping with the arguments and proposals that TÜSİAD advocated for years. Thus TÜSİAD strongly supported the program.[72]

The leading members of TÜSİAD also welcomed the IMF-induced reform package. Rahmi Koç, the CEO of the Koç Holding, Turkey's largest conglomerate, for instance, expressed his support, noting the "program as Turkey's last chance."[73]

The approach of the peak association of small- and medium-sized enterprises, TOBB, toward the reform program needs to be analyzed in two distinct phases. The first phase, which lasted until June 2001 under the chairmanship of Fuat Miras, refers to a period of "cautious support." TOBB, in this period, did not categorically reject the reform program. However, Miras criticized Derviş and his economic team on several occasions since, according to Miras, they declined to consult to TOBB representatives regarding the policy mix of the reform program. This reluctant stance, however, gradually changed after June 2001 with the election of Rifat Hisarcıklıoğlu as the new chairman. Hisarcıklıoğlu claimed that the responsibility of the crisis lays on the shoulders of all segments of the society, in particular the political elite and businessmen. He also interpreted the crisis as "a golden opportunity" to restructure the Turkish economy.[74] TOBB occupied a crucial position in the post-crisis context as it represents all small- and medium-sized enterprises in Turkey, which composes more than 65 percent of total employment. TOBB's role became more important in a context that another important representative of Anatolian capital, MÜSİAD, categorically rejected the program.[75] According to MÜSİAD representatives, the program was biased toward big business and international financial capital, thus offering no concrete benefits to the productive classes. MÜSİAD representatives also targeted Derviş since, according to them, Derviş refrained from informing them at the formulation and implementation stages of the program.[76] TOBB's institutional support increased the legitimacy of the reform measures in

[72] Interview with senior advisor to President, TÜSİAD, September 24, 2014.

[73] Milliyet Gazetesi, "Koç: Program Son Şansımız," May 18, 2001.

[74] Rifat Hisarcıklıoğlu, "57. Genel Kurul Konuşması, 2 Mayıs 2002" in Nart Bozkurt, *Başkanların Genel Kurul Konuşmaları*, Volume 3 (Ankara: TOBB Yayınları, 2011), 645–646.

[75] Interview with senior official of MÜSİAD, September 16, 2014.

[76] Interview with senior official of MÜSİAD, September 16, 2014.

the eyes of its members, which in turn, decreased the risks of untoward social incidents.[77]

The major institutional actors that ensure social control in crisis juncture were labor organizations. On the labor side, trade unions, in a stark contrast to the Greek case, did not categorically reject the reform program. Therefore, the labor class did not pour into the streets, though occasional and spasmodic protests took place.[78] It is also important to note at this point that trade unions' reactions were much weaker than their resistance to the stabilization measures put into implementation following the 1994 economic crisis. In fact, field research revealed that the two major trade unions developed a relatively consensus-prone approach in terms of the ownership of the reform program. As anticipated, trade unions claimed no responsibility in the emergence of the crisis. According to TÜRK-İŞ, Turkey's peak labor association, the crisis was the outcome of "corrupt banking system," "greedy political behaviour," and "misguided IMF policies imposed on Turkey."[79] Similarly, DİSK argued that the main responsibility lies on the shoulders of the financial elite and owners of capital that behaved irresponsibly to maximize their short-term interests at the expense of society, which was encouraged by uncontrolled neoliberal economic model.[80] That being said, trade unions seemed to be convinced that reform program was the only way to get out of the economic havoc in 2001.

> The crisis was a financial crisis, which emanated from the lax legal regulations, loopholes in the regulatory mechanisms, and political [shortsidedness]. Yet, the crisis pushed the entire country into difficulty. Thus we decided to do whatever it takes in order to overcome it.[81]

DİSK, for obvious reasons, was not a fan of the IMF policies. Historical record also suggests that DİSK representatives denounced the previous stand-by agreements. The debt of the 2001 crisis, however, forced DİSK to adopt a tolerant approach to the economic reform program as they deemed it the only way to restore economic recovery and avoid further job losses.

[77] Interview with senior official, Ministry of Economic Affairs, September 11, 2014.

[78] Interview with senior official of TÜRK-İŞ, September 10, 2014; interview with senior official of DİSK, September 9, 2014.

[79] Interview with senior official of TÜRK-İŞ, September 10, 2014.

[80] Interview with senior official of DİSK, September 9, 2014.

[81] Interview with senior official of DİSK, September 9, 2014.

> DİSK was aware that public finances bankrupted. Thus DİSK adopted a consensus-seeking and solution-based approach [to restore quick economic recovery]. We, of course, put primary emphasis on the wages and rights of the labour class.[82]

TÜRK-İŞ, Turkey's largest trade union and the major representative of civil servants adopted a more critical stance in the first instance.[83] The cuts in public expenditures and privatization of the SEEs constituted one of the cornerstones of the IMF-led reform program. Similar to all other stand-by agreements, the IMF officials requested sharp decline in public sector wages (see above). Therefore, TÜRK-İŞ strongly resisted the demands of the IMF on the wage issue. The resistance of TÜRK-İŞ, and to a certain degree DİSK, forced Derviş to renegotiate the policy mix of the program in regard to public sector wages. Following the softening stance of the IMF, a wage deal was cut off with labor unions, as a result of which they also softened their resistance.

> [Business associations, trade unions, and society in general] owned the reform program to a surprising degree. Trade unions showed us significant support. They rightly claimed that they were not responsible for the crisis. Yet, they did not reject reform measures in order to avoid further job losses. The wage deal we concluded with TÜRK-İŞ was a very successful example of a consensus-based adjustment.[84]

The regulation of the financial sector and tough measures taken against ailing banks increased the credibility of the reform program in the eyes of the labor unions because they perceived these measures as "sincere" steps in the right direction to overcome Turkey's deep-rooted fiscal and financial profligacy.

> Derviş promised [and succeeded] to create a rule-based financial system in Turkey. The lax and arbitrary credit policies of the banks were brought under strict regulation thanks to independent regulatory agencies. All these measures [that we also supported] disciplined Turkish economy.[85]

[82] Interview with senior official of DİSK, September 9, 2014.

[83] Interview with senior official of TÜRK-İŞ, September 10, 2014.

[84] Interview with senior official, Ministry of Economic Affairs, September 11, 2014.

[85] Interview with senior official of DİSK, September 9, 2014. Also, interview with senior official of TÜRK-İŞ, September 10, 2014.

What changed the preference functions of domestic policy coalitions in Turkey and how are they convinced to bear the immediate costs of massive economic adjustment? It appears that the depth of the economic crisis, the almost perfect narrative match at the domestic-external nexus, and the policy entrepreneurship effects mutually interacted so that a new fiscal regime was deemed inescapable. In addition to the factors highlighted above, one should also underline that Turkey took advantage of the double external actor in the post-crisis context, which unprecedentedly cemented the domestic ownership of new economic paradigm. The IMF was in fact not strong enough to play a permanent anchor role for Turkey. The previous IMF programs were failed not only because of the weak domestic ownership and crucial design failures but also because the IMF proved to be a relatively weak external anchor to ensure state's fiscal and financial prudence. In this sense, the EU further strengthened the hands of pro-reform coalitions and helped overcoming collective action problems toward implementation of the deep-seated reforms in the wake of economic crisis. In other words, the idea of EU membership had profound effects on the consolidation of dominant crisis narrative framed at the agency level.

The EU declared Turkey a candidate country in December 1999 Helsinki summit. The decision invited a series of political and economic reverberations because, for the first time in Turkey's long-lasting relationship with the EU, "the ball was placed in Turkey's court, meaning that the door to Europe is open to Turkey if it can meet the criteria for membership… including economic transparency and competitiveness."[86] Turkey was asked to instigate a set of comprehensive political and economic reforms so as to obtain a date to start negotiations with the EU. The incentive structures offered by the EU reinforced a virtuous cycle of reform activism unmatched in Turkey's recent history. The coalition partners, particularly DSP and ANAP, and the recently established future ruling party, the Justice and Development Party (AKP), adopted a "euro-enthusiastic" stance. In addition, the most active economic interest groups, such as TOBB and TÜSİAD exhibited strong interest in Turkey's EU vocation. TOBB defined the EU membership goal as "a social [and economic] transformation project."[87] TÜSİAD suggested that being part of the EU would boost "Turkey's eco-

[86] Paul Kubicek, "The Earthquake, the European Union, and Political Reform in Turkey," *Mediterranean Politics* 7, no. 1 (2002): 2.

[87] Rifat Hisarcıklıoğlu, "57. Genel Kurul Konuşması, 2 Mayıs 2002," 655.

nomic welfare, foreign direct investment, and growth performance," noting particularly that the creation of a regulatory state was sine qua non of the EU accession process.[88] In the words of TÜSİAD president:

> By achieving structural reforms in the way we govern our state [and economy], and to integrate with the EU, we have to prove the entire world that we are determined not to be 'a country of crises' anymore.[89]

The popular support was also fairly high, as some 75 percent of the public had had a positive perception on Turkey's EU bid.[90] In this context, as membership seemed a real possibility, the EU-leverage appeared as a strong asset to legitimize the reform packages. It is in this appropriate context that economic reforms were linked to the membership process as "necessary steps to converge with the EU."[91]

> Derviş narrated the reform agenda as the [only] way for Turkish economy to converge with the EU members in the fields of financial [and fiscal] regulations. It was possible to promulgate these reform bills only in such a context [i.e., in the heydays of EU membership process].[92]

The EU-factor reinforced many aspects of Turkey's post-crisis reform agenda because the prerequisites for EU membership overlapped with the IMF-sponsored reform program. A close examination of the EU progress reports reveals that state's fiscal discipline, independence of the Central Bank for an effective control of inflation,[93] the enforcement of a set of laws and institutions in charge of effective financial regulation, and massive privatizations,[94] inter alia, were recommended for Turkey to convergence with the EU standards. Thus, the EU endorsed the IMF-sponsored reform

[88] TÜSİAD, "Türkiye'nin AB Üyeliği: Doğrudan Yatırımlar ve Ekonomik Büyüme," *TÜSİAD Görüşler Dizisi*, no. 8 (2002).

[89] TÜSİAD, "TÜSİAD Yönetİm Kurulu Başkanı Tuncay ÖzİIhan'ın 5. SİAD ZirvesI Konuşması," 2.

[90] Kubicek, "The Earthquake, the European Union, and Political Reform in Turkey," *Mediterranean Politics*, 11.

[91] Undersecretariat of Treasury, *Strengthening the Turkish Economy: Turkey's Transition Program,* 34.

[92] Interview with senior official of DİSK, September 9, 2014.

[93] European Commission, *1999 Regular Report on* Turkey's *Progress Toward Accession* (Brussels: European Commission, October 1999): 26, 39.

[94] European Commission, *2000 Regular Report on Turkey's Progress Toward Accession* (Brussels: European Commission, November, 2000): 31, 47.

program, mentioning that the proper implementation of the measures would help Turkey comply with the accession criteria:

> [Following the economic crisis] a substantial number of laws, implementing aspects of the new economic plan, were adopted swiftly in the second quarter of 2001. *These reforms are intended to overcome the crisis, and to help meet the economic criteria for EU membership.*[95]

It is therefore fair to argue that the EU-anchor sturdily altered the interest functions and outlook of domestic policy coalitions and provided considerable leeway in the circulation of reform-oriented ideas at the domestic political economy landscape. Derviş skillfully exploited the EU-factor as a complementary anchor in order to broaden the scope of pro-reform coalitions and enfeeble the resistance points. In this sense, it is not coincidental that *Turkey's Transition Program* made explicit references to the Maastricht criteria and EU membership:

> Through structural reforms, Turkey will permanently reduce inflation to single digits, maintain public deficit at sustainable levels and satisfy other criteria for membership in the EU and EMU.[96]

The double IMF-EU anchor synergistically tilted the balance in disfavor of status quo so that the Turkish parliament swiftly adopted the laws and regulations envisaged in *Turkey's Transition Program* and *Banking Sector Restructuring Program* in the summer of 2001. That being said, certain difficulties were also encountered due to the fragility and knife-edge equilibrium of the coalition government. The two most controversial reforms were related to the tobacco law and the restructuration of Türk Telekom, Turkey's telecommunications giant. The minister of state in charge of privatization implementations, Yüksel Yalova, expressed his objection to the tobacco law mainly because of electoral concerns. He therefore refused sending the draft law to the parliament. The postponement laid the groundwork for a clash between Yalova and Derviş, since the latter thought that this step might put the entire credibility of the reform program into jeopardy. As a result of the intense pressures, Deputy Prime

[95] European Commission, *2001 Regular Report on Turkey's Progress Toward Accession*, SEC (2001) 1756 (Brussels: European Commission, November 2001): 14, emphasis added.

[96] Undersecretariat of Treasury, *Strengthening the Turkish Economy: Turkey's Transition Program*, 34.

Minister, Mesut Yılmaz, asked Yalova to leave his post. The tobacco law was then passed by the parliament just few days after the resignation of the minister.

The second incident, the Türk Telekom case, was even more critical. Derviş had a public argument with the minister of transportation, Enis Öksüz, backed by the MHP leader Devlet Bahçeli, over the appointments to the governing board of Türk Telekom.[97] Derviş claimed that the candidates proposed by the transportation minister did not comply with the criteria highlighted in the Letter of Intent, thus he opposed their appointments. The eventual political stalemate paved the way for a tacit crisis in the coalition government, which in turn, led to the postponement of the second tranche of the IMF credit support because of IMF's insistence "to verify that the newly appointed board of Türk Telekom meets the requirements set out in the [May 3 memorandum]."[98] The IMF's adamant stance and Derviş' pressures forced the MHP leader to ask for the resignation of the minister of transportation on July 17, 2001. Just ten days after the debate, Stanley Fischer paid a visit to Turkey to discuss the state of the program and to underscore IMF's strong support to Turkey's on-going reform agenda. Fischer and Derviş, in their joint press statement, declared that they are in full agreement regarding the design of the package and the progress so far achieved.[99]

Despite the most intense phase of the crisis was left behind as of late 2001, the reform agenda remained on knife-edge equilibrium since the consensus among pro-reform coalitions was still paper-thin. Furthermore, the political context took a turn for the worse starting from the second quarter of 2002 as the coalition government entered into deep turbulence. First, the Prime Minister Bülent Ecevit experienced serious health problems that impeded the proper functioning of the government. The imminent political instability and economic uncertainty adversely informed the expectations of the market actors. In such a parlous state of political environment, the coordination failures regarding the economic affairs amplified to such an extent that Derviş had to send a letter to the coalition leaders on April 4, 2002, seriously warning about a train wreck in the economy.

[97] MHP leader vociferously criticized Kemal Derviş by stating, "it is by no means acceptable that Derviş threatens the government in every bottleneck with his resignation and cut-off of the IMF support." Milliyet Gazetesi, "MHP: İstifa Etse Hiçbir Şey Olmaz," June 29, 2001.

[98] IMF, "IMF Postpones Board Meeting on Turkey," *News Brief no. 01/51*, July 2, 2001.

[99] IMF, "Statement on Turkey by IMF First Deputy Managing Director Stanley Fischer," *News Brief no. 01/66*, July 28, 2001.

Second, Derviş appeared as a potential leader in Turkish politics, which in turn, stroke a sensitive nerve among coalition partners.[100] On May 10, he overtly complained about the political instability and fingered out the early elections as an exit strategy. His decision to abandon his non-partisan position laid the groundwork for an unexpected challenge from within DSP ranks to Ecevit's leadership. Half of the parliamentarians, headed by Ecevit's close aid Hüsamettin Özkan, resigned from DSP to found a new political party. Upon the insistence of the MHP leader, the coalition government called for early elections scheduled for November 3, 2002. Not surprisingly, the limping macroeconomic balances turned upside down again, while the IMF decided to postpone the next trench of financial support.

4.7 Third Stage: The Consolidation of Regulatory State

The third stage refers to the consolidation of the reform program through the fortification of new winning coalitions. As it will be discussed in the Greek case, change in legal codes need not mean a real change in substance. What translates the former into the latter is the consolidation of pro-reform coalitions inspired by a strong political will. Thus, the difference is only discernible through a thorough analysis of the third stage of the three-stage framework. From this point of view, Turkey entered into a stable consolidation phase only after the elections held on November 3, 2002.

In the first national elections following the economic crisis, Turkish voters swept aside established parties. The election results were historic for a number of reasons. First, the whole cohort of political establishment was severely punished by the public. All three members of the coalition government (DSP, MHP, and ANAP) failed to pass the election threshold. Astonishingly, their combined vote share decreased from 53.4 percent in 1999 to 14.6 percent in 2002 elections. The opposition parties also fared very poorly as none of them succeeded to pass the election threshold. The election results reflected "electorate's anxious search for new options" as they got disenchanted with the corruption-tainted parties and clientelism-prone old spoils system.[101] Second, the AKP, a successor of previously

[100] Interview with senior official of MHP, September 4, 2014; interview with member of the Economic Advisors Committee to Bülent Ecevit, September 10, 2014.

[101] Özel, "After the Tsunami," *Journal of Democracy*, 81.

banned Islamist parties, gained a triumphant victory that generated earthquake-like political impacts. The AKP wound up two-thirds of the parliament (363 of the 541 elected seats), which put a decisive end to the long-lasted interlude of shaky coalition governments. Third, the election results posed a new critical juncture on the fortune of the economic reforms enacted in the aftermath of the economic crisis. As a matter of fact, in its pre-election party program, the AKP framed an avowedly pro-EU and pro-market rhetoric, clearly stated in AKP's election manifesto. Yet, the "party's questionable provenance" was still a source of anxiety for many, both at home and abroad, as there were grave doubts about the sincerity of AKP's conversion.[102] A sharp reversal of the reform processes and the reincarnation of the Islamist-cum-uncontrolled populism was still not-a-too-distant possibility in the context of late 2002 and early 2003. The AKP leadership, however, owned the IMF-induced reform program along with a zealous quest for EU membership, which in turn, paved the way for the consolidation of new economic paradigm.[103]

The AKP's adherence to the main contours of the regulatory state laid the groundwork for the enhancement of Turkey's state capacity in its first term in office. First, political context approximated to consensus-based policy-making under intense pressure of the double IMF-EU anchor. The successive weak coalition governments that lacked political will and capacity to impose economic discipline were replaced by single party governments functioning in line with the basic parameters of a regulatory state. Second, state economic bureaucracy benefitted from better coordination and increasing autonomy vis-à-vis the rent-seeking interest coalitions. The regulatory institutions performed their functions without major political interventions from the non-market forces, which in turn informed rule-based agency behavior. Third, intra-capital restructuration, especially in the banking sector, dismantled the previous networks that rely on rentier type of accumulation strategies. The fiscal discipline of the state, in this sense, forced capital holders to adopt more growth-oriented internationalization strategies. During 2002–2007, new winning coalitions emerged

[102] Ziya Öniş and E. Fuat Keyman, "Turkey at the Polls: A New Path Emerges," *Journal of Democracy* 14, no. 2 (2003): 96.

[103] I should note at this point that the leading economic figures of the AKP government do argue that they made substantial revisions in the IMF-sponsored reform program. A former minister stated in our interview that AKP government added strong social and industrial policy components to the existing program during its first term in office. Interview with former Minister of Industry and Trade, September 12, 2014.

in the sense that, hitherto isolated economic interest groups, primarily MÜSİAD and related capital circles, was also taken on board by the AKP government that further legitimized the new policy paradigm in the eyes of the conservative entrepreneurs spread across the Anatolia.[104] This also had deep-seated ramifications on Turkey's democratization experience and foreign policy performance.

The empirical outcomes of the virtuous cycle Turkey entered in the post-2002 are reflected in basic indicators: The state's fiscal house was put into order as the budget deficit was reduced to 1.6 percent from 11.5 percent and public debt declined to 40 percent from more than 90 percent of GDP in five years. Turkey also succeeded to overcome stubborn inflation problem as the annual inflation rate declined to 8.7 percent from 45 percent during 2002–2007. The strict regulation of the financial sector also laid the groundwork for the banks to perform their true intermediary roles between the savers and the investors, rather than banking on the government.

The regulatory shift in the fiscal and financial policies, however, was not complemented by a pronounced industrial transformation strategy. For instance, selective industrial policy reforms were not included in the economic policy mix to ensure the transformation of Turkey's import-dependent foreign trade structure.[105] It is therefore fair to argue that the AKP government in its first term put the emphasis on the regulatory rather than the developmental aspect of the state capacity. However, the transformations taking place in the global political economy following the 2008 financial crisis triggered a reshuffling in Turkish policy-makers' perspectives as well. Parallel to the neo-developmental turn in global political economy in the aftermath of the global financial crisis,[106] the Turkish government also tried to develop a hands-on industrial approach to improve Turkey's industrial base. The declared aim was to transform production and exports structures in a gradual manner toward high-technology products. The premier-turned-president, Recep Tayyip Erdoğan, even set an overambitious target for Turkish economy: "By 2023," declared Erdoğan, "we want Turkey to be one of the top ten economic areas of the world...

[104] Interview with senior official of MÜSİAD, September 16, 2014.

[105] Mustafa Kutlay, "Internationalization of Finance Capital in Spain and Turkey: Neoliberal Globalization and the Political Economy of State Policies," *New Perspectives on Turkey*, no. 47 (2012): 115–137.

[106] Gerard Strange, *Towards a New Political Economy of Development* (Basingstoke: Palgrave Macmillan, 2014).

Over the next 15 years we want to increase the per capita income from $10,500 to $25,000."[107] Furthermore, ambitious economic targets were linked to a proactive foreign policy to place Turkey as a regional economic power in the Middle East and Eurasia.[108]

The government took certain steps in this direction. First, the *Turkish Industrial Strategy Document* was adopted in 2011 under the auspices of the Ministry of Science, Industry, and Technology, along with the involvement of the relevant public and private bodies.[109] The long-term goal of the industrial plan is to position Turkey as "the production base of Eurasia in medium- and high-tech products." In line with this overall objective, three basic strategic targets have been determined: (1) to increase the ratio of mid- and high-tech sectors in production and exports, (2) to transition to high value-added products in low-tech sectors, and (3) to increase the weight of companies that can continuously improve their skills. Thus industrial policy objectives were designed to target Turkey's recalcitrant current account deficit through high value-added products, which is expected to decrease the dependence of exports on imports.

The second aspect of Turkey's industrial strategy involved generous investment stimulus packages. In 2012, the AKP government announced a new package to encourage investments that aims at reducing dependence on imported intermediate goods, thereby alleviating the current account deficit and improving the research and development (R&D) base of the national economy. The stimulus package, which divides Turkey into six regions, enables each region to receive different amounts of incentives in proportion to regional socio-economic inequalities, including corporate tax incentives, cuts in social security premiums, free land, and access to cheap credit. The investment stimulus packages complement already-existing R&D policies, whereby the AKP governments have poured considerable amounts of money into research and innovation over the last decade. However, the stagnation of Turkey's high-technology share in total manufactured exports, a point that shall be discussed in detail below, hints that there is a long way ahead for the Turkish economy to catch up the world averages in high value-added production. For instance, the

[107] Recep Tayyip Erdoğan, "Turkish Economy Meets EU Entry Criteria," *The Huffington Post,* November 28, 2012.

[108] Mustafa Kutlay, "Economy as a Practical Hand in Turkish Foreign Policy: A Political Economy Explanation," *Insight Turkey* 13, no. 1 (2011): 67–88.

[109] Republic of Turkey Ministry of Industry and Trade, *Turkish Industrial Strategy Document: Towards EU Membership (2011-2014)*, 2010.

share of high-tech goods in Turkey's total exports is just 2 percent as of 2016, which is obviously a very low ratio in comparison to world average that hovers around 17 percent.[110] Furthermore, the adverse developments in Turkish politics in the post-2011 put the entire economy into serious jeopardy. The following part aims to shed light on this turbulent episode in Turkish politics.

4.8 Turkish Political Economy in Flux (2011–2016)

If Turkey's rise during 2002–2011 is the bright side of the coin, the post-2011 is equally striking since it demonstrates the conditions under which reactive states can exponentially erode their capacity and undermine their own potential. Rather ironically, Turkey plunged into a vicious cycle in the post-2011 era. The reversal started with significant setbacks and retreats on the democratization front. The 2011 general elections proved to be a crucial turning point in this context. In June 2011, the AKP succeeded to outperform its rivals by obtaining almost half of the total votes, an exceptional achievement in Turkish political history. It was the first time for a political party to win three successive elections with increasing vote shares (Fig. 4.1). This is an unusual phenomenon compared with Western democracies, where incumbent powers have a tendency to lose their popularity over time as a result of governmental fatigue. This unprecedented success boosted the confidence of the AKP elites and generated overconfidence on part of the executive at a time when the checks and balance mechanisms that constrained the AKP and its powerful leader Recep Tayyip Erdoğan were progressively dismantled. Turkish democracy in the post-2011 suffered from the absence of effective opposition and powerful external anchors.

The AKP's victory signified an era of "electoral hegemony," in which the power of a party becomes so strong that "it exceeds simply being a strong majority government."[111] The AKP's third term is also qualitatively different as domestic politics tilted toward intense polarization and gradual

[110] For an in-depth discussion, see Ziya Öniş and Mustafa Kutlay, "Rising Powers in a Changing Global Order: Political Economy of Turkey in the Age of BRICs," *Third World Quarterly* 34, no 8 (2013): 1416–1417.

[111] Fuat Keyman, "The AKP: Dominant Party, New Turkey and Polarization," *Insight Turkey* 16, no. 2 (2014): 23–24.

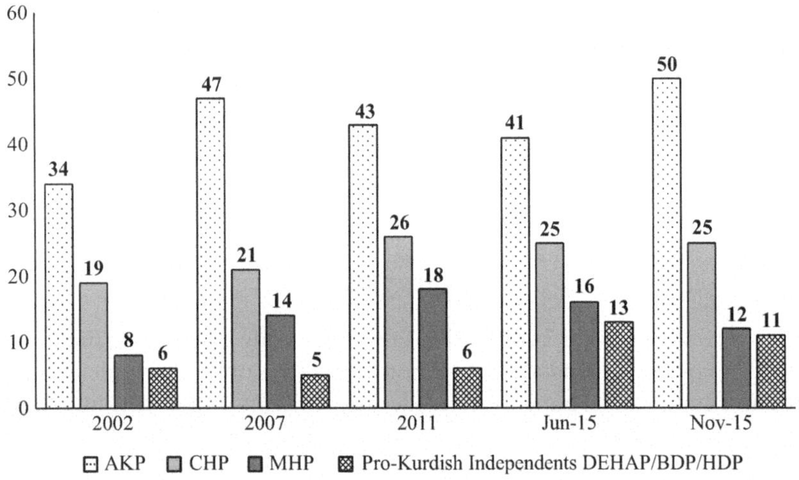

Fig. 4.1 Vote shares of Turkey's major parties

erosion of democratic institutions due to exclusive accumulation of political power. In fact, there appeared a chance on Turkey's political horizon in 2011 to craft a new constitution guaranteeing robust checks and balance mechanisms to replace the current 1982 constitution, which is promulgated by a military junta that hijacked Turkish democracy in 1980. All major political parties, including the AKP government, promised a new liberal constitution in their election campaigns. Despite the hopes were raised and civil society put great effort to draft alternative proposals the attempts were failed due to incommensurable interests of the parties represented at the parliament.[112]

The missed opportunity pushed Turkey into an equilibrium as a result of which excessive accumulation of power in the hands of the ruling party paved the way for considerable challenges in terms of democratic deepening. Given that the EU's anchor role also faded mainly due to the Cyprus problem and the internal crises of the European integration project, the government's understanding of democracy steadily drifted toward majoritarianism, in which, elections are constantly appreciated but little room is

[112] Burak Bilgehan Özpek, "Constitution-Making in Turkey After the 2011 Elections," *Turkish Studies* 13, no. 2 (2012): 153–167.

left for pluralist democratic practices. At a juncture when liberal democracy is in global retreat, Turkey also increasingly moved to a state of illiberalism. Özbudun argues that Turkey in this period approximated to a "delegative democracy," a type of democracy in which horizontal accountability, that is, "accountability to other autonomous institutions of the state such as the legislature or the courts," is almost non-existent.[113] It appears that the unassailable electoral hegemony of the ruling party under an influential leader injected high dose of self-confidence and resources to "rule in the way that they saw fit."[114] As a result, heavy-handed Turkish state was revitalized, with an intense polarization strategy to engineer the social and political life from above through a series of changes in the education system, religious affairs, and strict bureaucratic control. Also, significant setbacks in the realms of the freedom of expression, media freedom, and independence of the judicial system reduced the democratic space.

The majoritarian understanding of democracy and intentional polarization policies had deep effects on different segments of Turkish society. A clear sign of the uneasiness accumulated among the opposition circles was the Gezi protests erupted in May and June 2013. On May 28, 2013, a wave of civil unrest began in Gezi Park, a small area of trees abutting İstanbul's central place, Taksim Square. The protesters gathered together to contest the urban development plan for the park. The threatened demolition of the park and the violent eviction of the protesters by police forces sparked nationwide mobilization spreading around 79 cities in a very short time span. The protests lasted for about one month during which 2.5 million people joined the demonstrations according to the Ministry of Interior.[115] The protests were spontaneous and bottom-up in nature without any single group, political party or leader dominating the agenda. The composition of the participants also depicts a heterogeneous distribution. Accordingly, 56 percent of the participants in the first week hold undergraduate or graduate degrees. 51 percent of the participants were women. The protestors belong to various social, religious, and political groups with secular Turks, different segments of Kurds, and football

[113] Ergun Özbudun, "AKP at the Crossroads: Erdoğan's Majoritarian Drift," *South European Society and Politics* 19, no. 2 (2014): 162.

[114] Ziya Öniş, "Monopolising the Centre: The AKP and the Uncertain Path of Turkish Democracy," *The International Spectator* 50, no. 2 (2015): 26.

[115] Milliyet Gazetesi, "2.5 Milyon İnsan 79 İlde Sokağa İndi," June 23, 2013.

supporter groups were among the pioneers.[116] The protests were more than an expression of concern for the environment, rather an outburst of the social anxieties about the majoritarian and conservative turn in Turkish politics that was considered as a threat against the lifestyles of opposition and minority groups.

The excessive use of police force during Gezi movements also marked the expansion of the security state, which became more pertinent in the shifting dynamics of the Kurdish question. The AKP government took major steps to put an end to Turkey's long-lasting Kurdish question. The government initiated the Kurdish peace process as a major step never taken before in Turkish political history. However, an extraordinary chain of events led to the collapse of the peace process, which in turn, paved the way for the escalation of conflict between the Turkish state and the PKK (Kurdistan Workers' Party).[117] Thus, the historical identity-based cleavages in Turkish politics, once again, made a strong comeback in the third term of the AKP rule.

The critical watershed, however, was the failed coup attempt in July 2016. The coup attempt against Turkish democracy was thwarted thanks to the resistance of the Turkish citizens. While the failure of the coup attempt was a clear victory for democracy and civilian rule in Turkey, the aftermath was increasingly associated with a new illiberal wave under the imposition of state of emergency in a de facto hyper-presidential system. It is plausible to suggest that the extent of the clamp down was far bigger than any conceivable attempt to bring those responsible for the coup to justice. The prolonged "state of emergency" in the wake of the coup attempt and widespread detentions pushed Turkish politics into a permanent crisis. The scale of the purges involving journalists, academics, teachers, public sector employees, and business people further weakened rule of law and freedom of expression. The coup attempt also had deep impact on Turkey's relations with the West. The EU came under severe criticism from the government for its lukewarm reception of the massive popular reactions that helped to protect the civilian regime from a possible military intervention. On the other side, concerns were raised in both the US and Europe regarding the government's response and the scale of the purges

[116] Erdem Yörük and Murat Yüksel, "Class and Politics in Turkey's Gezi Protests," *New Left Review* 89 (2014): 103–123.

[117] Ziya Öniş, "Turkey's Two Elections: The AKP Comes Back," *Journal of Democracy* 27, no. 2 (2016): 141–154.

in the name of penalizing groups responsible for the attempt to overthrow the democratic regime. The worries expressed in the EU were interpreted as attempts to interfere in Turkey's domestic politics and an implicit endorsement of the coup attempt, generating strong nationalist sentiments in the process.

The Reversal of the Regulatory State Paradigm

The Turkish economy also encountered significant challenges starting from the third term of the AKP rule. Part of the problem with Turkey's reversing fortunes was external developments that took place following the global financial crisis. In the post-2009, the global markets entered into a sharp turbulence, in which, low growth rates, declining foreign investment, and shrinking space for trade has become defining parameters of the new normal. Not surprisingly, the global slump also hit the Turkish economy. Turkey's growth performance declined to 3.1 percent annually in the post-2011, from almost 7 percent during 2002–2008. Beyond the negative external influences, developments at the domestic level also hampered economic activity. In this period, the independence of regulatory institutions, which laid the institutional basis of the regulatory state paradigm, was gradually undermined. A good example was the growing interventionism in the operations of the Central Bank. This clearly made a sharp contrast with the early years of the AKP rule where independent regulatory institutions constituted the part and parcel of the new economic paradigm that contributed to economic success. Similarly, increasing politicization of public tenders and various new rent-extraction mechanisms jeopardized the rule-based governance. In fact, the state's role in the economy became increasingly non-transparent and shifted away from EU standards. The number and value of non-transparent public procurements, for instance, reached almost 45 percent, up from 34 percent in 2005.[118]

These forces altogether plunged the economy into stagnation. This is signified by the fact that Turkey's GDP per capita in current prices appeared to be stuck around $10,000 over the last five years (2011–2016), which suggest that Turkey entered middle-income trap. The middle-

[118] Daron Acemoğlu and Murat Üçer, "The Ups and Downs of Turkish Growth, 2002-2015: Political Dynamics, the European Union and the Institutional Slide," *NBER Working Paper*, no. 21608 (2015): 15–16.

income trap refers to the slowdown tendency for fast-developing countries after their GDP per capita has reached a certain threshold. Research on the middle-income trap reveals that it remains a serious challenge for countries to improve their GDP per capita from middle- to high-income levels. The World Bank's research estimates that of the 101 middle-income countries in 1960 only 13 reached high-income level status by 2008.[119] The overwhelming majority was unable to accomplish the jump and became stuck in the middle. As the economy moves from labor-intensive, low-cost exports toward capital-intensive production, labor is reallocated from agriculture to manufacturing sectors. This leads to the slowdown of economic output, because productivity growth from sectoral reallocation and technology import disappears. The most effective way to break out of the middle-income trap is the creation of market-enhancing inclusive institutions in the fields of democratic governance, education, industrial relations, judicial independence, and technology. This, again, implies that addressing Turkey's structural economic problems goes far beyond the economic realm. The creation of a genuinely pluralistic political order that feeds democratic practices, the reformation of the education system in order to promote free and creative thinking, and the consolidation of a legal system that guarantees political accountability and civil rights shall inform expansion of development-friendly inclusive institutions.[120]

Turkey's failure to break out of middle-income trap is closely related to the revival of the antagonistic relationship between state and domestic policy coalitions. The evidence suggests that state-business relations sharply deteriorated in the AKP's third term in office. The government directed harsh criticisms to TÜSİAD, Turkey's biggest business association representing the mainstream capitalist establishment of the country, since mid-2013 due to polarized political setting. This, in turn, hampered the kind of synergy needed to ensure reform-oriented institutional cooperation to overcome middle-income trap. On the other side, the government developed deeper relations with the newly emerging business elites in the inlands of Turkey, the so-called Anatolian Tigers. The new conservative business elite, particularly large-scale companies, took advantage of

[119] World Bank, *China 2030: Building a Modern, Harmonious, and Creative High-Income Society* (Washington, DC: World Bank Press, 2012), 13.

[120] For more on the relationship between inclusive institutions and economic development, see Daron Acemoğlu and James Robinson, *Why Nations Fail?* (London: Profile Books, 2012).

lucrative state incentives, public tenders, and extensive political support. However, these business actors have not demonstrated the expected performance in terms of transforming Turkey's import-dependent production and foreign trade structure. The government-backed "new capitalist class" mainly concentrated on low value-added sectors, with construction activities being the main engine of the expansion of their wealth.[121] The capital accumulation model over the last decade heavily relied on land and construction-related activities at the expense of technological and industrial production. This, in turn, exacerbates Turkey's current account deficits and creates imminent sustainability risks. Thus Turkish political economy is at a crossroads again, which suggests that Turkey, as a reactive state, seems to exhaust the extant policy paradigm.

4.9 Conclusion

This chapter set out to explore the dynamics of change in Turkish political economy following the 2001 crisis. The February 2001 turmoil was a critical juncture for Turkey as it put the socio-political and economic life into severe disarray. Despite its long-lasting hazardous impacts, the crisis opened up an opportunity window to reform the deeply flawed fiscal and financial regime of the reactive Turkish state. The depth of the crisis disturbed power balances and denounced well-entrenched rent-seeking coalitions. It, therefore, created room for reformist state agents to step through in, which was capitalized on to a significant extent. In the economic realm, regulatory state as a new paradigm was introduced. Based on the three-stage framework, this chapter argued that crisis did invite a paradigmatic change due to the complex mutual interplay of agents and institutions along domestic-external nexus.

Kemal Derviş stepped in as a capable reformist actor to mediate external dynamics and domestic coalitions in the wake of the crisis. Derviş narrated that the crisis emerged due to reactive state policies accumulated over the years. He coordinated economic bureaucracy and steered new pro-reform coalitions in support of the reform program. Derviş also succeeded in securing the urgently needed trust and credibility in the eyes of international community, thanks to which Turkey received an extraordinarily large amount of IMF assistance.

[121] Ayşe Bugra and Osman Savaskan, *New Capitalism in Turkey: The Relationship Between Politics, Religion and Business* (Cheltenham: Edward Elgar, 2014).

The chapter also maintained that domestic institutional players assumed enabling roles in the crisis context. The business associations, except MÜSİAD, threw their support behind the dominant crisis narrative as the content of the reform package resonated well with the changing interests of big business in Turkey. On the labor side, the roles played by the trade unions point to a stark contrast to the Greek case. In addition to their relatively weaker position in domestic power configuration, they also did not categorically reject the proposed package, which in turn, decreased the audience costs of a paradigm change. Finally, the EU-anchor turned into a crucial factor that complemented the IMF conditionality. The assumed benefits of a potential EU membership asymmetrically tilted the balance in favor of pro-change coalitions. The reform program was narrated as part of a broader economic strategy to converge with the EU standards. Thus, in the third phase of three-stage framework, the logic of regulatory state was consolidated during the first two terms of the AKP government.

The paradigm change in the wake of the 2001 crisis was not the only game-changing development in Turkish political economy. What is equally striking is the sharp reversal of the regulatory state paradigm and multiple challenges Turkey encountered in the post-2011. The over-accumulation of power in the hands of the ruling party and the gradual erosion of institutional checks and balance mechanisms marked the beginning of the end for regulatory state paradigm, which was underpinned by intentional polarization and institutional regression. The political turbulence during the AKP's third term in office also informed Turkey's economic slowdown. The capital accumulation model in this period mainly relied on construction-related activities and land at the expense of technological and industrial production. Thus, the extant development model creates imminent sustainability risks for Turkish politics and economy.

References

Acemoğlu, Daron and James Robinson. *Why Nations Fail?* London: Profile Books, 2012.

Acemoğlu, Daron and Murat Üçer. "The Ups and Downs of Turkish Growth, 2002–2015: Political Dynamics, the European Union and the Institutional Slide." *NBER Working Paper*, No. 21608 (2015).

Akyüz, Yılmaz, and Korkut Boratav. "The Making of the Turkish Financial Crisis." *World Development* 31, no. 9 (2003): 1549–1566.

Bakır, Caner. "Policy Entrepreneurship and Institutional Change: Multilevel Governance of Central Banking Reform." *Governance: An International Journal of Policy, Administration and Institutions* 22, no. 4 (2009): 571–598.

BDDK. *Towards a Sound Turkish Banking Sector*. Ankara: BDDK. May 2001.

Birand, Mehmet Ali. *Son Darbe 28 Şubat*. İstanbul: Doğan Kitap, 2012.

Bugra, Ayşe and Osman Savaskan. *New Capitalism in Turkey: The Relationship between Politics, Religion and Business*. Cheltenham: Edward Elgar, 2014.

Çelebi, Işın. *Türkiye'nin Dönüşüm Yılları: Yeniden Öğrenme Zamanı*. İstanbul: Alfa, 2012.

Derviş, Kemal. "Returning From the Brink: Turkey's Efforts at Systemic Change and Structural Reform." In *Development Challenges in the 1990s: Leading Policymakers Speak from Experience*, edited by Tim Besley, and Roberto Zagha, 62–81. Oxford: Oxford University Press, 2005.

DPT. *Dokuzuncu Kalkınma Planı (2007–2013): Finansal Hizmetler Özel İhtisas Komisyonu Raporu*. Ankara: Devlet Planlama Teşkilatı. 2007.

Erdoğan, Recep Tayyip. "Turkish Economy meets EU Entry Criteria." *The Huffington Post*, November 28, 2012.

European Commission. *1999 Regular Report on* Turkey's *Progress Toward Accession*. Brussels: European Commission, October 1999.

European Commission. *2000 Regular Report on Turkey's Progress Toward Accession*. Brussels: European Commission, November, 2000.

European Commission. *2001 Regular Report on Turkey's Progress Toward Accession, SEC (2001) 1756*. Brussels: European Commission, November 2001.

Fischer, Stanley. "Remarks by Stanley Fischer, First Deputy Managing Director of the IMF," April 25, 2001.

Gültekin-KarakaŞ, Derya. *Hem Hasımız Hem Hısımız: Türkiye'de Finans Kapitalin DönüŞümü ve Banka Reformu*. İstanbul: İletiŞim Yayınları, 2009.

Hisarcıklıoğlu, Rifat. "57. Genel Kurul Konuşması, 2 Mayıs 2002" in Nart Bozkurt, *Başkanların Genel Kurul Konuşmaları*, volume 3. Ankara: TOBB Yayınları, 2011.

IMF. *IMF Postpones Board Meeting on Turkey, News Brief no. 01/51*. Washington, DC: IMF Publication Services, 2001.

IMF. *Statement on Turkey by IMF First Deputy Managing Director Stanley Fischer, News Brief no. 01/66*. Washington, DC: IMF Publication Services, 2001.

Keyman, E. Fuat, and Berrin Koyuncu. "Globalization, Alternative Modernities, and the Political Economy of Turkey." *Review of International Political Economy* 12, no. 1 (2005): 105–128.

Keyman, E. Fuat. "The AK Party: Dominant Party, New Turkey, and Polarization." *Insight Turkey* 16, no. 2 (2014): 19–31.

Kubicek, Paul. "The Earthquake, the European Union, and Political Reform in Turkey." *Mediterranean Politics* 7, no. 1 (2002): 1–18.

Kutlay, Mustafa. "Economy as a Practical Hand in Turkish Foreign Policy: A Political Economy Explanation." *Insight Turkey* 13, no. 1 (2011): 67–88.

Kutlay, Mustafa. "Internationalization of Finance Capital in Spain and Turkey: Neoliberal Globalization and the Political Economy of State Strategies." *New Perspectives on Turkey*, no. 47 (2012): 115–137.

Miller, Calum. "Pathways Through Financial Crisis: Turkey." *Global Governance* 12, no. 4 (2006): 449–464.

Milliyet Gazetesi. "2.5 Milyon İnsan 79 İlde Sokağa İndi." June 23, 2013.

Milliyet Gazetesi. "Koç: Program Son Şansımız." May 18, 2001.

Milliyet Gazetesi. "MHP: İstifa Etse Hiçbir Şey Olmaz," June 29, 2001.

Oatley, Thomas, and Jason Yackee. "American Interests and IMF Lending." *International Politics* 41, no. 3 (2004): 415–429.

Öniş, Ziya, and Fikret Şenses. "Rethinking the Emerging Post-Washington Consensus." *Development and Change* 36, no. 2 (2005): 263–290.

Öniş, Ziya, and Fuat Keyman. "Turkey at the Polls: A New Path Emerges." *Journal of Democracy* 14, no. 2 (2003): 95–107.

Öniş, Ziya, and Mustafa Kutlay. "Rising Powers in a Changing Global Order: The Political Economy of Turkey in the Age of BRICs." *Third World Quarterly* 34, no. 8 (2013): 1409–1426.

Öniş, Ziya. "Monopolising the Centre: The AKP and the Uncertain Path of Turkish Democracy." *The International Spectator* 50, no. 2 (2015): 22–41.

Öniş, Ziya. "Turkey's Two Elections: The AKP Comes Back." *Journal of Democracy* 27, no. 2 (2016): 141–154.

Öniş, Ziya. "Varieties and Crises of Neoliberal Globalization: Argentina, Turkey and the IMF." *Third World Quarterly* 27, no. 2 (2006): 239–263.

Özbudun, Ergun. "AKP at the Crossroads: Erdoğan's Majoritarian Drift." *South European Society and Politics* 19, no. 2 (2014): 155–167.

Özilhan, Tuncay. "TÜSİAD Yönetim Kurulu Başkanı Tuncay Özilhan'ın 5. SİAD Zirvesi Konuşması." May 9, 2001.

Özpek, Burak Bilgehan. "Constitution-Making in Turkey After the 2011 Elections." *Turkish Studies* 13, no. 2 (2012): 153–167.

Republic of Turkey Ministry of Industry and Trade, *Turkish Industrial Strategy Document: Towards EU Membership (2011–2014)*, 2010.

Rodrik, Dani. "How to Save Globalization From its Cheerleaders." *The Journal of Trade and Diplomacy* 1, no. 2 (2007): 1–33.

Rodrik, Dani. *Has Globalization Gone Too Far?* Washington D.C.: Institute of International Economics, 1997.

Soli Özel, "Turkey at the Polls: After the Tsunami." *Journal of Democracy* 14, no. 2 (2003): 80–94.

Stiglitz, Joseph E. "More Instruments and Broader Goals: Moving Toward the Post-Washington Consensus." *Revista de Economia Politica* 19, no. 1 (1999): 94–120.

Strange, Gerard. *Towards a New Political Economy of Development*. Basingstoke: Palgrave Macmillan. 2014.

Thirkell-White, Ben. *The IMF and the Politics of Financial Globalization: From the Asian Crisis to a New International Financial Architecture*. Basingstoke: Palgrave Macmillan, 2005.

TÜSİAD. *Türkiye'nin AB Üyeliği: Doğrudan Yatırımlar ve Ekonomik Büyüme*. TÜSİAD Görüşler Dizisi, no. 8, 2002.

Ümit, Cizre, and Erinç Yeldan. "The Turkish Encounter with Neo-Liberalism: Economics and Politics in the 2000/2001 Crisis." *Review of International Political Economy* 12, no. 3 (2005): 387–408.

Undersecretariat of Treasury, *Strengthening the Turkish Economy: Turkey's Transition Program*. Ankara: TCMB. 2001.

Williamson, John. "What Washington Means by Policy Reform?" In *Latin American Adjustment: How Much Has Happened?*, edited by John Williamson. Washington DC: Institute for International Economics, 1990.

Woods, Ngarie. "Understanding Pathways Thorough Financial Crises and the Impact of the IMF: An Introduction." *Global Governance* 12, no. 4 (2006): 373–393.

World Bank, *China 2030: Building a Modern, Harmonious, and Creative High-Income Society* (Washington, DC: World Bank Press, 2012), 13.

Yörük, Erdem and Murat Yüksel. "Class and Politics in Turkey's Gezi Protests." *New Left Review* 89 (2014): 103–123.

CHAPTER 5

Political Economy of Greece (1974–2009)

This chapter delves into the institutionalization of a reactive Greek state in a neoliberal setting between 1974 and 2009. The post-1974 posed a new era in Greek politics as it demarcates the end of military regime and restoration of democracy in Greece. In addition, Greek political economy was gradually transformed toward a more neoliberal regime under the auspices of Europeanization and financial globalization. The end of the Colonels regime in 1974, a military junta that had ruled the country for seven years, opened a new phase in Greek politics. It posed a critical juncture to overhaul established state institutions and construct new ones in line with the changing power balances among political and economic interest groups. However, the new political context gradually underpinned an increasingly polarized and conflict-prone policy-making, which in turn, informed state bureaucracy and domestic policy communities in a mutually reinforcing manner.

Greece made a strikingly quick and peaceful transition to democracy with the collapse of the military regime. Following the fall of the junta, Konstantinos Karamanlis (1907–1998), a veteran statesman and former conservative prime minister from the days before the Colonels, returned from self-imposed exile in France and played maestro role during Greece's transition to democracy. After being elected as prime minister in November 1974 with a landslide electoral majority around 54 percent of the total votes, Karamanlis demonstrated outstanding political leadership to

M. Kutlay, *The Political Economies of Turkey and Greece*,
International Political Economy Series,
https://doi.org/10.1007/978-3-319-92789-3_5

reconstruct Greece's institutional architecture. In this regard, three major developments are of particular importance. First, as a sign of clear rupture from the past, Karamanlis ensured the legalization of the Communist Party together with other once-banned leftist parties; threw his political support behind the courts to prosecute junta leaders; and abolished the monarchy in December 1974 plebiscite, with the backing of the 70 percent of population.[1] Second, Karamanlis secured the parliamentary majority to promulgate a new constitution in June 1975. Third, and most important, Greece became a full member of the then European Economic Community in January 1981, five years earlier than Spain and Portugal.

Greece's integration into the European Community and neoliberalism, however, reflects certain patterns that weakened state capacity. This chapter explores these patterns from a historical-institutional perspective. The first part concentrates on 1974–1996 during which institutional fundamentals of reactive Greek state were laid down. The second part examines the Simitis era (1996–2004) in Greek political economy, and the final part deciphers the consolidation of reactive Greek state until the devastating Greek economic crisis.

5.1 Emergence of a Reactive State (1974–1996)

Post-authoritarian Greece poses striking paradoxes in the sense that notable increase in material wealth accompanied by a secular decline in state capacity. It is an unusual story that material wealth improved, while painful structural reforms were watered down. This, in turn, paved the way for Greece's enduring political and economic problems. Concentrating on the first-stage of three-stage framework, this part explores three major aspects that inform Greek state's capacity, that is, domestic political context, state bureaucracy, and domestic policy coalitions, during the era of neoliberal globalization.

Domestic Political Context

The immediate aftermath of 1974 provided a critical juncture for Greece to restructure the state-market relations and consolidate Greece's place in Europe. The historical opportunity window, however, could not be

[1] Dimitri A. Sotiropoulos, "The Authoritarian Past and Contemporary Greek Democracy," *South European Society and Politics* 15, no. 3, (2010): 450–452.

exploited to a significant extent in the economic realm. In the post-authoritarian period, political context took the form of "polarized pluralism,"[2] in which two major parties, right-wing New Democracy (ND) and left-wing Panhellenic Socialist Movement (PASOK), dominated the political landscape.[3] The two parties' share in total votes remained above 80 percent threshold between 1981 and 2009. Except a short interval of coalition governments formed during 1989–1990, ND and PASOK alternated in power with strong one-party majorities in the parliament.

The consolidation of PASOK and ND spawned an unusual pattern of cleavage politics that combined two-party competition with conflictual pluralism, which Pappas calls "polarized bipartism."[4] Accordingly, in the Greek case, constituency is kept at the polar opposites of the political spectrum and polarized policy-making has become the defining characteristics of domestic politics. Pappas argues that this was an "intentional polarization"[5] strategy deliberately pursued by the political elite to exploit the state's fiscal resources single-handedly and distribute it to their supporters in a populist fashion in return for electoral loyalty. It is obvious that the root causes of political polarization and populism can be traced back to the early days of the Greek state. Historically, Greece suffered from multiple national schisms: In the nineteenth century, the major dividing lines were drawn between "traditionalists"—the seminal political figure was Deliyannis—and "modernists"—the seminal political figure was Trikoupis. In the first quarter of the twentieth century, the struggle between liberals—gathered around Venizelos and the royalists—the supporters of monarchy—deeply divided Greek society. The long-lasting wounds of the Greek Civil War (1946–1949) further polarized the country in the first two decades of the post-World War II period.[6] Thus, the historical evolution of cleavage politics in Greece provided fertile grounds for constant reproduction of polarization-induced patronage relations. After the restoration of democracy, however, political context took a new

[2] Giovanni Sartori, *Parties and Party Systems: A Framework for Analysis* (Cambridge: Cambridge University Press, 1976).

[3] George Th. Mavrogordatos, "The Greek Party System: A Case of 'Limited but Polarized Pluralism'?" in Stefano Bartolini and Peter Mair, eds., *Party Politics in Contemporary Europe* (London: Frank Cass, 1984), 156–169.

[4] Takis Pappas, "Why Greece Failed?" *Journal of Democracy* 24, no. 2 (2013): 40–41.

[5] Ibid.

[6] John S. Koliopoulos and Thanos M. Veremis, *Modern Greece: A History Since 1821* (Oxford: Wiley-Blackwell, 2010).

form in the sense that the post-1974 exemplifies a qualitative transformation from traditional interpersonal patron-client relations to a group and institution, which is called "machine politics." Accordingly:

> A political party [becomes] a 'collective patron' [in] its relationship with voters... The party machine is fundamentally impersonal and its organizational core is a group, not an individual. Consequently, the political loyalty and identification of voters benefits the party as such, rather than individual politicians.[7]

The PASOK period deserves particular attention in this regard. Under Andreas Papandreou's charismatic leadership, PASOK governments (1981–1989) played instrumental role in the consolidation of a reactive state over the 1980s. As Kalyvas argues, Papandreou opted for not mere polarizing rhetoric but an "instance of polarized politics" that has long-lasting implications.[8] PASOK positioned itself as the representative of middle and lower strata of society, which Papandreou himself called "the people" against "privileged" establishment, whose legitimate representation had been thwarted in the past. Exploiting the historical cleavages of the country, Papandreou championed the left-wing populist policies and portrayed the society "as being split by the fundamental division between an all-embracing 'non-privileged' majority, which he claimed to stand for, and a tiny 'privileged' oligarchy, representing foreign interests and domestic monopolies, which were identified as the enemy."[9] Along these lines, expansionary distributive outlook guided the social and economic policies of PASOK governments to consolidate party's electoral base.

First, PASOK initiated new economic plans to underpin welfare state practices in the sectors such as healthcare, social security, and education to incorporate the previously excluded middle and lower strata of Greek society. In fact, by challenging the social base of the economic system that condition state-market relations, Papandreou aimed at changing the underlying power structures of and state's position in the Greek political

[7] George Th. Mavrogordatos, "From Traditional Clientelism to Machine Politics: The Impact of PASOK Populism in Greece," *South European Society and Politics* 2, no. 3 (1997): 2.

[8] Stathis N. Kalyvas, "Polarization in Greek Politics: PASOK's First Four Years, 1981–1985," *Journal of the Hellenic Diaspora* 23, no. 1 (1997): 83–104.

[9] Christos Lyrintzis, "PASOK in Power: From 'Change' to Disenchantment" in Richard Clogg, ed., *Greece, 1981–1989: The Populist Decade* (London: The Macmillan Press, 1993), 29.

economy. What he had in mind was a radical reformation. He unearthed this aim lucidly in his speech when he first appeared in Greek Parliament as prime minister on November 22, 1981:

> Our basic target is a self-sufficient economic and social development, using all the productive forces in combination with a fairer distribution of the national income and wealth... We seek the gradual reform of the structures of the economy so that the basic economic choices are made by the society as a whole. The strategic sectors of the economy must come under substantial social control without overlooking the positive role of private initiative. The crisis in the capitalist system on a world scale, with ever-increasing unemployment and inflation, intensified international competition, the increase in the degree of concentration and the monopolistic structure of many branches, have made the traditional means of economic policy ineffective.[10]

It was not coincidence that his election motto, *Allaghi* (change), touched a sensitive chord in the hearts and minds of ordinary Greek citizens. However, the uncontrolled expansion of state's fiscal reach created widespread inefficiency and accumulation of new economic problems in the medium-term, despite expansionary welfare policies proved beneficial for the well-being of society in the short-run.[11] The accumulation of fiscal problems during the 1990s and 2000s mostly emanated from the bankrupted pension system, social security system, and inefficient public sector practices that were institutionalized in this period (see below).

Second, as a Harvard-trained heterodox economics professor, Papandreou pursued a rather aggressive developmental strategy, especially in the first term of his premiership. His economic narrative relied on the assumption that the weakness, short-term and speculative character of Greek big business, which based their performance on state-dependent subsidies and assistance, led to the rent seeking and underdevelopment of Greek economy.[12] Thus, he targeted the small- and medium-sized entrepreneurs, cooperatives, and the public sector as the engines of Greece's

[10] Quoted in Theodore C. Kariotis, "Andreas G. Papandreou: The Economist," *Journal of the Hellenic Diaspora* 23, no. 1 (1997): 52.

[11] Christos Lyrintzis, "PASOK in Power: From 'Change' to Disenchantment," 27.

[12] Euclid Tsakalatos, "The Political Economy of Social Democratic Economic Policies: The PASOK Experiment in Greece," *Oxford Review of Economic Policy* 14, no. 1 (1998): 117.

economic development. PASOK designed a set of supply-side initiatives by providing lucrative subsidies, incentives, and fiscal support to the targeted firms in the private and public sectors. A new piece of legislation (Law 1262/1982) was enacted that identified the policy instruments, incentives, and subsidies, according to which state support would be utilized.[13] Yet, these reform initiatives hardly got off the ground, as public money could not be channeled into the productive capacity-enhancing investments due to populist stimuli and resistance of dominant economic policy communities. During the 1980s, state was controlling four-fifths of the total credits extended by the Greek financial system and, according to OECD reports, these credits were distributed without any particular attention to the banking and financial criteria.[14] Since discretionary politics guided state's economic behavior, political privileges rather than efficiency became the main criterion in the distribution of state subsidies and bank credits. This paved the way for the gradual consolidation of a self-reinforcing path that informed economic actors to opt for effortless gains. At the turn of the decade, therefore, state's fiscal balances were already on the brink of collapse.

The alternation of two populist parties in power informed the main contours of political context in which the ruling party in each term seized lucrative opportunities to control and distribute state rents to their supporters, as par excellence examples of machine politics. The voters, on the other side of the coin, have experienced and rationalized that "the state was up for grabs and that it was better to associate with the state through party contacts rather than venture into the market through competition."[15] The electorates also internalized the rules of the game in this majoritarian electoral system that their attachment to one of the two main parties would enable them to have rewarding opportunities when "their parties" would return to power.[16]

In this institutional setting, not surprisingly, politics was conceived as zero-sum game so that the incumbent state agents did not prioritize issue-based consensus-seeking attempts. Instead, the political agenda was

[13] Kostas Lavdas, *The Europeanization of Greece* (London: Palgrave Macmillan, 1997), 151–152.

[14] Tayfur, M. Fatih, *Semiperipheral Development and Foreign Policy: The Cases of Greece and Spain* (Aldershot: Ashgate, 2003), 96–97.

[15] Pappas, "Why Greece Failed?," *Journal of Democracy*, 42.

[16] Iosif Kovras and Neophytos Loizides, "The Sovereign Debt Crisis in Southern Europe: Majoritarian Pitfalls?," *Comparative Politics* 47, no. 1 (2014): 1–20.

permeated by pervasive party factionalism. As a result, more often than not, the urgently needed economic reforms were pushed back.[17] The adversarial political culture also generated negative feedback mechanisms beyond political sphere that weakened Greek state's internal and external capacities. On the internal aspect, uncontrolled populism permeated state administration in a way that undermined bureaucratic autonomy and meritocracy. On the external aspect, political setting and accompanied state policies motivated domestic policy communities to adopt rentier mode of behavior, which shall be discussed in the following parts.

State Bureaucracy

State capacity literature suggests that meritocratic and insulated bureaucracy characterized by "embedded autonomy" significantly improves state's reform credentials. The Greek bureaucracy, however, did not approximate to these qualities. In retrospect, Greek state's internal capacity could not be empowered because state bureaucracy increasingly became "a focus of discord, an arena of intense political party competition."[18] All three dimensions of state's bureaucratic capacity indicated secular decline in the Greek case. First, the public sector expanded in an uncontrolled and unplanned manner over the years. Since state was conceived as an arena to be captured by rival political parties, the governments approached the public bureaucracy through the lens of political patronage, which Lyrintzis called "bureaucratic clientelism."[19] In early 1980s, the Greek state was relatively small in size, employing about 510,000 people out of a population then numbering about ten million. During PASOK governments (1981–1989), total public sector employment reached 786,200 by 1990, an increase of more than 50 percent in a decade.[20] Between 1975 and 1990, the Greek public sector as a percentage of overall economy expanded from 35 percent to almost 60 percent, four-fifths of which belongs to the

[17] Dimitri A. Sotiropoulos, "The Remains of Authoritarianism: Bureaucracy and Civil Society in Post-Authoritarian Greece," *Cahiers d'Etudes sur la Méditerranée Orientale et le monde Turco-Iranien*, no. 20 (1995): 2.

[18] Dimitri A. Sotiropoulos, "A Description of the Greek Higher Civil Service," in Edward C. Page and Vincent Wright, ed., *Bureaucratic Elites in Western European States* (Oxford: Oxford University Press, 1999), 28.

[19] Christos Lyrintzis, "Political Parties in Post-junta Greece: A Case of 'Bureaucratic Clientelism?,' " *West European Politics* 7, no. 2 (1984): 99–118.

[20] Pappas, "Why Greece Failed?," *Journal of Democracy*, 38.

1980s.[21] Informed by long-lasting historical practices, governments used public sector for the allocation of spoils to consolidate their electoral base.

> In a country where the state has always played a crucial social and economic role, it was relatively easy for a well organized party to become a collective patron by using an intricate combination of party mechanisms and state structures. Needless to say, the overlapping of party and state structure is at the expense of the efficiency, modernization, and rationalization of the public sector. The proliferation of parasitic jobs and the creation of numerous state-controlled agencies exemplify the logic of organized and bureaucratic patronage.[22]

The expansionary practices exercised during the 1980s remained intact in the aftermath. As a result, except a short anti-populist interval in the late 1990, the total number of public employment finally reached to around 984,000 before 2009 economic crisis.[23] The reallocation of resources to inefficient public sector and the political motivations behind public sector appointments not only jeopardized public finance but also deteriorated the public-private balance that the Greek business community frequently criticized.

In fact, contrary to the popular arguments, the size of the Greek state per se does not pose a problem. One may even argue that the size of Greek state has always been reasonable in comparison to other OECD members.[24] The state capacity literature also suggests that sizeable public sector may even be an advantage for state's transformative, regulatory, and distributive capacities as it is the case in Nordic countries. Greece, however, suffers from the lack of bureaucratic meritocracy and embedded autonomy, which brings us to the second aspect of Greece's internal state capacity. The single most important variable that informed the degree of meritocratic credentials in state bureaucracy has been the political context that paved the way for politically motivated discretionary recruitments. More often than not, "political friends looking-for-jobs" have been

[21] Quoted in George Pagoulatos, "Economic Adjustment and Financial Reform: Greece's Europeanization and the Emergence of a Stabilization State," *South European Society and Politics* 5, no. 2 (2000): 193.

[22] Lyrintzis, "PASOK in Power: From 'Change' to Disenchantment," 32–33.

[23] OECD, *Greece: Review of the Central Administration* (Paris: OECD Publications Service, 2012), 71.

[24] According to OECD data, Greece has the tenth largest state measured in terms of the employment in public sector in comparison to total labor force in 2008.

appointed to key managerial positions at the fiscal and financial echelons.[25] As documented in comparative studies, over-politicized recruitments and appointments have taken place both "at the bottom" and "at the top" of the Greek state bureaucracy.[26] The absorption of new personnel was actualized through bypassing the competitive meritocracy-based entrance systems.[27] Therefore, loyalty, rather than meritocracy and technical capacity had become the main selection criterion. Also, key bureaucratic posts were dominated by top-down clientelism.[28] Thus, the higher echelons of fiscal bureaucracy had virtually no autonomy to impose budget discipline or challenge policy-makers if they perceived the political requests deleterious for state's fiscal performance. Several OECD reports assert "that political criteria have tended to weigh heavily on promotions, [which in turn] discouraged the recruitment of talented personnel."[29] In short, both the higher echelons and entry-level positions are predominantly linked with political parties that lead to the gradual deterioration of the bureaucratic autonomy at all levels and policy realms. Sotiropoulos bluntly puts "that the Greek public administration render service, for the most part [...] to its elected political masters, to the governing political party, and to favoured clienteles among prospective voters."[30] The lack of autonomy impeded state capacity to initiate and supervise economic reform measures in corporation with political executive and non-state economic interest groups.

Third, Greek state's internal capacity was also severely constrained due to policy fragmentation and incoherence. This is mainly because of the frequent changes in policy competencies with the alternation of governments and inter-ministerial rivalries even within the same governments. Bureaucratic positions were reshuffled, deactivated, and/or new ones were created with no respect to organizational coherence and insulation. OECD surveys reveal that the inter-ministerial cooperation in Greek eco-

[25] Tayfur, *Semiperipheral Development and Foreign Policy*, 105.

[26] Dimitri A. Sotiropoulos, "Southern European Public Bureaucracies in Comparative Perspective," *West European Politics* 27, no. 3 (2004): 411.

[27] Dimitri A. Sotiropoulos, "The Two Faces of Politicization of the Greek Civil Service: The Case of Contemporary Greece," in Guy Peters and John Pierre, ed., *Politicization of the Civil Service in Comparative Perspective: The Quest for Control* (London: Routledge, 2004): 256–265.

[28] Ibid.

[29] OECD, *Economic Surveys, Greece: 1990–1991* (Paris: OECD Publications Service, 1991), 63.

[30] Sotiropoulos, "A Description of the Greek Higher Civil Service," 29.

nomic bureaucracy remained very low and subject to ad hoc mechanisms.[31] Thus, bureaucratic feudalization posed considerable obstacles in terms of meticulous formulation and cogent implementation of long-term-oriented economic reforms.[32] For instance, fiscal bureaucracy in Greece remained parochial so that it could not overcome coordination problems in its relations with expert communities despite the fact that countless reform initiatives had taken place in the post-authoritarian era.[33] Similarly, Greek state—that is, the executive authority—lacks competence and capacity to pose common policy-making vision to the relevant ministries, including fiscal and financial issues. Featherstone and Papadimitriou define this fragmentation as "solitary centres amid a segmented government."[34] In short, all three aspects of Greek state's capacity suffered certain deficiencies and setbacks in a downward trend between 1980 and 1996, which further jeopardized in the post-2000 (see below).

Domestic Policy Coalitions

The political system in Greece not only undermined state bureaucracy but also informed the main features of the interest intermediation structures. Lavdas asserts that the mode of relationship between state, trade unions, and business associations reflect "disjointed corporatism"—lacking compromise, trust, and rule-based dialogue. Accordingly, disjointed corporatism denotes "the combination of a set of corporatist features and a prevailing political modality that lacks diffuse reciprocity and remains incapable of brokering social pacts."[35]

There are two strands to this argument. On the one hand, the "corporatist" element indicates strong state tradition capable of influencing the

[31] OECD, *Greece: Review of Central Administration*, 51.

[32] For example, for the ministry of finance alone, 2,890 competency changes through laws, 11,018 changes through presidential decrees, and 3,191 changes through ministerial degrees have taken place between 1996 and 2011. It refers to 1,140 changes of government competencies per year. Ibid.

[33] Monastiriotis, Vassilis, and Andreas Antoniades. "Reform That! Greece's Failing Reform Technology: Beyond 'Vested Interests' and 'Political Exchange'." In Stathis Kalyvas, George Pagoulatos, and Haris Tsoukas, eds., *From Stagnation To Forced Adjustment: Reforms in Greece, 1974–2010*, 31–47 (London and New York: Hurst Co. and Columbia University Press, 2012).

[34] Kevin Featherstone and Dimitris Papadimitriou, "The Emperor Has No Clothes: Power and Resources Within the Greek Core Executive," *Governance* 26, no. 3 (2013): 523–545.

[35] Lavdas, *The Europeanization of Greece*.

market dynamics thanks to buoyant fiscal and financial resources and lucrative arrangements at the disposal of the state. Historically, Greece's semiperipheral integration to world economy provided institutional and ideational background for the state to possess a dominant role in Greek political economy. Yet, Greek state's mode of economic intervention significantly diverged from the corporatist models of the western European states. Similar to other reactive states, Greek state's market interventions reflect an incoherent and spasmodic tendency mostly resulted in unproductive outcomes; thereby fell short of steering sustainable reform activism. On the other hand, state's relations with economic interest groups reflect a "disjointed" nature due to the lack of institutionalized negotiated relationship and limited ability of peak economic organizations to commit and ensure the compliance of their members: Such as the General Confederation of Labour (GSEE), the Confederation of Public Servants (ADEDY) on the labor side and the Hellenic Federation of Enterprises (SEV) on the capital side.

Main interest groups' interactions with the state have traditionally been adversarial, fragmented, and lopsided. Thus, interest groups remained relatively weak vis-à-vis the state so that non-state actors suffer from collective action problems in articulating, promoting, and defending their autonomous interests through interactive intermediation structures. They also suffer from internal fractionalization, norms of reciprocity, and commitment problems due to the lack of social capital and general trust.[36] This historical and socio-political background—once informed by polarized political context—magnified power asymmetries in state-labor and state-capital relations during neoliberal globalization. I stated previously that, in the post-authoritarian democratic environment, the political parties replaced the traditional interpersonal patron-client linkages with machine politics. Similar to the patronage-induced politics-bureaucracy interactions, unidirectional and top-down imposition of policy decisions permeated state-labor and state-capital relationships. In terms of the labor unions, an almost entirely state-dependent relationship dominated the policy-making processes. Accordingly, the labor unions were subject to party control and patronage politics, because of which institutional reciprocity was jeopardized during 1980s. As Mavrogordatos deciphers:

[36] Nikoleta Jones, Chrisovaladis Malesios, Theodoros Iosifides & Kostas M. Sophoulis, "Social Capital in Greece: Measurement and Comparative Perspectives," *South European Society and Politics* 13, no. 2 (2008): 175–193.

> Unions in Greece have served as Trojan Horses of PASOK populism and clientelism. This is due primarily to their complete penetration or even substitution by the corresponding specialized party organizations. The process was spearheaded by PASOK's own organization (PASKE) and perpetuated by PASOK legislation imposing proportional representation as the compulsory electoral system in trade union elections.[37]

Trade unions have suffered from frequent and direct state interventions.[38] Labor union activity had been subject to state control through a series of supervisory laws that constrained unions' financial independence, decision-making autonomy, and bargaining capacities.[39] However, post-authoritarian period brought a qualitative transformation in state-labor relations as machine politics became much more pervasive.[40] In this context, the imposition of "proportional representation" in the elections of the GSEE and ADEDY presidencies is a clear illustration of Greek state's patronage motivations during 1980s.[41] Proportional representation provided new tools to resurrect and perpetuate populist practices of the past in a more radical fashion since it enabled PASOK governments to control unions by "thinly-disguised party lists."[42] Schmitter, in his comparative study of state-labor relations in southern Europe underlines the over-politicized nature of union activity in Greece: "Parties, especially PASOK after it took over in 1981, have made concerted efforts to penetrate and capture leadership positions [in labor unions]."[43] The party competition

[37] Mavrogordatos, "From Traditional Clientelism to Machine Politics," *South European Society and Politics*, 21.

[38] Interview with high-level bureaucrat, Organization for Mediation and Arbitration in Greece, June 26, 2014.

[39] Christos Ioannou, "From Divided 'Quangos' to Fragmented 'Social Partners': Explaining the Absence of Mergers," in Waddington Jeremy, ed., *Restructuring Representation: The Merger Process and Trade Union Structural Development in Ten Countries* (Brussels: P.I.E-Peter Lang, 2005), 150–151.

[40] Christos Ioannou, *Trade Unions in Greece: Development, Structures and Prospects* (Athens: Friedrich Ebert Foundation, 1999).

[41] Dimitris Tsarouhas, "Social Partnership in Greece: Is There a Europeanization Effect?," *European Journal of Industrial Relations* 14, no. 3 (2008): 358.

[42] George Th. Mavrogordatos, "Civil Society under Populism," in Richard Clogg, ed., *Greece, 1981–1989: The Populist Decade* (New York: St. Martin's Press, 1993), 47–64.

[43] Philippe C. Schmitter, "Organized Interests and Democratic Consolidation in Southern Europe," in Richard Gunther, Nikiforos P. Diamandouros, Hans-Jürgen Puhle, eds., *The Politics of Democratic Consolidation: Southern Europe in Comparative Perspective* (Baltimore: Johns Hopkins University Press, 1995), 293.

inside the unions further aggravated in time as the alternating ND and PASOK governments followed the suit. Thus, labor unions turned into inefficient actors that help the formulation and implementation of concerted economic reforms.

The fragmented internal structures of peak labor organizations also hampered reform activism. At first glance, labor unions appear unitary at the peak level since two unions represent the entire working class in Greece. Greek trade unions, however, are characterized by intra-fractionalization that tends to underpin collective action and credibility of commitment problems as highlighted by the state capacity framework. The GSEE, for example, accompanied by more than 7000 primary (individual organizations and local branches) and more than 100 secondary (federations and labor centers) level units, which "operate independently of any links with the higher levels."[44] ADEDY also depicts very similar characteristics. Accordingly, ADEDY includes a total of 1264 primary-level units, organized in 52 federations[45] As one of the respondents suggested, the over-politicized, fragmented and state-dependent nature of labor unions create insurmountable challenges to any kind of substantive social dialogue and cooperation-based economic policy-making.[46]

On the capital side, the Greek business presents a contrast to labor unions because major business organization SEV enjoyed relative autonomy vis-à-vis the Greek state. However, the dominant mode of the relationship between the state and SEV had generally been antagonistic and conflictual.[47] In the post-1974 period, Andreas Papandreou's anti-capitalist and anti-European rhetoric, aggressive nationalization attempts, and expansionary fiscal policies pushed state-business relations into a slippery slope, particularly during the first half of 1980s. SEV overtly condemned the government's economic policies while Papandreou "responded publicly [and] accused businessmen of making use of semi-legal methods,

[44] Kostas Lavdas, "Interest Groups in Disjointed Corporatism: Social Dialogue in Greece and European 'Competitive Corporatism,' " *West European Politics* 28, no. 2 (2005): 302.

[45] Ioannou, "From Divided 'Quangos' to Fragmented 'Social Partners': Explaining the Absence of Mergers," 146.

[46] Christos Ioannou, "Odysseus or Sisyphus Revisited: Failed Attempts to conclude Social-liberal Pacts in Greece," in Philippe Pochet, Maarten Keune, and David Natali, eds., *After the Euro and Enlargement: Social Pacts in the European Union* (Brussels: Observatoire Social Europeen & ETUI, 2010), 83–108.

[47] Lavdas, "Interest Groups in Disjointed Corporatism," *West European Politics,* 302–303, 307.

manipulating public work contracts, defrauding public funds, and misusing investment loans."[48] In the 1990s, PASOK's changing discourse toward the EU and its softened tone about economic liberalization paved the way for relative normalization in state-business relations during the Simitis leadership (see below). However, the "disjointed" nature of state-business relations remained almost intact because governed interdependence institutions could not be established.[49]

On the other side of the coin, business elites associated with SEV also exploited state funds and subsidies rather than pushing for competition-enhancing reforms. Furthermore, SEV failed to encompass individual firms and local associations so that it also suffered from collective action problems despite the fact that it was more successful in terms of the organizational coherence and interest representation in comparison to the labor class.[50] The limited representative capacity of the SEV provided ample room for various "pockets of inefficiency," which "draw a significant advantage from their small size, as they do not contain free riders that could undermine their agenda or fail to contribute actively to their interests."[51] More than 130 professions, for instance, were shielded from real external and domestic competition.[52] However, state-business relations were not always confrontational. The initial antagonistic relationship between PASOK government and Greek business elite in early 1980s was gradually transformed into a kind of mutual dependence in the second half of the decade.[53] The emergent relationship, however, did not empower the capacity of the state to steer business communities. During 1980s, Greek state extended almost half of all grants and subsidies to uncompetitive rent-seeking finance capital mainly for political patronage motivations.[54] In this sense, financial system played crucial intermediary role in cementing the sub-optimal equilibrium in state-business relations. Tridimas

[48] Tayfur, *Semiperipheral Development and Foreign Policy*, 95.

[49] Orazio Lanza and Kostas Lavdas, "The Disentanglement of Interest Politics: Business Associability, the Parties, and Policy in Italy and Greece," *European Journal of Political Research* 37, no. 2 (2000): 203–235.

[50] Tsarouhas, "Social Partnership in Greece," *European Journal of Industrial Relations*, 359.

[51] Theodore Pelagidis and Michael Mitsopoulos, *Understanding the Economic Crisis in Greece: From Boom to Bust* (Hampshire: Palgrave Macmillan, 2011), 8.

[52] Pappas, "Why Greece Failed?," *Journal of Democracy*, 38.

[53] Lavdas, *Europeanization of Greece*, 170–185.

[54] Tayfur, *Semiperipheral Development and Foreign Policy*, 96.

reports that Greek financial sector funded three-quarters of the bloating public sector borrowing requirements during the Papandreou period.[55] Greek governments forced oligopolistic banking system to invest more than half of their assets in treasury bonds issued by the state, which in turn was used to shore up state's fiscal profligacy.

In the 1990s, rising tide of neoliberal globalization and the EU's single market regulations created external pressures to liberalize Greek financial system. Accordingly, Greece removed all restrictions on the capital movement as of 1994 along with the introduction of a more flexible and simplified regulatory framework (see below).[56] The financial liberalization, however, further informed the fiscal and financial profligacy due to two main reasons. First, oligopolistic structure of the Greek banking system was not overhauled before liberalization took place. Thus, the share of state-controlled banks (SCB) remained relatively high in the financial system. In a clientelistic political economy structure devoid of regulatory checks-and-balance mechanisms, "bad credits to good friends" turned into business-as-usual practices. As Pagoulatos points out, "the SCB acted like a second state budget and excessive ambiguity and lack of transparency surrounded the financial give-and-take between governments and state-controlled banks."[57] The SCB also served as political elites' backyards for patronage appointments and electoral purposes. Starting from early 1980s, the competitive entrance exams to the state banks, similar to fiscal bureaucracy, were de facto abolished.[58] As a result, the SCB bloated with non-qualified personnel. The state banks could operate with only half of their personnel in this period.[59]

Second, increasing public debt ratios generated crowding out effects by encouraging rent-seeking motivations of the private finance capital. The combination of state's fiscal profligacy and uncontrolled liberalization of the state-dominated financial system created a dangerous policy mix: On the one hand, Greek governments increasingly relied on treasury bills

[55] George Tridimas, "Greek Fiscal Policy and the European Union," in Kevin Featherstone and Kostas Ifantis, eds., *Greece in a Changing Europe: Between European Integration and Balkan Disintegration* (Manchester: Manchester University Press, 1996), 63.

[56] OECD, *Economic Surveys, Greece: 1992–1993* (Paris: OECD Publications Service 1993), 36–39.

[57] Pagoulatos, *Greece's New Political Economy*, 114.

[58] Mavrogordatos, "From Traditional Clientelism to Machine Politics," *South European Society and Politics*, 9–12.

[59] Ibid., 10.

yielding attractive real interest rates to finance swelling public deficits. On the other hand, financing Greek treasury opened up many opportunities for private finance capital because of the risk-free gains extracted through treasury bills and high intermediation commissions.[60] Moreover, close connections between industrial and financial elite and their deeply entrenched give-and-take relationships with the state exacerbated the problems in the financial system. In exchange for funding the governments, major Greek banks received privileges to enter into profitable public sector projects under favorable terms and conditions during 1980–1996. It is true that the state's share in the financial system substantially reduced after a series of privatization waves during the EMU process under intense pressures of the European Commission to adapt EU Banking Directives.[61] However, the ominous give-and-take relationship between the state and private interest groups reproduced itself by other means, a point to be discussed in the following pages.

5.2 A Self-Reinforcing Vicious Cycle

The discussion so far illustrates that state's reform capacity has been jeopardized in a path-dependent and self-reinforcing pattern in all three aspects between 1980 and 1996. The dominant mode of relations between the Greek state and major interest groups gradually reinforced resistance to change in a circular logic. In the initial phases, relevant institutional structures were crafted—or the already established ones were consolidated—in a way that served the immediate interests of the incumbent agents. The "locked-in" institutional structures, in turn, increasingly motivated agents to pursue rent-seeking economic strategies. The interaction between agents and institutional structures triggered a self-reinforcing vicious cycle that constantly hampered reform possibilities. As a result, urgently needed fiscal reforms were constantly delayed or watered down.

Two particular comprehensive reform attempts in the pre-1996 are illuminating in this regard. First, Papandreou launched a stabilization program at the beginning of his second term to curb the rising fiscal profligacy of the Greek state. As neoliberalism started to bite national economies and the EU became an increasingly important actor for the organization

[60] Pagoulatos, *Greece's New Political Economy*, 147.

[61] Ralph C. Bryant, Nicholas C. Garganas and George S. Tavlas, eds., *Greece's Economic Performance and Prospects* (Athens: Bank of Greece Printing Works, 2001): 85–91.

of the Greek economy within the context of single market regulations, a stabilization program (1986–1987) turned out to be an urgent necessity to keep competitive at the European level. The program aimed at curbing the exorbitant inflation, cutting down public sector expenditures and wages, and reducing the public sector borrowing requirements. The reform program was also underwritten by an EC loan of 1.75 billion ecus.[62] Despite a quick start, the program was halted abruptly, since Papandreou believed that PASOK was unlikely to keep its hold in power without a U-turn to distributive policies. Thus, in comparison to its first term, PASOK pursued even more populist and expansionary fiscal policies in the wake of 1989 elections.[63]

The ambitious pro-reformist turn of Constantine Mitsotakis, Greek prime minister during 1991–1993, is another illuminating case that demonstrates how change-oriented agents are constrained by institutional structures. A pro-European political rhetoric that advocated fiscal consolidation, massive privatizations, and financial reforms entered into Greek political agenda in early 1990s after ND's Mitsotakis assumed premiership. Representing the ND's progressive wing vis-à-vis the more traditional and conservative clique, Mitsotakis prepared a "Medium-Term Adjustment Programme" in 1991 targeting economic convergence with the core European countries.[64] Mitsotakis, however, could not succeed in achieving any of the program targets as he could not overcome the resistance of vested interests within ND and subsequently failed to achieve much-needed political consensus to deepen his reformist agenda even within his own party. Also, certain segments of the private business, labor unions, and state bureaucracy severely resisted the modernization objectives of the Adjustment Programme. As an external anchor, the EC did not play a strong anchor role because the monetary union was still seemed a distant objective in early 1990s. Tranditis portrays the besiegement of Mitsotakis in a rather stark manner: "The Mitsotakis agenda soon came under fire from both the opposition and the unions en bloc as well as from segments of the ND party associated with the employees of the public

[62] Sarantis E. G. Lolos, "Success and Failure of Economic Reforms: The Experience of Greece and Portugal," *Comparative Economic Studies* 40, no. 1 (1998): 79–81.

[63] Tsakalatos, "The Political Economy of Social Democratic Economic Policies," *Oxford Review of Economic Policy,* 118.

[64] Theodore Pelagidis and Michael Mitsopoulos, *Greece: From Exit to Recovery* (Washington, DC: Brookings Institution Press, 2014), 7–10, 13–15.

sector."[65] As a result, the targets of the Adjustment Programme were abandoned in 1992 and Papandreou's PASOK replaced Mitsotakis government in 1993 elections.

The costs of uncontrolled fiscal expansion reverberated through state's fiscal indicators in this period: General public expenditure increased from 27.6 percent of GDP in 1980 to 46 percent in 1995. Government revenue, on the other hand, increased from 25 percent to just 36 percent of GDP. Greek state's public debt also skyrocketed from 22.5 percent to almost 97 percent of economic output in the same period. Likewise, Greece's average budget deficit floated around 10 percent of GDP between 1980 and 1995.[66] Attached to weak conditionality, the EC assistance, in the same period, bolstered reform failures in Greece though in an unintended way. The potential cushioning impact of the EC funds was crucial for Greece because inflows reached more than $20 billion during Papandreou era.[67] In relative terms, net receipts from the EC increased from 0.5 percent to more than 5.5 of GDP annually.[68] That being said, however, PASOK governments followed the least-resistant path so that EC funds were used to shore up budget deficits and appease electoral constituency. As Verney puts, "Greek government appeared unable to absorb the financial support it was offered or to coordinate its use in a way that would help the country to adjust to the challenge of Community competition."[69] Hence, paradoxically, the EC became the sponsor of the reactive Greek state in this period.

Overall, Greece has gradually become *une société bloquée*, thwarting state's capacity to prudently craft and coherently implement economic adjustment policies in the normal course of politics.[70] Reform attempts, even if emboldened by reformist state agents, fell upon infertile ground.[71]

[65] Aris Tranditis, "Reforms and Collective Action in a Clientelist System: Greece During the Mitsotakis Administration (1990–1993)," *South European Society and Politics* 19, no.2 (2014): 215–234.

[66] Bryant, Garganas, and Tavlas, eds., *Greece's Economic Performance and Prospects,* 4.

[67] Tayfur, *Semiperipheral Development and Foreign Policy*, 98.

[68] Tridimas, "Greek Fiscal Policy and the European Union," 55.

[69] Susannah Verney, "From the 'Special Relationship' to Europeanism: PASOK and the European Community, 1981–1989," in Richard Clogg, ed., *Greece, 1981–1989: The Populist Decade* (London: The Macmillan Press, 1993), 150.

[70] Kevin Featherstone, "The Greek Sovereign Debt Crisis and EMU: A Failing State in a Skewed Regime," *Journal of Common Market Studies* 49, no. 2 (2011): 197–198.

[71] Antigone Lyberaki and Euclid Tsakalotos, "Reforming the Economy without Society: Social and Institutional Constraints to Economic Reform in post-1974 Greece," *New Political Economy* 7, no. 1 (2002): 110.

5.3 Kostas Simitis Case (1996–2004): A Break with the Past?

An important opportunity window was opened with the election of Kostas Simitis as prime minister in 1996. Simitis was a dedicated reformist agent and potential policy entrepreneur, whose aim was to overhaul Greek political economy comprehensively. His technocratic background, non-populist personality, and conciliatory leadership style also signified a clear divergence from his predecessor, Andreas Papandreou. Thanks to his education as a law and economics professor, and intellectual competencies, Simitis appeared as a key figure keen on offering issue-based technical solutions to specific problems; it is not coincidental that his nickname was "accountant."[72] He was also a respected figure among different segments of Greek society and politics. Simitis was known as "an individual without a spot of corruption" on his past[73]; and enjoyed high level of popularity hovering around 60 percent of the population when he assumed premiership, according to public surveys.[74] He was also a respected figure among international epistemic communities. Simitis represented Greece at the EU platforms for many years at different posts and became an esteemed person among his colleagues due to his compatible technical and diplomatic credentials. He was acknowledged in the European circles as "a safe pair of hands."[75] As Ludrow asserts, Simitis was seen as a skillful statesman and "one of the most senior members of the European Council with a quiet authority that his colleagues respect."[76] Simitis had a sound understanding of the major problems Greece encountered at the time. He was aware of the fact that "state capture" was at the heart of Greece's persistent economic reform failures. In one of his earliest speeches, for instance, he self-reflectively acknowledged the very problems created by his own party in the post-authoritarian period:

[72] The Economist, "Kostas Simitis, Greece's Cautious Helmsman," April 13, 2000.

[73] Koliopoulos and Veremis, *Modern Greece: A History since 1821*, 190.

[74] Athens News Agency, "Polls Favour New Simitis Government," January 29, 1996.

[75] Dionyssis G. Dimitrakopoulos and Argyris G. Passas, "The Greek Presidency: In the Shadow of War," *Journal of Common Market Studies* 42, Annual Review (2004): 43.

[76] Peter Ludlow, "The Greek Presidency," Briefing note no. 9 (Brussels: Euro Comment), 2.

> Our political practice followed the same track as that of the right-wing governments; many times we implemented ad hoc policies; we maintained clientelistic relations between the government and the voters; we made selective allocation of funds and we introduced measures benefitting specific groups. The principle governing our political practice [*sic*] was that the party and the government were always right and that their actions had to be justified… We do not need attractive slogans that create rising expectations but systematic programming and well planned action.[77]

Rather than opting for expansionary fiscal policies, uncontrolled populism, and conflictual zero-sum politics, Simitis framed an avowedly reformist rhetoric with repeated emphasis on the concepts of "modernization" and "Europeanization" to "prepare Greece for the 21st century."[78] Along these lines, first, he tried to overcome internal fractionalization in PASOK. His first cabinet (1996–2000) included leading pro-European figures such as Yiannos Papantoniou responsible for national economy and finance, and George Papandreou responsible for EU affairs as deputy foreign minister.[79] The highly technocratic character of Simitis government launched an ambitious economic modernization project to position Greece as a core European country in the Balkans, rather than an inferior Balkans state at the periphery of Europe. The guiding logic of his government program, which was entitled "Building a Strong Greece," was to launch a new national development and reform strategy in order to construct a sustainable fiscal regime.[80]

The time of Simitis' advent into premiership was ripe because the EU possessed strong legitimizing role to empower Simitis government in the second half of 1990s. Simitis' first term coincided with intense Europeanization in wider European politics due to the final stage of European Monetary Union (EMU). In the 1990s, creation of a single currency regime turned out to be one of the most ambitious projects had ever experienced in the history of European integration. It is in this context that Simitis narrated and communicated his reformist agenda as a

[77] Quoted in Lyrintzis, "PASOK in Power: From 'Change' to Disenchantment," 41–42.

[78] Athens News Agency, "Hard Work the Recipe for Success, Simitis Tells New Government," January 23, 1996.

[79] Simitis also kept these figures in their positions in his second cabinet. Athens News Agency, "Simitis Unveils New Government," April 13, 2000.

[80] Athens News Agency, "Simitis Presents New Government Programme: 'Building a Strong Greece,' " January 30, 1996.

compulsory recipe for integrating Greece into the grand European project. In PASOK's official program, he claimed, "that the unshakable target of the government's economic policy is Greece's participation in EU developments and the final stage of EMU."[81] Accordingly, adopting euro was narrated not only as the most efficient way of improving state's fiscal discipline but also as the only way to have a voice in the emerging architecture of European political economy.[82]

Simitis also reframed the EU's role in the domestic consumption of Greek politics. This reshuffling refers to a clear departure from PASOK's antagonizing tradition with the EU during the Papandreou era. In that sense, the EU factor strengthened Simitis' hands to foster his reformist agenda, which further informed the normalization of Greek politics to initiate consensus-based economic reforms with private interest groups and enabled to overcome the old age left-right cleavages in the country.[83] The main opposition party, ND, supported Greece's single currency membership and backed the fiscal reforms associated with EMU membership.[84] The conservative political elite rendered the cost of non-compliance with the Maastricht criteria and the eventual exclusion of Greece from the monetary union unbearable. Thus, an ostensibly broad-based coalition at the political level assembled around a reformist narrative.[85] The change in PASOK's rhetoric regarding the EU factor enhanced the capacity of Simitis to build new winning coalitions that encompasses certain interest groups aligned with the main opposition party.

The ideological convergence among the rival political camps also informed the preference functions of dominant interest groups including labor and business unions. Greek financial and industrial capital increasingly threw support behind the fiscal convergence reforms. The first and foremost supporter was financial elite. The industrial elite also

[81] Ibid.

[82] Quoted in Christos Dimas, "Privatization in the Name of 'Europe': Analysing the Telecoms Privatization in Greece from a 'Discursive Institutionalist' Perspective," GreeSE Paper No. 41 (Hellenic Observatory Papers on Greece and Southeast Europe, 2010), 34.

[83] Tayfur, *Semiperipheral Development and Foreign Policy*, 123–128.

[84] Athens News Agency, "Karamanlis Hails Greece's Entry into EMU," June 20, 2000. Also see, European Parliament Task Force on Economic and Monetary Union, "EMU and Greece," prepared by the Directorate General for Research Economic Affairs Division, 1998, 14.

[85] Panos Kazakos, "Europeanization, Public Goals and Group Interests: Convergence Policy in Greece, 1990–2003," *West European Politics* 27, no. 5 (2004): 906.

welcomed the membership decision since they perceived it as an opportunity to integrate with core European production structures.[86] The Greek labor unions also softened their stance toward euro membership as "[labor unions] thought that euro membership would help consolidating welfare state policies in Greece and foster economic convergence at the European level."[87]

On the external side, Simitis succeeded garnering the support of other member states partially thanks to his connections at the European epistemic communities. Simitis directly contacted with European leaders. For instance, he got Hans Tietmeyer, the then head of Germany's central bank, and Theo Waigel, the then finance minister of Germany to support Greece's entry into the exchange rate mechanism in 1998. It is ironic in retrospect that Germany's political backing proved crucial for Greece's acceptance into single currency regime.[88] In fact, initially, Greece was excluded from participating in final stage of the EMU. The European Commission and European Monetary Institute gauged in their 1998 report that Greece could not sustain high degree of convergence in none of the fiscal and financial criteria. Following the political support threw behind Simitis government at the European level, however, the atmosphere changed dramatically. In 2000, European Commission report concluded "Greece has achieved striking progress towards convergence" and gave its positive opinion regarding Greece's entry despite the same Commission highlighted just two years ago that none of the convergence criteria were fulfilled by Greece.[89] Having taken the membership process into consideration, it seems reasonable to argue at this point that Greece's adhesion into the euro area was primarily the outcome of the country's geopolitical importance for the core EU member states. Thus, the fiscal discipline imposed on Greece was dressed up in a dangerous euphemism that opened up Greek political and economic elites to synthesize accession rules with their traditional political modus operandi.

[86] Interview with former senior official, SEV, June 25, 2014; interview with senior official, SEV, June 24, 2014.

[87] Interview with senior official, GSEE-ADEDY, June 24, 2014.

[88] The Economist, "Greece: The Painful Road to Modernity," March 19, 1998.

[89] European Commission, *Report from the Commission: Convergence Report 2000*, COM (2000), 277 final (Brussels: European Commission, May 2000), 10.

5.4 Persistence of Status Quo: An Assessment of Simitis Period

Simitis' ambitious reform activism produced some initial results at the fiscal realm. Between 1996 and 2000, Greek economy grew 3.5 percent annually, higher than the EU averages (2.9 percent), the budget deficit decreased to 1.7 percent, and the government revenue/expenditure ratio improved from 0.8 to 0.92. Inflation, a historically recalcitrant problem for the Greek economy, was also reduced to 3 percent from double-digit numbers. Greek government's initial reform attempts impressed the markets that the interest rate differential had fallen dramatically: In 1992, long-term interest rates in Greece were about 16 percentage points higher than the EU average; by 2000 the difference was less than 1 percentage points. The record on public debt remained poor, however. The public debt was far from being close to the relevant Maastricht criterion (60 percent of GDP), nevertheless it was stabilized around 100 percent of the GDP.

Simitis also embarked on a set of reforms in the financial realm to comply with the European Commission directives. Lucas Papademos, a close advisor of Simitis and the future prime minister of Greece, played a crucial role in the pre-EMU process as the governor of the Greek Central Bank, namely the Bank of Greece (BoG). In this regard, the independence of the BoG and the establishment of new financial regulatory institutions were proved as significant changes.[90] In 1997, BoG was granted institutional independence, that is, the legal status to operate independently from the instructions and advices of the government, in line with the single currency program that established the European System of Central Banks. In pursuant of the pertaining legal framework, "price stability" became the main objective of the BoG. After 2001, the monetary policy was transferred to the discretion of the independent European Central Bank.

Simitis was successful in ensuring nominal convergence in the first term of his premiership and building pro-reform coalitions toward common currency membership. However, Simitis failed to initiate a sustainable cycle of reform activism that improved state capacity. Therefore, medium-term implications of Simitis era remained ephemeral. There are two strands to this argument. First, fiscal reforms initially targeted one-off convergence toward Maastricht criteria rather than structural transformation in

[90] OECD, *Economic Surveys: Greece, 1997–1998* (Paris: OECD Publication Service, 1999), 42–48.

state's fiscal regime. In this sense, it is not possible to refer to a paradigm shift in state's role in the economy because supposedly reformist policy coalitions, which backed Simitis government in the initial phases, approached the reform processes through the lens of nominal convergence.[91] Accordingly, achieving the technical criteria on budget deficit, inflation, and long-term interest rates were perceived as a goal in itself. The underlying structural problems, however, were not addressed.

Second, in the absence of an exogenous shock that alters power balances and dominant ideational paradigms, the reform-biased institutional structures remained almost intact. Although Simitis himself deemed fiscal reforms necessary to ensure Greek state's fiscal sustainability, he could not overcome the resistance of domestic policy coalitions.[92] Thus reform inertia perpetuated in the major structural problem areas of the Greek economy, the seeds of which were planted during PASOK governments in the 1980s, including labor markets, pension system, privatizations, tax regime, and public administration. For instance, Simitis aimed to reform the labor markets to underpin fiscal consolidation and competitiveness of the Greek economy. In 1997, he launched social dialogue with employers and labor unions, entitled "Confidence Pact Between the Government and Social Partners Towards the Year 2000." The aim of the Pact was to set a reform agenda including labor market flexibility and openness to ensure Greece's competitiveness in the euro area. The negotiations, however, plunged into deadlock as GSEE abstained from social dialogue. The government, in turn, introduced a far too limited Labour Reform in 1998 (Law 2639/98), leaving all burning problems on the flexibility and efficiency of labor markets untouched. OECD report pointed, "that an opportunity to address key rigidities was missed in Greece."[93] In 2000, following the introduction of the Lisbon agenda at the European Council Helsinki Summit (1999, see below) Simitis government reintroduced the reform bills on labor markets. The domestic policy coalitions, however, harshly reacted. GSEE, once again, opposed the

[91] Pagoulatos, "Economic Adjustment and Financial Reform," *South European Society and Politics*, 199.

[92] Kevin Featherstone, "Introduction: 'Modernisation' and the Structural Constraints of Greek Politics," *West European Politics* 28, no. 2 (2005): 237.

[93] OECD, *Economic Surveys: Greece, 1997–1998* (Paris: OECD Publication Service, 1999), 10, 69–78.

reform bill.[94] ADEDY, the union of public servants, also joined the anti-reform coalitions since it did not have interest in labor market flexibility. Featherstone notes that "in effect, [labor unions] are protected from job insecurity, have little interest in job creation, and seek to protect their privileges. Their interests are also short-term and defensive."[95]

The institutional representatives of the Greek finance capital also did not demonstrate a genuine willingness to support reform initiatives promoted by Simitis beyond the nominal convergence targets. SEV, for instance, did not back the labor reform proposals because its membership base, which was dominated by traditional state-protected entrepreneurs, found the transition to market competition difficult. The attempts to alter the parlous state of pension system, which was acting like a black hole in Greece's fiscal accounts, also shared alike destiny. Despite a quasi-certain consensus emerged that pension system was one of the main problems increasingly "threatening the fiscal sustainability" of state budget as highlighted in various OECD reports,[96] the well-entrenched pro-status quo forces succeeded blocking the process by a series of strikes and street demonstrations as never before since the end of the military dictatorship.[97] As a result, Simitis relented and shelved the implementation of labor markets and pension system reforms. Similarly, Simitis government pursued an incremental stop-go strategy regarding privatizations, tax reforms, and public administration reforms in fear of electoral costs.

5.5 Consolidation of a Reactive State (2004–2009)

The post-Simitis period refers to the consolidation period of the reactive Greek state. In fact, the empowerment capacity of the EU ceased to exist after Greece adopted euro in 2001. The "hard" conditionality of convergence criteria was replaced by "soft" conditionality principles after the

[94] Kazakos, "Europeanization, Public Goals and Group Interests," *West European Politics*, 906.

[95] Kevin Featherstone, "Greece and EMU: Between External Empowerment and Domestic Vulnerability," *Journal of Common Market Studies* 41, no. 5 (2003): 935.

[96] OECD, *Economic Surveys: 2000–2001* (Paris: OECD Publication Service, 2001), 45–48.

[97] Athens News Agency, "GSEE Calls New Strike despite Government Freeze of Proposed Social Security Reforms," April 28, 2001.

membership.[98] At Helsinki in December 1999, the European Council established a process to review progress on structural fiscal reforms across member states. One year later, Lisbon Strategy was launched. The common focus included the improvement of member states' competitiveness through a set of structural reforms. Open Method of Coordination, an intergovernmental voluntary cooperation mechanism based on benchmarking and sharing best practices among EU member countries, was determined as the ultimate driver of the reform processes. However, the "soft" conditionality of Lisbon agenda proved inadequate to ensure economic discipline in member states, including Greece. During 2000–2009, economic reforms came to a complete halt in the strict sense of the word.

With the rise of ND's Kostas Karamanlis as the new prime minister in 2004, traditional petty-politicking made a strong comeback in Greek political context. Despite Karamanlis' main election motto was the "re-foundation of the state"[99] and then the finance minister Alogoskoufis promised "efficiency, moderation and economic reforms based on consensus,"[100] Greek state's poor governance performance perpetuated during the ND governments (2004–2009). On the fiscal side, Karamanlis government overlooked the uncontrolled expansion of the state. Despite he labeled the public sector as "great invalid" lacking meritocracy and efficiency[101]; he still followed the reform-biased path mainly for electoral calculations. The OECD survey reports that the number of public employees continued to increase about 61,000 during 2002–2008, which was just 6000 in 1997–2002.[102] Contrary to its pre-election promises and party program, the Karamanlis government, in coordination with its trade union faction in GSEE, bypassed the independent regulatory agency, Supreme Council for Civil Personnel Selection (ASEP) that was established to recruit public servants. Karamanlis frequently reappointed part-

[98] Kevin Featherstone, " 'Soft' Co-ordination Meets 'Hard' Politics: the European Union and Pension Reform in Greece," *Journal of European Public Policy* 12, no. 4 (2005): 733–750.

[99] Athens News Agency, "New Interior Minister Says 'State to be Re-established with Spirit of Unity,' " March 11, 2004.

[100] Athens News Agency, "Government Seek Balanced Economic Growth, FinMin Says," March 30, 2004.

[101] Nikos Konstandaras, "Kostas Karamanlis's Deafening Silence," *Kathimerini*, September 5, 2013.

[102] OECD, *Greece: Review of the Central Administration, 2011* (Paris: OECD Publishing, 2012), 71.

time positions that need not go through ASEP for furthering his political patronage.[103] The wider public sector employment, including general government and public corporations, increased from 19.3 percent of total employment in 2000 to 20.7 in 2008.[104]

The wages in the public sector also increased spectacularly during his terms in office. According to the European Central Bank report, the cumulative wage increase in the state sector per employee was 108.7 percent in 1998–2009 period, well above the euro area average (34.9) with the highest rate after Ireland (110.8).[105] According to OECD, just before the economic crisis, public sector wages were 30–40 percent above the private sector averages. As a result, the total government expenditure in 2000–2008 increased from 46.7 percent to 50.6 percent of GDP. The government revenue, on the other hand, declined from 43 percent to 40.7 due to massive tax evasion.[106]

Similar to the Simitis period, Greek economy grew at relatively high rates during Karamanlis government, around 3.1 percent annually in 2004–2008. The fundamentals of economic growth, however, were somewhat superficial and absolutely fragile. It was a debt-driven growth model heavily relied on foreign inflows in the form of foreign loans extended to Greek government bonds and domestic banking system mainly for consumption and housing credits (see below). In fact, in the post-EMU process, Greek state played a shock-absorber role because the Greek firms could not keep pace with breath-taking competition in the euro area. The divergence in the competitive performance of the Greek economy triggered new fault-lines, which further obliged Greek state to pursue an expansionary fiscal outlook. Greece, in the post-2000, became entrapped in a vicious cycle again. The expansion of public sector due to uncontrolled populism, the deterioration of the private sector competitiveness due to postponement of structural reforms, and the continuance of clientelistic relations between state and social partners created a dangerous policy mix, which is aptly summarized by Katsimi and Moutos as follows:

[103] Athens News Agency, "Prime Minister Vows to Keep Election Pledges," March 22, 2004.

[104] OECD, *Greece: Review of the Central Administration*, 71.

[105] Fédéric Holm-Hadulla et al., "Public Sector Wages in the Euro Area: Towards Securing Stability and Competitiveness," *European Central Bank Occasional Paper Series*, no. 112 (2010): 14.

[106] OECD, *Economic Surveys, Greece: 2011* (Paris: OECD Publication Service, 2011), 89.

> Increases in public employment and tax rates, without attendant increases in publicly provided goods and in tax revenue, along with the shouldering of the financial obligations of inefficient private-sector firms, led to both public debt accumulation and increased wage demands by private-sector workers and a weakening of private-sector performance and employment opportunities, which in turn induced the 'nanny' state to intervene (as an employer and lender of last resort) in order to alleviate what it was co-responsible for creating in the first place, thus leading to further debt accumulation and providing new impetus to the vicious circle.[107]

The cost of "nanny state" was unbearable for Greece: Budget deficit increased from 3.7 percent in 2000 to 15.7 percent of GDP in 2009. Public debt jumped from 104.4 percent to 130 percent of the GDP. The accumulation of the public debt went hand in hand with the skyrocketed private debt. The ample credit opportunities encouraged the private sector borrowing in an unprecedented fashion that private debt over GDP ratio increased from 57.5 to 123.1 percent.

Given the scope of fiscal and financial problems, a puzzling question emerges: How did it become possible to make the "unsustainable sustainable" in the Greek case? How did the Greek state perpetuate a debt-ridden model for such a long period? The EU, as an external actor, planted the seeds of grave moral hazard problems that reinforced "state capture" in Greece during the post-Simitis era. Stated differently, Greece's integration into wider institutional setting of the monetary union without adequate state capacity exacerbated ubiquitous fiscal failures. Thus, Greece's accumulating economic problems in the post-2000 is closely linked to the perverse incentive structures and moral hazard problems emanated from the reversal of the EU's anchor role due to two main dimensions.

The first dimension relates to the architecture of the currency union. The intellectual forebears of the euro area acknowledged that, for a sustainable monetary union, fiscal discipline was sine quo non. However, having realized the political impossibility of the creation of a federal fiscal state, Stability and Growth Pact (SGP) was designed in 1997 to provide a benchmark for fiscal discipline among euro countries. The SGP set upper limits for member states to keep their budget deficit and public debt within acceptable thresholds—60 percent of GDP for public debt and 3 percent of GDP for budget deficits. The SGP, however, proved insufficient to ensure

[107] Margarita Katsimi and Thomas Moutos, "EMU and the Greek Crisis: The Political Economy Perspective," *European Journal of Political Economy* 26, no. 4 (2010): 572.

fiscal prudence since the core countries, primarily Germany and France, breached the Pact several times. The Council of Economic and Finance Ministers (Ecofin) decided to suspend the Excessive Deficit Procedure component of the SGP on November 25, 2003, due to the insistence of Franco-German axis. In a rather paradoxical way, by doing so, Germany undermined the foundations of the very fiscal regime it had created in the first instance. Once the fiscal discipline was hollowed out, the hands of the peripheral states were untied. Hence, peripheral states, especially Greece, compensated external competitiveness losses with increasing state borrowing rather than initiating supply-side reforms. Accordingly, Greek state continued to expose lucrative and non-transparent subsidies to privileged private sector firms and inflated public employment. Not surprisingly, in 2000–2008, Greece never complied with the criteria (see Fig. 5.1).

It appears that the EU, once again, turned into the "sponsor" of Greece's fiscal profligacy, albeit this time easy-money also channeled through the private markets in addition to the structural EU funds. The perverse setting, that is, the abundance of Ponzi-cum-funding opportunities, enabled state to postpone necessary reform measures in an already status quo biased domestic environment. In the post-membership era, the Greek state had an exclusive opportunity to borrow through very low interest rates as credit rating agencies and the international investors perceived Greece as a country that is not different from Germany. EMU membership, in this sense, provided de facto bail out guarantee to the Greek state and private business.[108] Benign expectations of the markets, which were in fact unrelated to the economic fundamentals, put a downward structural break in Greek real interest rates. The long-term rates fell to 6.1 percent in 2000 from 14.4 percent in 1996; government bond yields further slumped to 3.6 percent in mid-2005 and remained less than 5 percent in the pre-crisis period. The difference between German and Greek sovereign spreads, for instance, fell precipitously between 2001 and 2008. The unprecedentedly cheap credit opportunities and lax fiscal and financial policies motivated the Greek elites to opt for Ponzi strategies. Thus, the post-2000 exhibits textbook examples of pervasive moral hazard problems.

Second factor that informed economic profligacy in Greece was rapid financialization of European economies. The abolition of capital controls

[108] Michael G. Arghyrou and John D. Tsoukalas, "The Greek Debt Crisis: Likely Causes, Mechanics and Outcomes," *The World Economy* 34, no. 2 (2011): 180.

	2001	2002	2003	2004	2005	2006	2007	2008	2009	2010	2011	2012
Government deficit (% of GDP)												
Greece	-4.5	-4.8	-5.6	-7.5	-5.2	-5.7	-6.5	-9.8	-15.7	-10.7	-9.5	-9
Spain	-0.5	-0.3	-0.3	-0.1	1.3	2.4	2	-4.5	-11.1	-9.6	-9.6	-10.6
Ireland	0.9	-0.4	0.4	1.4	1.6	2.9	0.2	-7.4	-13.7	-30.6	-13.1	-8.2
Portugal	-4.8	-3.4	-3.7	-4	-6.5	-4.6	-3.1	-3.6	-10.2	-9.8	-4.3	-6.4
Germany	-3.1	-3.8	-4.2	-3.8	-3.3	-1.6	0.2	-0.1	-3.1	-4.2	-0.8	0.1
Italy	-3.1	-3.1	-3.6	-3.5	-4.4	-3.4	-1.6	-2.7	-5.5	-4.5	-3.8	-3
France	-1.5	-3.1	-4.1	-3.6	-2.9	-2.3	-2.7	-3.3	-7.5	-7.1	-5.3	-4.8
EU average	-1.5	-2.6	-3.2	-2.9	-2.5	-1.5	-0.9	-2.4	-6.9	-6.5	-4.4	-3.9
Gross public debt (% of GDP)												
Greece	104.7	102.6	98.3	99.8	110	107.8	107.3	112.9	129.7	148.3	170.3	156.9
Spain	55.6	52.6	48.8	46.3	43.2	39.7	36.3	40.2	54	61.7	70.5	86
Ireland	34.5	31.8	31	29.5	27.2	24.6	24.9	44.2	64.4	91.2	104.1	117.4
Portugal	53.8	56.8	59.4	61.9	67.7	69.4	68.4	71.7	83.7	94	108.2	124.1
Germany	59.1	60.7	64.4	66.2	68.5	68	65.2	66.8	74.5	82.5	80	81
Italy	108.3	105.4	104.1	103.7	105.7	106.3	103.3	106.1	116.4	119.3	120.7	127
France	57.1	59.1	63.3	65.2	66.8	64.1	64.2	68.2	79.2	82.4	85.8	90.2
EU average	83	80.1	74.5	62.2	58.9	61.6	62.9	62.3	61.9	60.4	61	61.8
Current account deficit (%of GDP)												
Greece	-7.2	-6.5	-6.5	-5.8	-7.6	-11.4	-14.6	-14.9	-11.2	-10.1	-9.9	-2.4
Spain	-3.9	-3.3	-3.5	-5.2	-7.4	-9.0	-10.0	-9.6	-4.8	-4.5	-3.8	-1.1
Ireland	-0.6	-1.0	0.0	-0.6	-3.5	-3.6	-5.3	-5.6	-2.3	1.1	1.2	4.4
Portugal	-10.3	-8.2	-6.4	-8.3	-10.3	-10.7	-10.1	-12.6	-10.9	-10.6	-7.0	-2.0
Germany	0.0	2.0	1.9	4.7	5.1	6.3	7.4	6.2	6.0	6.3	6.2	7.0
Italy	0.3	-0.4	-0.8	-0.3	-0.9	-1.5	-1.3	-2.9	-2.0	-3.5	-3.1	-0.4
France	1.7	1.0	0.4	0.5	-0.5	-0.6	-1.0	-1.7	-1.3	-1.3	-1.8	-2.2

Fig. 5.1 The widening gap between "north" and "south" in the EU

in the 1990s and the complete external liberalization of financial markets set the foundations for a full-fledged financialization in Europe.[109] The single currency regime amplified the moral hazard problems thanks to the emergence of complex financial interdependence devoid of robust prudential regulatory mechanisms. During 2000–2008, parallel to other European economies, Greek financial sector unprecedentedly bloated. For instance, credit institutions' assets over GDP increased from 107 percent

[109] George Pagoulatos, "State-driven in Boom and in Bust: Structural Limitations of Financial Power in Greece," *Government and Opposition* 49, no. 3 (2014): 452–482.

to 190 percent in 2008. The Greek banks extended huge volumes of credits to the Greek state and private business. Furthermore, the banks in core European countries willingly exposed massive credits to the Greek state and households. As Crouch argues in a rather more general context, "privatised Keynesianism" laid the groundwork for lucrative opportunities to satisfy consuming aspirations of the society.[110] Private sector borrowing, primarily the banking system, played intermediary role to sustain the debt-ridden economic model. The ECB data reveals that annual bank lending for housing purchases increased from 15 percent to 35 percent of total bank lending during 1998–2007. Similarly, consumer credit increased from 6.5 percent to 16 percent in the same period.[111] As Pagoulatos puts, "credit-driven, demand-led growth was politically popular, and the high growth rates achieved up to 2008, combined with the low interest rates, generated the kind of complacency that allowed governments to eschew necessary supply-side structural reforms."[112] These perverse dynamics at the domestic and international level, in turn, paved the way for the most catastrophic economic crisis in the history of modern Greece.

5.6 Conclusion

This chapter discussed the consolidation of a reactive state in Greece during post-authoritarian period. Accordingly, weakening capacity of the Greek state was informed through path-dependent interactions between agents and institutional structures along the domestic-international nexus. All three aspects of Greece's state capacity declined over the years. First, Greek political context took a shape of polarized bi-party competition. Thus, conflict-prone and uncontrolled populism occupied political sphere. Similar to other reactive states, the Greek state was perceived as an arena to be captured—rather than governed—by competing interest groups. Second, state bureaucracy remained fragmented and dependent on patronage politics. Third, deterioration of the Greek state's internal capacity influenced the organization of the interest intermediation structures.

[110] Colin Crouch, "Privatized Keynesianism: An Unacknowledged Policy Regime," *The British Journal of Politics and International Relations* 11, no. 3 (2009): 382–399.

[111] European Central Bank, *Structural Indicators for the EU Banking Sector* (Frankfurt: European Central Bank Publications, 2008), Table 4, Table 5, and Table 6; European Central Bank, *Structural Analysis of the EU Banking Sector* (Frankfurt: European Central Bank Publications, 2003), Table 7, Table 8, and Table 9.

[112] Pagoulatos, "State-driven in Boom and in Bust," *Government and Opposition*, 463.

Economic and political opportunities, which were structured by the state, led to self-reinforcing processes for further entrenchment of rent-seeking coalitions.

Kostas Simitis tried to launch a new policy path for Greece in mid-1990s. Simitis was in a suitable position to couple the problems, policies (i.e., solutions), and the politics to address Greece's economic calamities. Simitis, however, could achieve limited success due to two main reasons. First, despite the fact that Simitis assumed his post in a critical juncture, the EU factor failed to play a genuine trigger role in instigating a virtuous cycle of reform activism because the criteria to be admitted to the euro membership were far from having long-lasting transformative impacts on candidate states. The second reason that explains Simitis' failure to accomplish his agenda is related to the adverse role played by domestic institutional players. Simitis failed to receive a genuine support from the political parties, trade unions, and business associations to steer pro-chance coalitions. Despite the emergence of a consensus on Greece's membership in the euro area, the scope of necessary reforms to achieve this goal was limited to the nominal convergence criteria.

The Greek case demonstrates that the EU factor is also context-specific. There are three major episodes with regard to the EU factor in the Greek case. In the first episode, Greece's early membership to the Community retarded reform capacity during the 1980s. The EU, even in an unintended manner, financed reactive state practices through massive influx of fiscal transfers. In the second episode, the EU's role changed during mid-1990s thanks to the acceleration of the EMU project. However, the flawed design of convergence reforms and the poor implementation of Maastricht criteria enabled Greece to become single currency member without instigating a compatible fiscal regime. In the third episode, the EU totally ceased to be a reform-encouraging factor for Greece. Perverse incentive structures informed state agents' behavior in a way that economic reforms were constantly watered down. Karamanlis governments enjoyed moral hazard problems emanated from the structure of the monetary union and financialization of European economies. In summary, economic problems of the Greek state were exacerbated that led to the 2009 Greek debacle. The crisis, ultimately, opened up a new episode in contemporary political economy of Greece.

References

Arghyrou, Michael G., and John D. Tsoukalas. "The Greek Debt Crisis: Likely Causes, Mechanics and Outcomes." *The World Economy* 34, no. 2 (2011): 173–192.

Athens News Agency. "Government Seek Balanced Economic Growth, FinMin Says", March 30, 2004.

Athens News Agency. "GSEE Calls New Strike despite Government Freeze of Proposed Social Security Reforms," April 28, 2001.

Athens News Agency. "Hard Work the Recipe for Success, Simitis Tells New Government," January 23, 1996.

Athens News Agency. "Karamanlis Hails Greece's Entry into EMU," June 20, 2000.

Athens News Agency. "New Interior Minister Says 'State to be Re-established with Spirit of Unity,'" March 11, 2004.

Athens News Agency. "Polls Favour New Simitis Government," January 29, 1996.

Athens News Agency. "Prime Minister Vows to Keep Election Pledges," March 22, 2004.

Athens News Agency. "Simitis Presents New Government Programme: 'Building a Strong Greece,'" January 30, 1996.

Athens News Agency. "Simitis Unveils New Government," April 13, 2000.

Bryant, Ralph C., Nicholas C. Garganas, and George S. Tavlas, eds. *Greece's Economic Performance and Prospects*. Athens: Bank of Greece Printing Works, 2001.

Crouch, Colin. "Privatized Keynesianism: An Unacknowledged Policy Regime." *The British Journal of Politics and International Relations* 11, no. 3 (2009): 382–399.

Dimas, Christos. "Privatization in the Name of 'Europe': Analysing the Telecoms Privatization in Greece from a 'Discursive Institutionalist' Perspective." GreeSE Paper No. 41, Hellenic Observatory Papers on Greece and Southeast Europe, 2010.

Dimitrakopoulos, Dionyssis G., and Argyris G. Passas. "The Greek Presidency: In the Shadow of War." *Journal of Common Market Studies* 42, Annual Review (2004): 43–46.

European Central Bank. *Structural Analysis of the EU Banking Sector*. Frankfurt: European Central Bank Publications, 2003.

European Central Bank. *Structural Indicators for the EU Banking Sector*. Frankfurt: European Central Bank Publications, 2008.

European Commission, *Report from the Commission: Convergence Report 2000*, COM (2000), 277 final. Brussels: European Commission, May 2000.

Featherstone, Kevin, and Dimitris Papadimitriou. "The Emperor Has no Clothes: Power and Resources within the Greek Core Executive." *Governance* 26, no. 3 (2013): 523–545.

Featherstone, Kevin. "'Soft' Co-ordination Meets 'Hard' Politics: the European Union and Pension Reform in Greece." *Journal of European Public Policy* 12, no. 4 (2005): 733–750.

Featherstone, Kevin. "Greece and EMU: Between External Empowerment and Domestic Vulnerability." *Journal of Common Market Studies* 41, no. 5 (2003): 923–940.

Featherstone, Kevin. "Introduction: 'Modernisation' and the Structural Constraints of Greek Politics." *West European Politics* 28, no. 2 (2005): 223–241.

Featherstone, Kevin. "The Greek Sovereign Debt Crisis and EMU: A Failing State in a Skewed Regime." *Journal of Common Market Studies* 49, no. 2 (2011): 193–217.

Holm-Hadulla, Fédéric et. al. "Public Sector Wages in the Euro Area: Towards Securing Stability and Competitiveness." *European Central Bank Occasional Paper Series*, no. 112, 2010.

Ioannou, Christos. "From Divided 'Quangos' to Fragmented 'Social Partners': Explaining the Absence of Mergers." In *Restructuring Representation: The Merger Process and Trade Union Structural Development in Ten Countries*, edited by Waddington Jeremy, 139–164. Brussels: P.I.E-Peter Lang, 2005.

Ioannou, Christos. "Odysseus or Sisyphus Revisited: Failed Attempts to conclude Social-liberal Pacts in Greece." In *After the Euro and Enlargement: Social Pacts in the European Union*, edited by Philippe Pochet, Maarten Keune, and David Natali, 83–108. Brussels: Observatoire Social Europeen & ETUI, 2010.

Ioannou, Christos. *Trade Unions in Greece: Development, Structures and Prospects.* Athens: Friedrich Ebert Foundation, 1999.

Jones, Nikoleta, Chrisovaladis Malesios, Theodoros Iosifides, and Kostas M. Sophoulis. "Social Capital in Greece: Measurement and Comparative Perspectives." *South European Society and Politics* 13, no. 2 (2008): 175–193.

Kalyvas, Stathis N. "Polarization in Greek Politics: PASOK's First Four Years, 1981–1985." *Journal of the Hellenic Diaspora* 23, no. 1 (1997): 83–104.

Kariotis, Theodore C. "Andreas G. Papandreou: The Economist." *Journal of the Hellenic Diaspora* 23, no. 1 (1997): 33–59.

Katsimi, Margarita, and Thomas Moutos. "EMU and the Greek Crisis: The Political Economy Perspective." *European Journal of Political Economy* 26, no. 4 (2010): 568–576.

Kazakos, Panos. "Europeanization, Public Goals and Group Interests: Convergence Policy in Greece, 1990–2003." *West European Politics* 27, no. 5 (2004): 901–918.

Konstandaras, Nikos. "Kostas Karamanlis's Deafening Silence." *Kathimerini*, September 5, 2013.

Kovras, Iosif and Neophytos Loizides. "The Sovereign Debt Crisis in Southern Europe: Majoritarian Pitfalls?" *Comparative Politics* 47, no. 1 (2014): 1–20.

Lanza, Orazio, and Kostas Lavdas. "The Disentanglement of Interest Politics: Business Associability, the Parties, and Policy in Italy and Greece." *European Journal of Political Research* 37, no. 2 (2000): 203–235.

Lavdas, Kostas. "Interest Groups in Disjointed Corporatism: Social Dialogue in Greece and European 'Competitive Corporatism'." *West European Politics* 28, no. 2 (2005): 297–316.

Lavdas, Kostas. *The Europeanization of Greece.* London: Palgrave Macmillan, 1997.

Lolos, Sarantis E. G. "Success and Failure of Economic Reforms: The Experience of Greece and Portugal." *Comparative Economic Studies* 40, no. 1 (1998): 72–102.

Ludlow, Peter. "The Greek Presidency." *Briefing note*, no. 9. Brussels: Euro Comment.

Lyberaki, Antigone, and Euclid Tsakalotos. "Reforming the Economy without Society: Social and Institutional Constraints to Economic Reform in post-1974 Greece." *New Political Economy* 7, no. 1 (2002): 93–114.

Lyrintzis, Christos. "PASOK in Power: From 'Change' to Disenchantment." In *Greece, 1981–1989: The Populist Decade*, edited by Richard Clogg, 26–46. London: The Macmillan Press, 1993.

Mavrogordatos, George Th. "From Traditional Clientelism to Machine Politics: the Impact of PASOK Populism in Greece." *South European Society and Politics* 2, no. 3 (1997): 1–26.

Mavrogordatos, George Th. "The Greek Party System: A Case of 'Limited but Polarized Pluralism'?" In *Party Politics in Contemporary Europe*, edited by Stefano Bartolini, and Peter Mair, 156–169. London: Frank Cass, 1984.

Monastiriotis, Vassilis, and Andreas Antoniades. "Reform That! Greece's Failing Reform Technology: Beyond 'Vested Interests' and 'Political Exchange'." In *From Stagnation To Forced Adjustment: Reforms In Greece, 1974–2010*, edited by Stathis Kalyvas, George Pagoulatos, and Haris Tsoukas, 31–47. London and New York: Hurst Co. and Columbia University Press, 2012.

OECD, *Economic Surveys, Greece: 1990–1991.* Paris: OECD Publications Service, 1991.

OECD, *Economic Surveys, Greece: 1992–1993.* Paris: OECD Publications Service, 1993.

OECD, *Economic Surveys, Greece: 2011.* Paris: OECD Publication Service, 2011.

OECD, *Economic Surveys: 2000–2001.* Paris: OECD Publication Service, 2001.

OECD, *Economic Surveys: Greece, 1997–1998.* Paris: OECD Publication Service, 1999.

OECD, *Greece: Review of the Central Administration, 2011.* Paris: OECD Publishing, 2012.

Pagoulatos, George. "Economic Adjustment and Financial Reform: Greece's Europeanization and the Emergence of a Stabilization State." *South European Society and Politics* 5, no. 2 (2000): 191–216.

Pagoulatos, George. "State-driven in Boom and in Bust: Structural Limitations of Financial Power in Greece." *Government and Opposition* 49, no. 3 (2014): 452–482.

Pappas, Takis S. "Why Greece Failed?" *Journal of Democracy* 24, no. 2 (2013): 31–45.

Pelagidis, Theodore, and Michael Mitsopoulos. *Greece: From Exit to Recovery.* Washington, D.C.: Brookings Institution Press, 2014.

Pelagidis, Theodore, and Michael Mitsopoulos. *Understanding the Economic Crisis in Greece: From Boom to Bust.* Hampshire: Palgrave Macmillan, 2011.

Sartori, Giovanni. *Parties and Party Systems: A Framework for Analysis.* Cambridge: Cambridge University Press, 1976.

Schmitter, Philippe C. "Organized Interests and Democratic Consolidation in Southern Europe." In *The Politics of Democratic Consolidation: Southern Europe in Comparative Perspective*, edited by Richard Gunther, Nikiforos P. Diamandouros, and Hans-Jürgen Puhle, 284–314. Baltimore: Johns Hopkins University Press, 1995.

Sotiropoulos, Dimitri A. "A Description of the Greek Higher Civil Service." In *Bureaucratic Elites in Western European States*, edited by Edward C. Page, and Vincent Wright, 13–31. Oxford: Oxford University Press, 1999.

Sotiropoulos, Dimitri A. "Southern European Public Bureaucracies in Comparative Perspective." *West European Politics* 27, no. 3 (2004): 405–422.

Sotiropoulos, Dimitri A. "The Authoritarian Past and Contemporary Greek Democracy." *South European Society and Politics* 15, no. 3, (2010): 449–465.

Sotiropoulos, Dimitri A. "The Remains of Authoritarianism: Bureaucracy and Civil Society in Post-Authoritarian Greece." *Cahiers d'Etudes sur la Méditerranée Orientale et le monde Turco-Iranien*, no. 20 (1995).

Sotiropoulos, Dimitri A. "The Two Faces of Politicization of the Greek Civil Service: The Case of Contemporary Greece." In *Politicization of the Civil Service in Comparative Perspective: The Quest for Control*, edited by Guy Peters, and John Pierre, 256–265. London: Routledge, 2004.

Tayfur, M. Fatih. *Semiperipheral Development and Foreign Policy: The Cases of Greece and Spain.* Aldershot: Ashgate, 2003.

The Economist. "Greece: The Painful Road to Modernity," March 19, 1998.

The Economist. "Kostas Simitis, Greece's Cautious Helmsman." April 13, 2000.

Tranditis, Aris. "Reforms and Collective Action in a Clientelist System: Greece during the Mitsotakis Administration (1990–93)." *South European Society and Politics* 19, no.2 (2014): 215–234.

Tridimas, George. "Greek Fiscal Policy and the European Union." In *Greece in a Changing Europe: Between European Integration and Balkan Disintegration*, edited by Kevin Featherstone, and Kostas Ifantis. Manchester: Manchester University Press, 1996.

Tsakalatos, Euclid. "The Political Economy of Social Democratic Economic Policies: The PASOK Experiment In Greece." *Oxford Review of Economic Policy* 14, no. 1 (1998): 114–138.

Tsarouhas, Dimitris. "Social Partnership in Greece: Is There a Europeanization Effect?" *European Journal of Industrial Relations* 14, no. 3 (2008): 347–365.

Verney, Susannah. "From the 'Special Relationship' to Europeanism: PASOK and the European Community, 1981–1989." In *Greece, 1981–1989: The Populist Decade*, edited by Richard Clogg, 131–153. London: The Macmillan Press, 1993.

CHAPTER 6

Greek Crisis and Aftermath (2009–2016)

The accumulation of economic problems in Greece abruptly surfaced with the crisis erupted in October 2009, which George Papandreou, the prime minister at the time, described as the most tragic and hardest times in Greece's post-war history. The crisis endured deep social, political, and economic pains. The cumulative decline in GDP reached almost one-third of Greek economy with an astonishing unemployment rate that led to a massive wave of brain drain. The crisis also disturbed the power balances in a number of ways. The bi-party majoritarian model that defined the characteristics of post-authoritarian Greek politics collapsed and the peripheral parties assumed a more central role in Greek politics. The crisis also provided historical opportunity to restructure inefficient state institutions and introduce a new economic regime. The IMF and the EU involved in the post-crisis adjustment programs with an unmatched level of bargaining leverage.

This opportunity, however, could not be exploited to a significant extent. In fact, the opposite turned out to be the case: Despite presence of a single party government and strong external anchors encouraging reform packages in the wake of the crisis, Greece decisively plunged into a deadlock in which multi-level blame games have dominated the post-crisis policy-making agenda. Even the most optimistic accounts on Greece's economic performance acknowledge that there are considerable lags and notable reform failures. Why crisis did not lead to the creation of new

M. Kutlay, *The Political Economies of Turkey and Greece*,
International Political Economy Series,
https://doi.org/10.1007/978-3-319-92789-3_6

winning coalitions and give leeway to a reform-oriented paradigm change? This chapter offers a comprehensive political economy account of the Greek crisis and its aftermath to address this question. Second part provides a brief history of the Greek economic turmoil. Third part discusses the agency and institutional-level dynamics that paved the way for fragmented crisis narratives and multiple blame games. The fourth part assesses the meteoric political rise of the Coalition of the Radical Left (SYRIZA) with particular reference to its approach to the Greek crisis. The final part concludes the chapter.

6.1 Greek Crisis and Bailouts: A Brief Overview

The structural causes of the Greek economic crisis, which were discussed in detail in Chap. 5, accumulated over the years. The proximate causes, however, surfaced after the election of George Papandreou as the new prime minister on October 4, 2009, with 44 percent of the popular votes in the elections. Just two days after his ascendance to the premiership, in a private meeting with George Provopoulos, the then governor of the Central Bank of Greece, Papandreou was informed that the budget deficit was heading toward double digit figures instead of 3.7 percent of the GDP as previously declared by the outgoing center-right ND government. On October 18, 2009, Papandreou admitted that the previous government covered up the real budget deficits and declared the "true" figures to be around 12.5 percent of the GDP, more than tripling the previous projections.[1] As the new government's spokesperson put, the "unrealistic data" published by the previous government created "exceptionally negative reaction" among European circles.[2]

Combined with Greece's very high government debt—around 115 percent of GDP and net external debt almost 100 percent of GDP—and skyrocketed current account deficit—around 13.1 percent of GDP, the revision in budget figures triggered an unprecedented wave of panic. Since it became apparent that Greece was in fact suffering from triple deficits (budget, current account, and credibility) the markets and credit-rating agencies harshly and even punitively reacted. Fitch Ratings downgraded Greece's credit notch sharply, which was followed by other leading

[1] Athens News Agency, "Government Submits New Deficit Figure," October 22, 2009.

[2] Athens News Agency, "Government Blames ND for 'Credibility Deficit' at EU," October 22, 2009.

agencies, first such downgrading in a decade. Given the acute crisis atmosphere in global economy, in early 2010, market sentiments vis-à-vis Greece deteriorated precipitously. Papandreou had to announce an anti-crisis plan on March 4, 2010, to alleviate market pressures. The government's anti-crisis measures introduced increase in taxes, freeze on pensions, and cap on civil servants' pay, bonuses, and recruitments. The target was to reduce the country's fiscal deficit by a total of 4 percent in 2010. However, the plan was perceived neither comprehensive nor bold enough to decisively arrest the expansion of the crisis. Following the initial measures, PASOK government announced a new small set of cost-cutting measures totaling 0.5 percent of GDP. Further revenue-increasing and cost-cutting measures totaling 2 percent of GDP was also introduced in the third wave. Despite counter-crisis policy responses, Greece's economic outlook continued to worsen.

The Papandreou government's stop-go nature of anti-crisis measures injected further uncertainty rather than sending credible signals to the market players. The increasing credibility gap pushed the Greek economy into a virtual deadlock and Greek state's bonds were downgraded to "junk" status in a very short period. Bond yields surged to almost 15 percent, which resulted in Greece's cut-off from the markets in the first quarter of 2010. With no other viable policy options at hand, Papandreou officially requested the EU-IMF support as a "lender of last resort" on April 23 after a turbulent period of informal negotiations behind the closed doors, which also spawned subverting speculations. A joint European Commission, European Central Bank, and International Monetary Fund (EC-ECB-IMF) mission, called "troika," was sent to Athens to negotiate the scope of the bailout package and the conditionality measures attached to the program. Agreement at the technical level was reached on May 2, 2010, on a comprehensive multi-year program covering three years between 2010 and 2013.[3]

The bailout pledged a total of €110 billion, unprecedented in the history of the IMF and the EU. The then IMF director, Dominique Strauss-Kahn, pointed out that Greece retained "an exceptional level of access" to the IMF resources, "largest access granted to a member country."[4] The bailout package was attached to strict conditionality specified in two

[3] IMF, "IMF Reaches Staff-Level Agreement with Greece on €30 Billion Stand-By Arrangement," *Press Release*, no. 10/176, May 2, 2010.

[4] Ibid.

official documents: Memorandum of Economic and Financial Policies (MEFP) and a more detailed Memorandum of Understanding (MoU) providing a roadmap to reform Greek economy.[5]

The program was an ambitious document standing on three pillars: Fiscal reforms, financial reforms, and structural reforms that fortify the sustainability of Greece's macroeconomic balances. On top of the measures already taken by the Papandreou government, MEFP targeted fiscal adjustment amounting to 11 percent of the GDP as of 2013, which was pointed out as the "cornerstone of the program."[6] Accordingly, expenditures should be cut by 7 percent and revenues should be increased by 4 percent to reduce the budget deficit "well below" 3 percent of GDP by 2014.[7] The program urged the commitment of the Greek government to strengthen the national fiscal policy framework and fiscal institutions by keeping primary balance in a sizeable surplus (minimum 5 percent of GDP). The fiscal strategy also targeted the decline of the debt-GDP ratio starting from 2013. For achieving program targets, a front-loaded fiscal adjustment was prioritized by the troika to "avoid reform fatigue."[8] The fiscal reforms outlined in the program covered a wide range of items including tax reform, pension reform, health sector reform, debt management framework, and public administration.

In the financial pillar, the program envisaged two major adjustments. The immediate concern was to provide liquidity to the financial sector since, in the first quarter of 2010, Greek banks lost wholesale market access. In 2008, Karamanlis government extended bank assistance package around €28 billion to intercept the shock waves of global financial turmoil. However, the amount proved inadequate. The financial sector, which was not in fact the primary problem in the initial phases, was drawn into the Greek debacle following the fiscal insolvency of the Greek state. For instance, the non-performing loans reached at 7.7 percent of the total loans disbursed in 2009. In this environment, Greece's cut-off from the markets further exacerbated the financial woes in the banking system. Hence, the MEFP envisioned liquidity mechanisms for the financial sector

[5] European Commission, *The Economic Adjustment Programme for Greece* (Brussels: European Commission Directorate-General for Economic and Financial Affairs Publications, 2010).

[6] Ibid., 40.

[7] Ibid. Also see IMF, *Greece: Staff Report on Request for Stand-By Agreement* (Washington, DC: IMF Publication Services, May 2010), 10–11.

[8] European Commission, *The Economic Adjustment Programme for Greece*, 42.

via the ECB and the Central Bank of Greece. Second, the medium-term concern was to provide stability in the financial system. To this end, the program requested the Greek government to establish a fully independent Hellenic Financial Stability Fund (HFSF) through specific legislation in consultation with the troika. The HFSF was endowed with €10 billion from the bailout package to recapitalize the Greek banks, "if and when such needs arouse."[9] The Bank of Greece (BoG) committed itself to "implement intensified supervision and increase the resources dedicated to banking supervision."[10]

In the structural pillar, the MEFP specified ambitious reform targets to transform the fundamentals of the Greek state. The structural reforms were deemed necessary to ensure "internal devaluation" in the absence of an exchange rate lever. According to the program, the ultimate medium-term goal of the structural reforms was to construct a competitive Greek state by way of arresting state's fiscal profligacy and ensuring fiscal sustainability. The impediments weakening Greek state's capacity, which were specifically addressed in the plan, can be broken down into three titles. First, public administration was to be overhauled through thorough reorganization of the recruitment procedures, establishment of the independent external institutions to review the public administration, and the reduction of the number of civil servants. Second, state-owned enterprises were to be reformed and divested within the context of a comprehensive privatization program. Third, labor and production markets were to be liberalized by introducing further flexibility in employment and wage policies. Given the scope of reforms listed in the program, Greece faced with the most coercive conditionality over the previous three decades. A Technical Memorandum of Understanding (TMoU) was attached to the program that specified the quantitative performance criteria, indicative targets, structural benchmarks, quarterly program reviews (to be published by European Commission) and consultation clauses.

In retrospect, however, it is apparent that Greece is far from being a success story. The hard data suggests that bailout programs did not yield the expected/targeted outcomes. Unemployment reached 28 percent; real GDP shrank around 25 percent; the public debt ratio skyrocketed to 175 percent of the GDP; and real domestic demand declined around 30

[9] IMF, *Greece: Ex-Post Evaluation of Exceptional Access Under the 2010 Stand-By Arrangement* (Washington, DC: IMF Publication Services, 2013), 11.

[10] European Commission, *The Economic Adjustment Programme for Greece*, 24, 47.

percent. The field research also suggests that the domestic interest groups shared the strong opinion that the troika program mostly failed, despite the views of the respondents significantly diverge regarding the reasons that lead to the failure of the program.[11]

Greece could not return to the path of economic recovery despite a total of €210 billion disbursed as of June 2013 in addition to a sizeable debt restructuration involving private sector.[12] Furthermore, non-performing over total loans ratio skyrocketed to 36.6 percent in consumer loans and 24.5 percent in corporate loans. The failure of the first program necessitated a second bailout package around €130 billion.[13] However, the second adjustment program also suffered from significant failures and implementation gaps. The third troika review, for instance, asserted that "several important reform actions being delayed," "fiscal outlook remains subject to high uncertainty," "concerns remain about the willingness and capacity of the Greek administration to implement [scheduled] public finance reforms," and "limited progress [achieved] in privatization."[14] Finally, Greece and creditors agreed on a third bailout package around €86 billion in 2015, which shall be discussed in the following parts.

The Greek case poses intriguing puzzles. An unprecedented economic crisis leveled the socio-political and economic landscape for a paradigmatic change by exhausting prevailing policy paradigms. The IMF-EU anchor also stepped in as strong disciplinary anchors in the wake of the crisis. Attached to strict conditionality, the bailout programs offered huge amounts of financial assistance to alleviate the distributional pressures. Hence, both "carrots" and "sticks" were available to ensure efficient implementation of economic reforms. Then, what went wrong in Greece? Why reform program did not generate the expected outcomes and domestic ownership could not be generated toward a new paradigm? The rest of the chapter delves into the crisis narratives along domestic-external nexus and try to elucidate how the responses of domestic institutional players informed reform dynamics in post-crisis Greece.

[11] For the full list of semi-structured in-depth interviews, see Appendix.

[12] European Commission, *The Second Economic Adjustment Programme for Greece: Third Review* (Brussels: European Commission Directorate-General for Economic and Financial Affairs Publications, 2013), 47.

[13] European Commission, *The Second Economic Adjustment Programme for Greece* (Brussels: European Commission Directorate-General for Economic and Financial Affairs Publications, 2012).

[14] European Commission, *The Second Economic Adjustment Programme for Greece: Third Review*, 1–8.

Agency-Level Dynamics: Diverging Crisis Narratives

One of the crucial factors that explain Greek stalemate is related to the commitment and domestic ownership problems. Reformist state agents play crucial roles during crisis episodes to steer new policy coalitions throwing their full support to the new paradigms. In the Greek case, the commitment problems mainly emanated from the diverging crisis narratives. In particular, Papandreou's crisis narrative diverged from those of the German leadership and the troika. In fact, unbridgeable gaps emerged between the parties regarding the sources of the Greek turmoil and the measures to be taken to overcome it. With the deepening of the economic crisis, narrative mismatch further widened. Since fragmented crisis narratives occupied the policy-making agenda, the proposed reform program suffered from serious ownership and legitimacy gaps in the eyes of domestic constituency.

Newly elected prime minister, George Papandreou, found himself as the key state agent to handle the Greek economic crisis. Papandreou period (October 2009–November 2011) deserves particular attention because the basic parameters of the bailout programs and the dominant mode of relations among key stakeholders were set up during his term in office, which in turn created a path-dependent process for the incoming governments. Therefore, this part discusses Papandreou's crisis narrative in an interactive perspective with external actors and domestic stakeholders. There are two distinct phases in this regard: In the first phase, Papandreou could not reckon the true depth of the crisis and could not develop a coherent crisis narrative. Thus, up to March 2010, Papandreou sent mixed signals to the domestic and international players. On the one hand, he continued to remain loyal to his pre-election promises regarding government spending and subsidy guarantees. On the other hand, he promised to reduce hefty budget deficits and public debt. Papandreou repeatedly denied that Greece was on the brink of insolvency. Papandreou's underestimation of the gravity of the situation and his apparent denial, however, received harsh response from the markets so that government spreads skyrocketed in early 2010.[15] He reckoned the severity of the situation when the markets harshly responded to the hazy messages of the Greek government. From this point onward, a second phase started in

[15] Dimitris Tsarouhas, "The Political Origins of the Greek Crisis: Domestic Failures and the EU Factor," *Insight Turkey* 14, no. 2 (2012): 92.

Papandreou's approach to the crisis. In this stage, he tried to frame the Greek crisis as "a test case for Europe," composed of domestic, but especially international dimensions. On the domestic side, in most of his speeches, Papandreou accepted that the Greek state had structural problems that necessitate substantial economic reforms:

> [We have a] political system built on clientelism, patronage, inequality and injustice, captive to special interest groups with special privileges, and along with it a huge, over-centralized, inefficient and bureaucratic state, lacking transparency, meritocracy and accountability.[16]

Papandreou was aware of the fact that Greece was suffering from serious credibility and commitment problems; thereby he tried to send strong signals to his European counterparts and financial markets. Along these lines, Papandreou argued that his government was dedicated to offset Greece's credibility deficit. He constantly argued, however, that his government was not part of the problems accumulated over the years.[17] Hence, Papandreou based his credibility-building strategy on a dichotomic portrayal of the "old" and "new" Greece. He blamed the previous government due to "the lack of transparency/accountability in governance and mismanagement of the Greek economy."[18] The underlying motivation was to convince the international markets and the European political elite that his government was "different" from the previous ones.[19]

On the external side, Papandreou blamed international speculators. He narrated the Greek crisis, at least partially, as a product of the unfettered international financial speculators. PASOK leader tried to place Greek turmoil into a structural context to counterbalance financial panic and speculative attacks. He later argued "Greece was only a symptom of much deeper structural problems in the euro zone and vulnerabilities in the wider global economic system."[20] In this sense, Papandreou criticized

[16] George Papandreou, "Re-inventing Greece: A Leadership Vision," Speech at the Economist Conference http://papandreou.gr/en/speech-at-the-economist-conference/ (arrived on February 27, 2016).

[17] Christiane Amanpour, "Interview with George Papandreou," http://papandreou.gr/en/interview-on-cnn/ (arrived on February 27, 2016).

[18] Ibid.

[19] Andrew Marr, "Interview with George Papandreou," http://news.bbc.co.uk/1/hi/uk_politics/8526880.stm (arrived on February 27, 2016), emphasis added.

[20] George Papandreou, "Imagine a European Democracy Without Borders," TED Speech, http://www.ted.com/talks/george_papandreou_imagine_a_european_democracy_without_borders/transcript (arrived on February 27, 2016).

unleashed financial speculation and claimed that his government's "radical reforms" were not appreciated:

> Our [Greek] crisis has exposed deep flaws in the international economic system, flaws that savage cuts to salaries will not cure. Despite the radical reforms my government has launched, opportunistic traders have forced interest rates on Greek bonds to record highs. Some of these speculators are making a fortune by betting on our nation's misfortune.[21]

Papandreou, therefore, asked for the establishment of European-level fiscal cohesion and solidarity mechanisms to "protect European democracies and people against unfettered financial speculators."[22] PASOK government tried to convince European counterparts to act in a coordinated way to avoid "Greece's scapegoating" by the markets as the weakest chain in Europe.[23] Thus, Papandreou framed the Greek crisis as a "test case" for European unity:

> We're in a laboratory right now and let us hope that this test case is a successful one for Europe by in fact putting to the test the unity of Europe in a positive way. Europe has a lot of strength. We need to pool that strength…[24]

As the crisis evolved, however, it became apparent that Papandreou's perspective diverged from his European counterparts, notably from Germany's approach to the Greek crisis. Germany consolidated its regional hegemonic power position thanks to unbeatable export capacity and current account surplus that outperformed other euro area countries in the post-2000. For instance, Germany's trade surplus quadrupled in the decade following the introduction of the single currency. All southern European countries, without any exception, suffered from chronic current account deficits after their membership to the euro area and none of them had current account surplus even in a single year in the post-2000 period. Hence, Germany stood out as the most resourceful but "reluctant hege-

[21] George Papandreou, "Greece Is Not an Island," *The New York Times*, March 9, 2010.
[22] Ibid.
[23] Interview with Member of Parliament, PASOK, June 19, 2014.
[24] Marr, "Interview with George Papandreou."

mon" capable of providing public goods in crisis-torn Europe.[25] Concomitantly, Germany became the predominant country to determine the form and content of rescue packages in crisis-ridden euro area economies. Thus, main parameters that shaped Germany's approach to the Greek crisis deserve in-depth analysis.

6.2 Diverging Interests and Ideas: The Logic of Extreme Austerity

Germany's response to the Greek crisis requires a multi-dimensional analysis along the interests-ideas nexus because neither "interests" nor "ideas" per se explicate the dominant crisis narrative adopted by the German ruling elite. In the initial phases, Merkel interpreted the Greek problem as an outcome of Greece's fiscal profligacy; thereby perceived Greece as a "special" and "exceptional case." Moreover, Papandreou's initial fragmented and lax response to the crisis exacerbated Greece's already grave credibility problems in the eyes of the German policy-makers. Based on this background, German chancellor backed the anti-crisis measures taken by the Greek government but denied any kind of European rescue on the ground of moral hazard problems. Merkel claimed, in early 2010, "that financial help [to Greece] is not on the agenda. I don't think it's advisable to upset the markets by raising false expectations."[26] Greece, however, completely failed to ensure the trust of the markets as of April 2010. Thus, a disorderly default became inescapable in the absence of a European rescue.

A possible Greek default was against Germany's interests for two main reasons. First, the German and French banks' exposure to Greece and neighboring markets was large enough to spark a wave of instability in the German financial system. German and French banks at the time carried a combined $119 billion in exposure to the Greek borrowers.[27] If Athens were to default, it was possible for markets to question whether French and German banks could withstand the potential losses, sparking a panic that could reverberate throughout the euro system. Second, and more

[25] William E. Paterson, "The Reluctant Hegemon? Germany Moves Centre Stage in the European Union," *Journal of Common Market Studies* 49, Annual Review (2011): 57–75.

[26] Ambrose Evans-Prichard, "Greece Accuses Germany of 'Squalid Game' in Debt Crisis," *The Telegraph*, March 22, 2010.

[27] Vanessa Fuhrmans and Sebastian Moffett, "Exposure to Greece Weighs on French, German Banks," *The Wall Street Journal*, February 17, 2010.

importantly, Merkel reckoned that a possible Greek default would create negative domino effects in other southern European economies, mainly Spain and Italy, which were also sitting on the sharp edge of the knife due to the dense interconnectedness of their financial markets. According to Bank of International Settlements, the German and French banks' exposure to southern European countries were around $970 billion at the time. Given the precariousness of the situation, Merkel had to change her position in April 2010 as the contagion risk turned into a real possibility. Hence, for Merkel, bailing Greece out was perceived "as a necessary evil."[28]

The negotiations over the first bailout package took place in a very tense environment. Germany insisted on a strict conditionality program including harsh austerity measures to overcome Greece's notorious credibility of commitment problems. Papandreou, on the other hand, asked for a "united European response" with a more flexible bailout package spanning a longer time horizon and less austere package while he also accepted that Greece was in need of substantial reforms. Just before the bailout agreement, Papandreou asked for "time, patience, and calmness":

> We [as Greek government] show determination while making painful decisions and changes. [From Germany and troika] we are asking for time, patience, calmness; to be given a chance to put things in order and get back on the path of normality and sustainable development.[29]

Papandreou, as the leader of social democrat PASOK and the president of Socialist International, did not agree with the spirit of the austerity program because he later admitted that the "people who were not responsible for the crisis [in Greece] were paying the price for [extreme austerity]. There was a sense of injustice [in the bailout program]."[30] However, Germany stood firm on a very strict austerity program from the outset. Consequently, since there was no alternative, Papandreou signed the memorandum, the main elements of which were discussed in the previous part. Merkel's crisis narrative was quite rigid and the balance was incomparably asymmetric between the parties that Greece had little bargaining leverage vis-à-vis Germany. The following excerpt eloquently captures

[28] Sebastian Dullien and Ulrike Guerot, *The Long Shadow of Ordoliberalism: Germany's Approach to the Euro Crisis* (London: European Council of Foreign Relations, 2012), 4.

[29] Papandreou, "In the Face of a Crisis for Greece and the EU."

[30] Neil Macdonald, "Papandreou Talks Greece's Debt," http://www.cbc.ca/news/papandreou-talks-greece-s-debt-1.954851 (arrived on February 27, 2016).

how difficult the situation was for the Greek prime minister during the April 2010 negotiations in Brussels:

> [When Greek army launched a coup in 1967], military trucks drive up to our house. Soldiers storm the door. They find me up on the top terrace. A sergeant comes up to me with a machine gun, puts it to my head, and says, "tell me where your father is or I will kill you." [Years later in] Brussels, in April 2010, this time it was not the military, but the markets, that put a gun to our collective heads. What followed were the most difficult decisions in my life, painful to me, painful to my countrymen.[31]

The austerity program was exceptional in the post-war OECD history. As Wolf suggests Greece was asked to do what Latin American countries did in the 1980s, "a lost decade—the beneficiaries being foreign creditors."[32] Many analysts also contended that this was a "crisis of design" rather than a mere fiscal profligacy case sparked by irresponsible Greek state.[33] Therefore, as the argument went, disproportionate imposition of austerity measures would not relief the pressure over Greek economy and would not strengthen the hands of pro-change forces in Greece.[34]

Even the IMF officials were skeptical about the success of the program. Serious concerns were raised on the fragility of the situation stemming from over-optimistic and ambitious targets that were set in the first place. An internal IMF document, highlighting the extreme austerity imposed on Greece, was leaked on May 9, 2010. According to "strictly confidential" Office Memorandum, "the exceptionally high risks of the program were recognized by [the IMF] staff itself, in particular in its assessment of debt sustainability."[35] Thus, the retrospective evidence suggests that the fundamentals of the bailout package were shaky and the derailment possibility is very high to overlook with devastating consequences to the entire euro area economy.

[31] Papandreou, "Imagine a European Democracy Without Borders."

[32] Martin Wolf, "A Bail-Out for Greece Is Just the Beginning," *Financial Times*, May 4, 2010.

[33] Vassilis K. Fouskas and Constantine Dimoulas, *Greece, Financialization, and the EU* (Basingstoke: Palgrave Macmillan, 2013).

[34] Wolfgang Münchau, "Greece's Bail-Out only Delays the Inevitable," *Financial Times*, April 18, 2010.

[35] IMF, *Office Memorandum: Board Meeting on Greece's Request for an SBA*, May 9, 2010. Available at http://online.wsj.com/public/resources/documents/Greece-IMF-2010-Bailout-Minutes.pdf (arrived on February 1, 2016), 2.

The German chancellor, however, argued that "the austerity program is sustainable [and] there is no other way."[36] At this point, one should question the ordering logic that informed Germany to develop a crisis narrative putting exclusive emphasis on very strict austerity measures. This book maintains that Germany's excessive response could not be explained with reference to German interests per se. In a rather paradoxical way, a possible deepening of the economic recession in Greece and its contagion into the wider euro area was against the immediate interests of export-oriented Germany. Therefore, deflationist risks associated with the memorandum were posing considerable risks for Germany as well. There was also an imminent risk that front-loaded harsh austerity measures may empower the anti-change coalitions in Greece and across Europe by diverting the attention. Then, why did the German policy-makers insist on extreme measures?

In order to address this puzzle, we need to refer to the constitutive roles of ideas at crisis moments, characterized by intense uncertainty. The ideational paradigm that informed the parameters of Germany's crisis narrative was ordoliberalism, which has historical roots in the German economic thinking and reflects a cross-party compromise in Germany. Bonefeld defines ordoliberalism as "the theory behind the German social market economy [which argues] that free economy presupposes the exercise of strong state authority."[37] The central tenet of ordoliberalism is that the state should regulate the markets in such a way that economic outcomes approximates to perfectly competitive markets. To that end, it calls for a state-centric approach to provide a constitutional-legal framework, an *ordo*, "which obliges countries to adhere to strict fiscal discipline and for automatic sanctions if the constitutional framework is violated."[38] Apart from state's legal-based regulatory function, however, ordoliberalism rejects the Keynesian demand-side expansionary fiscal and monetary policies to stabilize the economy even during recessions on the ground

[36] Angela Merkel, "Greece's Austerity Programme 'Ambitious and Sustainable,' " https://www.bundesregierung.de/ContentArchiv/EN/Archiv17/Artikel/2010/05/2010-05-02-griechenland-hilfen_en.html (arrived on February 27, 2016).

[37] Werner Bonefeld, "Freedom and the Strong State: On German Ordoliberalism," *New Political Economy* 17, no. 5 (2012): 633.

[38] Volker Berghahn and Brigitte Young, "Reflections on Werner Bonefeld's 'Freedom and the Strong State: On German Ordoliberalism' and the Continuing Importance of the Ideas of Ordoliberalism to Understand Germany's (Contested) Role in Resolving the Eurozone Crisis," *New Political Economy* 18, no. 5 (2013): 775.

that it would create moral hazard problems and lack of will to implement necessary economic reforms.

There are three main aspects of ordoliberal paradigm that conditioned the main contours of Germany's crisis narrative. First, ordoliberal paradigm considers government deficits and public debts as the only area that rule-based cooperation is required. The coordination on the supply-side policies such as wages, social security policies, and labor market reforms are not the primary concerns. In this respect, Germany insisted that euro area countries should emulate and follow the best model rather than asking for supply-side coordination and financial assistance to mitigate transnational economic imbalances. In a similar view, the worsening current account balances of the peripheral countries are interpreted as their own faults because they did not avoid a loss of competitiveness and excessive consumption. Hence, the recipes that Merkel eagerly proposed to Greece was outright wage cuts, reduction in expenditures, and increases in taxes. Second, German ordoliberal paradigm argues that harsh austerity measures do not necessarily lead to depression and negative growth prospects. On the contrary, it would mitigate moral hazard problems and credibility gaps, which in turn positively inform debt dynamics and growth projections. Accordingly, the fiscal discipline and extreme austerity is the most cogent way to improve debt dynamics because it would send strong signals to the markets by increasing the credibility of debtor countries' commitments and thereby boosting private sector confidence. It is because of this reasoning that Merkel indirectly sidelined Papandreou's "financial speculation" thesis and primarily approached the bailout issue from a moral hazard perspective.

Third, Germany challenged the idea of debt mutualization and the introduction of Eurobonds from the very beginning of the crisis due to the same ordoliberal perspective. Merkel's determined rejection of Papandreou's—and other European leaders—solidarity requests is a clear reflection of Germany's adherence to a system of rule-based fiscal and monetary prudence. Based on this logic, rather than mutualization of member states' public debt to demonstrate "European solidarity," Germany proposed a fiscal compact to promote "culture of stability." Along these lines, Merkel stipulated a constitutionally mandated debt brake "with which the member states cannot simply run up debts but rather must strive for economic strength and financial stability."[39]

[39] Angela Merkel, "Speech by Federal Chancellor Angela Merkel at the Opening Ceremony of the College of Europe on November 2, 2010," https://www.bundesregierung.de/

The debate so far reflects that not only conflicting interests but also the incommensurability of diverging ideas informed the mismatch of the two sides' crisis narratives. Social democrat and Keynesian Papandreou asked for longer time frame, more flexible bailout package, more EU-level coordination, and more accommodative fiscal and monetary policies. Christian democrat and ordoliberal Merkel, in return, proposed a bailout package attached to excessively austere conditionality measures. It appears that German leadership was very clear about the accuracy of ordoliberal principles and had no suspicion whether they would work in the Greek context. Therefore, May 2010 bailout program emerged as a sub-optimal deal in the first place. Papandreou admitted latter that Greece was "punished by Germany" in Brussels in May 2010. "Merkel said very clearly to me," claimed Papandreou, "someone has to be seen to be punished, so others don't do this in the future."[40]

In summary, the narrative mismatch along domestic-external nexus created insurmountable obstacles in terms of the ownership of the reform program. Papandreou found himself in a position to implement a program while denouncing it at the same time. Not surprisingly, as a result, Papandreou government started to depict serious deviations. Troika's third review, in a much sterner tone of warning, highlighted many crucial "delays" and "disappointing" reform performance in the fiscal and structural realms envisioned in May 2010 program.[41]

6.3 Institutional Structures: Constraining Factors at Work

The narrative mismatch at the agency level, however, constitutes just one side of the coin. Institutional structures at the Greek domestic scene further constrained the instigation of a virtuous cycle of reform activism in the post-2010 period. The institutional players also exacerbated the collective action problems and constrained proper implementation of the reform program in the Greek context. In fact, the ways in which institu-

ContentArchiv/EN/Archiv17/Reden/2010/2010-11-02-merkel-bruegge.html (arrived on February 10, 2016).

[40] Gavin Hewitt, *The Lost Continent: Europe's Darkest Hour Since World War Two* (London: Hodder & Stoughton, 2013), 84.

[41] European Commission, *The Economic Adjustment Programme for Greece: Third Review* (Brussels: European Commission Directorate-General for Economic and Financial Affairs Publications, 2011).

tional structures and agents interacted triggered a vicious cycle in Greece, as a result of which blame games and muddling through triumphed the consensus-based policy-making in the third phase of the three-stage framework.

Political Context

The conflictual and polarized political culture, which has historically been an integral aspect of reactive Greek state, continued to play a constraining role in the post-2009. The main opposition party, ND, questioned the logic and legitimacy of the reform program in the first instance.[42] As discussed in the previous part, blaming the previous ND government as the architect of Greece's economic havoc constituted the backbone of Papandreou's credibility-building strategy. However, this policy backlashed in the post-memorandum process because he lost a critical opportunity to implement the reforms in a consensus-based political environment. On the other side of the coin, ND opted for traditional intentional polarization strategy for the sake of short-term political calculations. The support of the ND was quite crucial to legitimize the reform packages in the eyes of large segments of the society, especially for those located at the right of the political center. Yet, ND voted against the troika program in the Parliament on May 6, 2010. Antonis Samaras, the leader of the ND, declared that they would not show "tolerance" for PASOK's policies during the implementation of the MEFP:

> We vote against it not because we refuse the financing support, which (the ruling) PASOK rendered indispensable now, but because we disagree with the policies that led us up to here as well as with the government's economic strategy for handling the crisis. The government does not need our vote to pass the relevant bill. It simply wants a 'vote of tolerance' for its policies.[43]

ND took a very ambivalent stance vis-à-vis the bailout package. On the one hand, Samaras assured the troika, European Parliament, and German and French leaders that his party would "commit itself to the agreements

[42] Interview with the Member of Parliament, New Democracy, June 25, 2014; interview with senior advisor to Lucas Papademos, June 24, 2014.

[43] Athens News Agency, "ND to Vote Against Greece's EU-IMF Financing," May 5, 2010.

that are signed by the Greek state, because the Greek state has continuity"[44]; on the other hand, Samaras severely criticized the harsh austerity measures attached to the MEFP and Papandreou's handling of the crisis. Aware of the potential popular backlash against the memorandum, Samaras exploited the fragile political context to consolidate its own electoral base via confrontational political maneuvers rather than interpreting the crisis as an opportunity to change Greece's wrecked economic system within the framework of a consensus-based national strategy. Other critical political stakeholder at the time, which even became more important thereafter, SYRIZA, categorically rejected the memorandum, burned all bridges with the Papandreou government, and adopted a full-fledged anti-austerity rhetoric.[45] Papandreou also experienced insurmountable difficulties in ensuring intra-party discipline.[46] During the election campaign, PASOK promised to expand state expenditure through a rationalized and better-governed social welfare system. Consistent with its pre-election promises, Papandreou government pursued expansionary policies in the initial months. The necessity to implement savage wage cuts after May 2010, however, disturbed the balances within PASOK. Some members of Papandreou's party, primarily traditionalist wing, staunchly opposed to the drastic cuts and reform proposals of the troika program.[47]

Gradually intensifying political tug-of-wars, lack of effective political leadership, and intra and inter-party coordination failures jointly hampered the coherent supply and consistent implementation of counter-crisis measures in the wake of the crisis. In their research, Vasilopoulou, Halikiopoulou, and Exadaktylos report that more than one-third of Samaras' speeches and more than half of SYRIZA leader's speeches had a direct blaming tone toward other political parties, IMF, troika, and Germany during 2009–2011.[48] Furthermore, Greek political landscape took a turn for the worse and depicted an entirely fragile equilibrium in the post-Papandreou period (see below).

[44] Athens News Agency, "ND Leader Phone Contacts with Commission, EPP Chiefs," May 6, 2010.

[45] Interview with representative of SYRIZA, June 7, 2014.

[46] Interview with senior policy analyst, ELIAMEP, June 24, 2014; interview with senior advisor to Lucas Papademos, June 24, 2014.

[47] Interview with senior advisor to Lucas Papademos, June 24, 2014.

[48] Sophia Vasilopoulou, Dafne Halikiopoulou, and Theofanis Exadaktylos, "Greece in Crisis: Austerity, Populism and the Politics of Blame," *Journal of Common Market Studies* 52, no. 2 (2014): 395–396.

Domestic Policy Coalitions

As discussed in Chap. 5, trade unions, business associations, and other small but deeply entrenched rent-seeking interest coalitions have been integral aspects of mainstream economic paradigm in Greece. Hence, their response to the MEFP was as critical as the reactions of the political parties. The major trade unions and small interest groups categorically rejected the policy mix of the adjustment program. The two leading peak associations ADEDY, the public servants trade union, and GSEE, the umbrella organization of the Greek labor class, organized a series of mass strikes and public demonstrations. One of the cornerstones of the troika program was to overhaul the public administration to improve state's fiscal capacity. The public bureaucracy immediately rejected the reform proposals and public servants' institutional representative ADEDY dismissed bailout program due to "the lack of proper dialogue and consultation." ADEDY in cooperation with GSEE asked for "renegotiating the [austerity program] to alleviate the negative impacts and social tensions."[49] The GSEE's initial reaction was also identical. GSEE challenged the austerity measures on the ground that reform program was unilaterally imposed on Greek people without any prior consultation to the social partners. ADEDY and GSEE severely criticized the Papandreou government and troika because of "top-down imposition of reform program."[50] According to GSEE representatives, "necessary coordination and consensus toward the implementation of the fiscal reforms was not launched."[51] The GSEE president, Yannis Panagopoulos, published a declaration, which claimed that Germany's unilateral imposition of the austerity measures would cause irrevocable harm on working classes and social fabric in Greece.[52]

On the business side, SEV, Hellenic Federation of Enterprises, initially supported the reform program.[53] SEV Chairman, Dimitris Daskalopoulos, challenged the trade unions in SEV annual meeting on May 11, 2010, by arguing, "painful measures we are called to undergo are not some interna-

[49] Zoe Lanara, *The Impact of Anti-crisis Measures and the Social and Employment Situation: Greece* (Brussels: European Economic and Social Committee, 2012), 9.

[50] Interview with senior official, Labour Institute (INE)/GSEE-ADEDY, June 24, 2014.

[51] Interview with senior official, GSEE, June 26, 2014.

[52] The General Confederation of the Greek Workers, "Declaration: President of GSEE Yannis Panagopoulos," available at http://www.ucbf.org/modules/news/article.php?storyid=129&sel_lang=english (arrived on February 10, 2016).

[53] Interview with senior official, SEV, June 24, 2014.

tional conspiracy for the oppression of our country [...] they are a much-needed therapy" to overhaul profligate state structures, fiscal irresponsibility, and pervasive vested interests.[54] Nevertheless, SEV also took a cautionary tone on the sub-optimal nature of policy mix proposed by the program. In fact, in a short time, SEV also raised its criticism to the troika program because of its "anti-growth bias." As austerity measures started to bite the private sector and contracted economic output and private consumption, SEV sent a memo with an accompanying report to the Papandreou government and troika representatives, which suggested amendments on the program. However, according to SEV officials, "their suggestions fall on deaf ears."[55] Therefore, SEV became a critic of the program as well. The absence of a coherent crisis narrative along domestic-external nexus and the unilateral imposition of the harsh austerity measures exacerbated the ownership problems. It, therefore, proved very difficult for Papandreou to create new winning coalitions vis-à-vis the entrenched policy communities.

On May 5, 2010, ADEDY and GSEE called for "strong social struggles" against austerity measures and organized a general strike in Athens. In response to government's approval of the spending-cuts, public sector layoffs and tax increases, more than 100,000 people marched through the Parliament building in Athens, which was the largest public protest since the restoration of democracy in Greece. The protestors were coming from different political and sociological backgrounds but they all believed that they were treated unfairly and were not themselves to blame for the crisis. The two targets in their blame attribution were the "corrupt" Greek political establishment and German leadership as the chief architect of the unjust and unfair measures imposed on Greek people.[56] The sense of widespread injustice and relative deprivation, combined with a strong protest culture, triggered a series of demonstrations that paralyzed the economic and socio-political life during Papandreou's premiership.[57] Between 2010 and 2011, 14 general strikes took place, a number far beyond the south

[54] Dimitris Daskalopoulos, "Hellenic Federation of Enterprises Annual General Assembly, May 11, 2010," Speech of the Chairman, http://www.sev.org.gr/online/viewNews.aspx?id=1721&mid=8&lang=en (arrived on February 20, 2014).

[55] Interview with senior advisor to the president of SEV, June 23, 2014.

[56] Interview with advisor to GSEE/ADEDY, June 26, 2014.

[57] For historical-institutional origins of protest culture in Greece, see Aikaterini Andronikidou and Iosif Kovras, "Cultures of Rioting and Anti-Systemic Politics in Southern Europe," *West European Politics* 35, no. 4 (2012): 707–725.

European averages. In addition to general strikes, a total of 7123 demonstrations organized just in 2010, in which "about 30 per cent of the entire population engaged."[58] In the aftermath of May 2010, the government was stuck between a rock and a hard place. Papandreou found himself in a position to implement an extremely austere package despite his disagreement on many aspects of it. Lack of a coherent crisis narrative in the initial phases also jeopardized his reputation and credibility at home. Moreover, major institutional players entered into a vicious cycle of tug-of-wars and blame games, which dominated the third stage in my conceptual framework.

6.4 Third Stage: Blame Games and Muddling Through

The narrative mismatch at the agency level, troika's insistence on harsh front-loaded austerity measures, Papandreou's leadership failures, and the resistance of domestic institutional players paved the way for a sub-optimal equilibrium, that is, blame games and muddling through in the third phase of the three-stage framework. In this phase, worsening macroeconomic conditions and deepening recession due to austerity measures informed domestic reform dynamics in a spiraling way that plunged Greek political economy into an ultimate deadlock. In fact, growth-biased reform program had rather unintended consequences for the Greek economy: The costs of domestic adjustment in Greece unexpectedly but exorbitantly aggravated. Since internal devaluation was imposed as the only acceptable strategy for Greece to stay in the euro area, the adjustment burden remained on the shoulders of the Greek people, which further undermined the legitimacy and credibility of the reform agenda.

Front-loaded strict fiscal consolidation created a strong deflationary bias starting from 2011. Greece's growth performance gradually worsened, which in turn diverted attention from structural reforms and strengthened the hands of anti-memorandum coalitions.[59] In 2011, Greek economy shrank 7.1 percent, which was projected to be just 2.6 in the May 2010 program. The contraction in GDP also derailed other program targets. For instance, public debt-to-GDP ratio, which was a crucial indi-

[58] Wolfgang Rüdig and Georgios Karyotis, "Who Protests in Greece? Mass Opposition to Austerity," *British Journal of Political Science* 44, no. 3 (2014): 487–513.

[59] Interview with senior member, Hellenic Observatory, LSE, June 11, 2014.

cator in the eyes of international investors, increased to 170 percent rather than 145.2 percent as projected. The failure in achieving the program targets, however, did not lead to a revision and compromise because creditors did not deviate from the ordoliberal crisis narrative. On the contrary, Germany insisted on the implementation of a new wave of austerity measures. As a result, Papandreou government approved the Medium Term Fiscal Strategy 2012–2015 (MTFS). The MTFS outlined new measures that worth €28.3 billion, including 6.4 billion euros to make up for the deviations in 2011. Of these, €13.5 billion come from the revenue side, while the remaining 14.8 billion euros come from the expenditure side. It included the dismissal of 30,000 public sector workers and cuts of 20 percent on pensions. The MTFS also included an ambitious privatization program designed to bring €50 billion by 2015.

The European Commission and the IMF reports in 2011 revealed that the program suffered from severe delays. The international market players also convinced that the program had already failed in its first year. The deterioration of the macroeconomic situation and the declining credibility of the reform program in the eyes of market actors sparked a new round of blame games between Greece and its European partners. Domestic institutional stakeholders, including SEV, claimed that the failure of the program was due to the deflationary effects of the austerity measures and the policy inaction of the EU and the ECB, which was unacceptable in a monetary union.[60] Creditors, on the other hand, blamed Greek government for delaying the reforms and for failing to ensure the political credibility vis-à-vis international investors. Similarly, in the absence of a coherent response to the crisis, markets convinced that there was no substantial progress in Greece's reform process and default was an increasingly likely option. The failure of the first bailout program necessitated another rescue package amidst "Grexit" debates in mid-2011. Hence, a new round of bargaining was kicked-off for the second bailout package. The new package was "estimated €109 billion with lower interest rates and extended maturities [which were] very closely [attached to] the strict implementation of the program based on the regular assessment by the Commission in liaison with the ECB and the IMF."[61] The program also envisioned

[60] Interview with senior official, SEV, June 25, 2014.

[61] "Statement by the Heads of State or Government of the Euro Area and EU Institutions," Brussels, July 21, 2011, http://europa.eu/rapid/press-release_DOC-11-5_en.htm (arrived on February 27, 2016).

Private Sector Involvement around €37 billion to restructure the Greek debt. Furthermore, in order to meet the conditionality criteria, Papandreou government was asked to implement more austerity measures in addition to the ones that were already indicated but postponed in the original program. Not surprisingly, the public outrage against further austerity measures and the political tug-of-war between Merkel and Papandreou exponentially intensified in 2011.

On the domestic side, Papandreou criticized domestic opposition forces on the ground that they did not own the reform program.[62] He argued that business associations, trade unions, and opposition parties categorically rejected his cooperation offers. Squeezed between troika's relentless austerity demands and the increasing opposition at home, Papandreou called for an unexpected referendum. PASOK government representatives argued that the critical situation that Greece had reached necessitated all domestic stakeholders to place their support behind the program.[63] However, Papandreou also conceded that pro-change coalitions could not be established. Papandreou's surprising decision increased the fever of the markets and aroused severe reaction of the Franco-German leadership. Under intense pressures from the Franco-German tandem, on October 6, 2011, Papandreou revoked his referendum decision and submitted his resignation to the president. His decision to step down demarked the incoming deadlock in Greek political economy, which could not be overcome in the post-Papandreou period.

6.5 Post-Papandreou Era: Greek Politics in Turmoil

Greek politics experienced major transformations following the resignation of Papandreou government. The stable majoritarian two-party system, which defined the parameters of Greek politics for more than three decades, suddenly collapsed. As the calamity seemed unending and the mainstream parties appeared inept in putting the country back on track, the electorates signaled major realignment toward alternative political alliances that emerged to capture the widespread discontent. The economic shock gave birth to heterogonous and spontaneous anti-memorandum movements, which ultimately led to a populist ruling alliance

[62] Interview with Member of Parliament, PASOK, June 19, 2014.
[63] Interview with Member of Parliament, PASOK, June 19, 2014.

orchestrated by SYRIZA. In the meantime, however, Greece tried different combinations of collation governments to hold the center of Greek politics.

National Unity Government

Lucas Papademos, the former BoG governor (1994–2002) and vice president of the ECB (2002–2010), was appointed as new prime minister to lead the "national unity government" three days after Papandreou's resignation on November 11, 2011. PASOK, New Democracy, and small right-wing party, Popular Orthodox Rally (LAOS), supported the Papademos government. Papademos was a policy entrepreneur in the strict sense of the term. He was a respected above-the-party figure in Greece. Graduated from MIT, he was also a renowned professor of economics with Europe-wide recognition. Papademos had ample experience on the Greek economy as well as his expertise on how the euro area works. Thanks to his BoG and ECB duties, he developed close connections with domestic and transnational epistemic communities. Papademos had personal comradeships with leading policy-making figures in the EU, including the ECB governor, Mario Draghi. As Kouvelakis asserts, "Papademos government was the natural incarnation of a ruling bloc that is entirely dominated by the interests of European finance."[64] Merkel also placed her full support behind Papademos. Given the strong support he received from European circles, Papademos succeeded to secure the second bailout package in February 2012, which was around €137 billion. He also orchestrated the largest debt restructuring in the history of modern Greece that involved private sector actors.

Beyond the implementation of pre-determined policy targets, however, Papademos could not fulfill the expectations to instigate a new virtuous cycle toward economic recovery and develop domestic ownership of the reform program. Having considered the timing and context of Papademos' rise, there were several constraining factors at work. First, Papademos lacked the political cloud to push the reform process in the parliament due to perverse political environment.[65] This was mainly because of the half-hearted support demonstrated by coalition partners. The leader of the ND, Samaras, for instance, called for early elections in a short period after the formation of the "national unity government" rather than seeking for

[64] Stathis Kouvelakis, "The Greek Cauldron," *New Left Review*, no. 72 (2011): 26.
[65] Interview with advisor to Lucas Papademos, June 23, 2014.

much-needed cross-party compromise.[66] Second, Papademos government lacked popular democratic legitimacy in the eyes of domestic constituency. The public outrage against Germany and austerity program significantly restricted his mandate. Papademos was conceived as the representative of troika and therefore suffered from extensive credibility deficits.[67] Neither timing nor context was suitable for Papademos to develop a coherent crisis narrative and mobilize the pro-change coalitions toward a particular direction because a path-dependent process had already been set in motion and restricted Papademos' choices before his ascendance to premiership. Furthermore, the strict imposition of Germany-led troika conditionality left no virtual space for Papademos to maneuver. In a rather sub-optimal context, Papademos fell short of making a lasting impact on Greece's reform performance. As a result, a new coalition government replaced Papademos under the premiership of ND's Samaras in June 2012, after two elections in one month.

ND-PASOK-DIMAR Coalition

The June 2012 elections were very tense since, they were considered as a referendum about Greece's euro area membership. The ND under the leadership of Samaras succeeded to secure 29.7 percent of the total votes, which provided an opportunity to form a coalition government with PASOK (12.28 percent) and the small Democratic Left Party (DIMAR). The leading representative of the anti-memorandum camp, SYRIZA became the main opposition party by increasing its vote share to 26.9 percent. The far-right neo-Nazi Golden Dawn party, which exploited the migration issue, increased its vote share from 0.3 percent in 2009 to almost 7 percent. It was ironic that Samaras, who built his political career against the austerity program, formed a coalition government with PASOK and DIMAR to implement the troika program.

The coalition government's main mission was to keep Greece in the euro area amidst "Grexit" debates. The government implemented certain economic reforms to secure bailout tranches. According to OECD report published in 2013, the implementation of the pension reform, certain improvements in tax system and expansion in tax base, and the partial restructuration of labor markets stand out as some notable transforma-

[66] Interview with senior advisor to Lucas Papademos, June 24, 2014.

[67] Interview with senior policy analyst, ELIAMEP, June 24, 2014.

tions.[68] Euro Plus Monitor also reports that Greece achieved substantial fiscal adjustment for 2009–2012 among euro area countries with a decline in general government deficit by 9.3 percent and a reduction in the primary budget deficit by 9.1 percent.[69] In November 2012, the euro area ministers agreed on the Greek debt in more favorable conditions. The macroeconomic prospects seemed to take a positive turn. Greece even succeeded to return to the markets and sell government bonds in April 2014.

The overall balance, however, was not encouraging. Despite all efforts, the targets of the reform program failed substantially. First, GDP growth projections of the first memorandum deviated 20.7 percent. In 2008–2013, Greece's GDP contracted almost 25 percent. Second, all debt reduction attempts and haircut of private sector debt notwithstanding, debt-to-GDP ratio increased to 174 percent, more than 25 percent deviation of the program projections. Third, unemployment ratio skyrocketed to 28 percent. In this adverse environment, the social havoc created by the economic crisis and harsh austerity measures imposed by troika hollowed out any substantial reform possibility.[70]

The disenchantment of Greek citizens grew exponentially. The overwhelming majority of the population started to draw analogies between the protectorates of foreign powers in country's debt-ridden history and Greece's present misery. The Greek state bankrupted several times during its modern history and each time major Western powers stepped in to ensure the rollover of the Greek sovereign debt due to the geopolitical importance of the country, but they established strict surveillance mechanisms in return. Germany, after 1890s in particular, turned out to be the most uncompromising creditor among the great powers that bailed out Greece. The Greek people interpreted the post-crisis intervention of the troika as "a new German occupation by other means," which revitalized the memoirs of the Weimar Republic during the inter-war period.[71] Hence, frequent street protests against Germany and the troika dominated the political agenda. Between May 2010 and March 2014, 20,201 legal dem-

[68] OECD, Economic Policy Reforms, 2013: Going for Growth (Paris: OECD Publishing, 2013), 155–159.

[69] Euro Plus Monitor, *The 2013-Euro Plus Monitor: From Pain to Gain*, The Lisbon Council Policy Brief, 2013.

[70] Interview with senior member of European Studies Centre, University of Oxford, June 13, 2014.

[71] Interview with senior official, GSEE, June 26, 2014.

onstrations took place in Greece.[72] ADEDY and GSEE organized 34 general strikes in the same period. The strikingly high number of protests indicates that established political parties, conventional approaches, and the reform program lost their entire credibility and legitimacy. According to European Commission surveys, for instance, the Greek citizens' trust in national government declined to 8 percent, trust in the national parliament to 17 percent, and trust in political parties to 5 percent as of 2013.[73]

6.6 SYRIZA's March to Power

The extraordinary conditions triggered by the Greek crisis led to the spectacular rise of anti-systemic radical left SYRIZA party. SYRIZA, right from the beginning of the Greek conundrum, adopted an anti-austerity and anti-memorandum stance. SYRIZA members took part in all protests, strikes, and mass movement of "the squares" without trying to patronize them.[74] Right from the inception of the crisis, SYRIZA leader Tsipras lamented that the "reform program itself is the crisis, not the solution" and blamed creditors for creating a humanitarian disaster in Greece.[75] In fact, SYRIZA gained its popularity by denouncing the "Greek exceptionalism" argument. For instance, Laskos and Tsakalotos, two SYRIZA members and economic advisors to Tsipras, dismissed this narrative as "Merkel's Calvinist fable."[76] SYRIZA's critical approach to neoliberalism as-the-main-cause of the Greek debacle captured thousands of demonstrators that poured into the streets. SYRIZA promised an alternative reform program that relied on six interrelated pillars: (a) terminating humanitarian crisis, (b) meeting the social needs, (c) reconstructing productive sectors, (d) reinvigorating democracy, (e) redistributing wealth, and (f) expanding social and collective rights.[77]

Alexis Tsipras, the young and charismatic leader of the party, targeted the establishment from the outset of the crisis in defense of "the people."

[72] Kathimerini, "More Than 20,000 Protests since 2010 Bailout," April 24, 2014.

[73] European Commission, Eurobarometer Interactive Search System, available at http://ec.europa.eu/ public_opinion/cf/index_en.cfm (arrived on December 14, 2016).

[74] Interview with member of SYRIZA, June 7, 2014.

[75] Interview with representative of SYRIZA, June 16, 2014.

[76] Christos Laskos and Euclid Tsakalotos, *Crucible of Resistance: Greece, the Eurozone, and World Economic Crisis* (London: Pluto Press, 2013), 3.

[77] Giorgos Katsambekis, "Radical Left Populism in Contemporary Greece: Syriza's Trajectory from Minoritarian Opposition to Power," *Constellations* 23, no. 3 (2016): 398.

The party declaration before the 2012 general election clearly put this point:

> Now is the time for the struggles of our people to be vindicated, for two-partism to be punished and defeated, for the memoranda and the troika to be condemned. A new social and political majority, with the radical Left in its core, can overthrow the rotten two-party political system and create alternative governance structures, where the people will be a protagonist.[78]

The results of early elections in January 2015 created an opportunity for SYRIZA to implement its program. The elections were an outcome of the Greek constitutional requirement. According to the Greek constitution, the Parliament elects the president by two-thirds majority in the first two rounds or by a three-fifths majority in the third round. In case the Parliament fails to elect a president, it is dissolved to renew national elections. The ND-PASOK government nominated Stavros Dimas as their presidential candidate,[79] but SYRIZA refused to provide its support to the government's candidate. The failure to elect a new president, as a result, led to the early elections held on January 25. The election outcome, though not unexpected, was a real shock for the established parties. SYRIZA defeated all rivals and became the largest party in the Hellenic Parliament, receiving 36.3 percent of the total vote shares (see Fig. 6.1).

Though SYRIZA could not have the absolute majority to form a single party government, Tsipras succeeded to form a coalition government with the right-wing Independent Greeks (ANEL). The SYRIZA-ANEL coalition was an unusual combination given that the parties had substantial ideological and programmatic differences. However, the ways in which both parties narrated the Greek crisis overlapped significantly. Similar to SYRIZA, ANEL adopted an overtly anti-austerity and populist rhetoric rejecting the bailout agreements and severely criticized the Greek political establishment. Both SYRIZA and ANEL argued that the policies implemented by troika had pushed the Greek economy into depression and led to the accumulation of public debt despite ferocious cuts in wages and pensions. Thus, the argument went, insisting on the same path would not bring economic recovery. As a logical consequence of this narrative,

[78] Ibid., 399.

[79] The junior partner, DIMAR, left the coalition in June 2013 after the unilateral closure of the state broadcasting corporation.

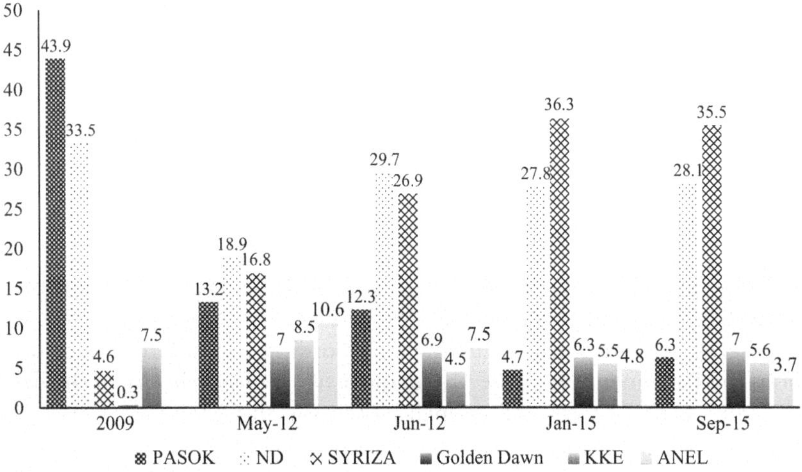

Fig. 6.1 Vote shares of Greece's major parties

SYRIZA-ANEL coalition promised to terminate the previous deal and negotiate a new one that would enable Greece to pay its mounting public debt. Tsipras, therefore, refused to meet the demands of the troika paired to the final installment of the second program. Instead, the government decided to negotiate a new one with a debt relief component. In response to SYRIZA's anti-memorandum rhetoric, however, creditors remained loyal to the ordoliberal austerity-oriented recipe. Hence, Eurogroup ministers insisted on the extension of the previous program with similar terms and conditions.

The immediate clash between SYRIZA government and the troika attracted widespread global attention. Once again, Greece's future in the euro area turned into an issue of intense debate. The SYRIZA government's negotiation style further exacerbated these concerns. Following elections, Tsipras appointed Yanis Varoufakis as finance minister and chief negotiator. Varoufakis, an economics professor and popular media figure, was a fierce critique of the dominant crisis narrative adopted by the creditors. The allegedly confrontational approach of Varoufakis incensed his counterparts in Eurogroup meetings as "EU officials treated his arguments as those of a death row inmate who claims to be against the death penalty."[80] On top of this, Tsipras' attempts to overcome the monolithic resistance in the Eurogroup also failed. Tsipras tried to set one-to-one meetings with euro area leaders to gain new political allies sympathetic to SYRIZA's narrative by way of increasing the government's bargaining leverage at the top-level. However, his strategy did not yield any concrete results.

The stalemate following the acrimonious negotiations put SYRIZA government between a rock and hard place. On the one hand, Tsipras tried to honor his commitments at home by taking legislative measures to tackle "humanitarian crisis." On the other hand, Tsipras struggled to convince creditors to adopt a more flexible negotiating position and ensure the steady flow of much-needed liquidity into the Greek economy. Given that troika was very critical toward the content of the SYRIZA's alternative narrative and SYRIZA officials' negotiation style at the EU meetings, negotiations plunged into a deadlock in mid-2015. To overcome this impasse, Tsipras decided to hold a snap referendum regarding the program proposed by troika on June 27, 2015.[81] The referendum decision sent shockwaves across Europe as, once again, the fragility of the economic situation exacerbated. Following SYRIZA's referendum move, the ECB cut off liquidity to the Greek financial system. The ECB's decision, combined with previous capital outflows due to political instability in the first half of the year, pushed the government to impose capital controls on June 28.

The referendum decision triggered a new round of framing contests in Greece and Europe. Despite SYRIZA never officially questioned Greece's euro area membership, the creditors and international community interpreted the referendum as a decision on the question whether Greece would stay in the euro area. Tsipras declared that the government would respect the outcome and act accordingly, though he clearly encouraged Greek citizens to say "no" to the troika program. Along with SYRIZA, ANEL and Golden Dawn also urged their supporters to reject the program. The Communist Party of Greece (KKE) also boycotted the referendum. On the other side of the political spectrum, ND, PASOK and To Potami urged their supporters to vote "yes" in the referendum. These

[80] George Tsebelis, "Lessons from the Greek Crisis," *Journal of European Public Policy* 23, no. 1 (2016): 30.

[81] Myrto Tsakatika, "SYRIZA's Electoral Rise in Greece: Protest, Trust and the Art of Political Manipulation," *South European Society and Politics* 21, no. 4 (2016): 519–540.

parties altogether argued that a possible "no" would force Greece to leave the euro area with catastrophic consequences for Greek economy and society.

The referendum outcomes were surprising for many observers. Accordingly, 61.3 percent of the voters rejected the troika program whereas 38.7 percent sided with the opposition forces and EU institutions. The July 5, therefore, marked a new turning point in the protracted crisis in Greece. The "Grexit" scenario, once again, hit the headlines of international press and occupied the agenda of the policymakers across Europe. In retrospect, it appears that the SYRIZA government was ill-prepared for the outcomes of the referendum, which meant exiting the euro area in practice. In a rather striking manner, Tsipras adopted a conciliatory tone vis-à-vis the creditors, given that SYRIZA did not have a credible alternative plan. Tsipras removed Varoufakis from the finance ministry post and signed a new deal with troika just one week after the referendum, which was around €86 billion. Despite the conditions of the third bailout program were harsher than the previous ones because of larger pension cuts and tax increases, Tsipras, who previously stated that he would "tear up the memorandum," made a U-turn to avoid an economic havoc.

Tsipras stroke a sensitive nerve within SYRIZA with his decision to sign the troika program in harsher conditions. On August 14, 2015, 44 SYRIZA members voted against the referendum in the Parliament, which led to a split from SYRIZA coalition. The third bailout package approved thanks to the support of the opposition parties, but Tsipras became the target of fierce criticisms. Lapavitsas, for instance, later argued, "SYRIZA has sold its soul for power."[82] Tsipras called a snap general election on September 20, to renew its mandate. However, SYRIZA proved more resilient than many Greeks and international observers had expected as it succeeded to won 35.5 percent of the total votes (see Fig. 6.1).[83] Tsipras quickly resumed cooperating with ANEL. SYRIZA's political elites did not change their main crisis narrative and continued to argue that the

[82] Costas Lapavitsas, "Syriza Has Sold Its Soul for Power," *The Guardian*, January 25, 2016.

[83] For an analysis of SYRIZA's election strategy, see Emmanouil Tsatsanis and Eftichia Teperoglou, "Realignment under Stress: The July 2015 Referendum and the September Parliamentary Election in Greece," *South European Society and Politics* 21, no. 4 (2016): 427–450.

government would fight against austerity, widespread corruption, and vested interests harming Greek citizens. However, the tone of the government had gone soft due to the pressure of the troika.

6.7 Conclusion

The 2009 Greek crisis constitutes a critical juncture in terms of its political and economic outcomes as the Greek economy teetered on the brink of total collapse. The humanitarian consequences of the turmoil were also unmatched in the peacetime history of the country. However, the crisis created an opportunity to overhaul the deeply flawed economic institutions of the Greek state, given that the depth of the crisis disturbed domestic power balances and delegitimized existing paradigms in favor of pro-change forces. Yet, this opportunity could not be exploited. The economic crisis did not lead to consensus-based reform activism due to the interplay of a set of factors at the domestic-external nexus, which resulted in fragmented crisis narratives and protracted implementation of sub-optimal reform programs. The Greek crisis sparked a wave of never-ending domestic and external blame games, which paved the way for muddling through and several deadlocks.

The Greek political elite narrated the Greek crisis as a "test case" for European integration. The Papandreou government, while acknowledging the fundamental flaws in Greek economy, also suggested that the problem was far more than a single country and an effective response to the crisis requires European-level response. The German-led troika, on the other hand, narrated the Greek crisis mostly as an "exceptional case" and imposed a very strict ordoliberal paradigm, which suffocated all possibilities to craft an exercisable reform program at the outset. The domestic state agents and pro-change coalitions had no virtual space to contribute to the policy mix of the memoranda, which not surprisingly, amplified domestic ownership problems. The data suggest that inflexible stance of the IMF-EU anchor due to the negative external perception of Greece reduced the space to communicate mutually acceptable reform packages. Greece's membership to the euro area also complicated the design and implementation of the bailout packages. Furthermore, Greek authorities could not alleviate the impact of the crisis through accommodative monetary policy strategies due to the skewed architecture of the euro area. Thus, adjustment policies were associated with very high costs in Greece.

The economic crisis also led to the collapse of the majoritarian two-party system in Greece. The anti-systemic far-right and far-left movements moved to the center stage of Greek politics, which further complicated the post-crisis politicking. The meteoric rise of SYRIZA from a peripheral position to power is a clear example of Greek voters' massive realignment. The election of the far-left SYRIZA opened a new episode in protracted Greek crisis. SYRIZA framed the crisis as a deleterious outcome of neoliberal forces and promised to reverse the austerity policies. The party's policies in government, however, did not clear a path to economic recovery. The antagonistic policies and serious narrative mismatch between SYRIZA and the EU officials triggered a series of events that would probably force Greece out of the euro area. SYRIZA had gone soft to avoid a potential clash but could not square the circle. Thus, Greece failed to overcome the vicious cycle of blame games it was entrapped.

References

"Statement By the Heads of State or Government of the Euro Area and EU Institutions," Brussels, 21 July 2011, http://europa.eu/rapid/press-release_DOC-11-5_en.htm (arrived on February 27, 2016).

Amanpour, Christiane. "Interview with George Papandreou," February 15, 2010, http://papandreou.gr/en/interview-on-cnn/ (accessed February 27, 2016).

Andronikidou, Aikaterini, and Iosif Kovras. "Cultures of Rioting and Anti-Systemic Politics in Southern Europe." *West European Politics* 35, no. 4 (2012): 707–725.

Athens News Agency. "Government Blames ND for 'Credibility Deficit' at EU." 22 October 2009.

Athens News Agency. "Government Submits New Deficit Figure." 22 October 2009.

Athens News Agency. "ND Leader Phone Contacts with Commission, EPP Chiefs." May 6, 2010.

Athens News Agency. "ND to Vote against Greece's EU-IMF Financing." May 5, 2010.

Berghahn, Volker, and Brigiette Young. "Reflections on Werner Bonefeld's 'Freedom and the Strong State: On German Ordoliberalism' and the Continuing Importance of the Ideas of Ordoliberalism to Understand Germany's (Contested) Role in Resolving the Eurozone Crisis." *New Political Economy* 18, no. 5 (2013): 768–778.

Bonefeld, Werner. "Freedom and the Strong State: On German Ordoliberalism." *New Political Economy* 17, no. 5 (2012): 633–656.

Daskalopoulos, Dimitris. "Hellenic Federation of Enterprises Annual General Assembly," May 11, 2010, http://www.sev.org.gr/online/viewNews.aspx?id=1721&mid=8&lang=en (accessed February 20, 2014).

Dullien, Sebastian, and Ulrike Guerot. *The Long Shadow of Ordoliberalism: Germany's Approach to the Euro Crisis*. London: European Council of Foreign Relations, 2012.

Euro Plus Monitor. *The 2013-Euro Plus Monitor: From Pain to Gain*. The Lisbon Council Policy Brief, 2013.

European Commission, *The Economic Adjustment Programme for Greece*. Brussels: European Commission Directorate-General for Economic and Financial Affairs Publications, 2010.

European Commission. *The Economic Adjustment Programme for Greece: Third Review, March 2011*. Brussels: European Commission Directorate-General for Economic and Financial Affairs Publications, 2011.

European Commission. *The Second Economic Adjustment Programme for Greece*. Brussels: European Directorate-General for Economic and Financial Affairs Publications, 2012.

European Commission. *The Second Economic Adjustment Programme for Greece: Third Review, July 2013*. Brussels: European Commission Directorate-General for Economic and Financial Affairs Publications, 2013.

Evans-Prichard, Ambrose. "Greece Accuses Germany of 'Squalid Game' in Debt Crisis." *The Telegraph*, March 22, 2010.

Fouskas, Vassilis K., and Constantine Dimoulas. *Greece, Financialization, and the EU*. Basingstoke: Palgrave Macmillan, 2013.

Fuhrmans, Vanessa and Sebastian Moffett. "Exposure to Greece Weighs On French, German Banks." *The Wall Street Journal*, February 17, 2010.

Hewitt, Gavin. *The Lost Continent: Europe's Darkest Hour Since World War Two*. London: Hodder & Stoughton, 2013.

IMF. *Greece: Ex-Post Evaluation Of Exceptional Access Under The 2010 Stand-By Arrangement*. Washington DC: IMF Publication Services, 2013.

IMF. *Greece: Staff Report on Request for Stand-by Agreement*. Washington D.C.: IMF Publication Services, 2010.

IMF. *IMF Reaches Staff-level Agreement with Greece on €30 Billion Stand-By Arrangement, Press Release, no. 10/176*. Washington DC: IMF Publication Services, 2010.

IMF. *Office Memorandum: Board Meeting on Greece's Request for an SBA*, May 9, 2010, http://online.wsj.com/public/resources/documents/Greece-IMF-2010-Bailout-Minutes.pdf (accessed February 1, 2016).

Kathimerini. "More than 20,000 Protests since 2010 Bailout." April 24, 2014.

Katsambekis, Giorgos. "Radical Left Populism in Contemporary Greece: Syriza's Trajectory from Minoritarian Opposition to Power." *Constellations* 23, no. 3 (2016): 391–403.

Kouvelakis, Stathis. "The Greek Cauldron." *New Left Review*, no. 72 (2011): 17–32.

Lanara, Zoe. *The Impact of Anti-crisis Measures and the Social and Employment Situation: Greece*. Brussels: European Economic and Social Committee, 2012.

Lapavitsas, Costas. "Syriza has Sold its Soul for Power." *The Guardian*, 25 January 2016.

Laskos, Christos and Euclid Tsakalotos. *Crucible of Resistance: Greece, the Eurozone, and World Economic Crisis*. London: Pluto Press, 2013.

Macdonald, Neil. "Papandreou Talks Greece's Debt", June 21, 2010, http://www.cbc.ca/news/papandreou-talks-greece-s-debt-1.954851 (accessed February 27, 2016).

Marr, Andrew. "Interview with George Papandreou," February 21, 2010, http://news.bbc.co.uk/1/hi/uk_politics/8526880.stm (accessed February 27, 2016).

Merkel, Angela. "Greece's Austerity Programme 'Ambitious and Sustainable.'" May 2, 2010, https://www.bundesregierung.de/ContentArchiv/EN/Archiv17/Artikel/2010/05/2010-05-02-griechenland-hilfen_en.html (arrived on February 27, 2016).

Merkel, Angela. "Speech by Federal Chancellor Angela Merkel at the Opening Ceremony of the College of Europe on November, 2, 2010." https://www.bundesregierung.de/ContentArchiv/EN/Archiv17/Reden/2010/2010-11-02-merkel-bruegge.html (arrived on February 10, 2016).

Münchau, Wolfgang. "Greece's Bail-out only Delays the Inevitable." *Financial Times*, April 18, 2010.

OECD. *Economic Policy Reforms: Going for Growth*. Paris: OECD Publications Service, 2013.

Papandreou, George. "Greece is not an Island", *The New York Times*, March 9, 2010.

Papandreou, George. "Re-inventing Greece: A Leadership Vision," May 17, 2011, http://papandreou.gr/en/speech-at-the-economist-conference/ (accessed February 27, 2016).

Paterson, William E. "The Reluctant Hegemon? Germany Moves Centre Stage in the European Union." *Journal of Common Market Studies* 49, Annual Review (2011): 57–75.

Rüdig, Wolfgang, and Georgios Karyotis. "Who Protests in Greece? Mass Opposition to Austerity." *British Journal of Political Science* 44, no. 3 (2014): 487–513.

The General Confederation of the Greek Workers, "Declaration: President of GSEE Yannis Panagopoulos" May 3, 2010, http://www.ucbf.org/modules/news/article.php?storyid=129&sel_lang=english (accessed February 10, 2016).

Tsakatika, Myrto. "SYRIZA's Electoral Rise in Greece: Protest, Trust and the Art of Political Manipulation." *South European Society and Politics* 21, no. 4 (2016): 519–540.

Tsarouhas, Dimitris. "The Political Origins of the Greek Crisis: Domestic Failures and the EU Factor." *Insight Turkey* 14, no. 2 (2012): 83–98.

Tsatsanis Emmanouil, and Eftichia Teperoglou. "Realignment under Stress: The July 2015 Referendum and the September Parliamentary Election in Greece." *South European Society and Politics* 21, no, 4 (2016): 427–450.

Tsebelis, George. "Lessons from the Greek Crisis." *Journal of European Public Policy* 23, no. 1 (2016): 25–41.

Vasilopoulou, Sophia, Dafne Halikiopoulou, and Theofanis Exadaktylos. "Greece in Crisis: Austerity, Populism and the Politics of Blame." *Journal of Common Market Studies* 52, no. 2 (2014): 388–402.

Wolf, Martin. "A Bail-out for Greece is just the Beginning." *Financial Times*, May 4, 2010.

CHAPTER 7

Toward a Comparative Political Economy of Reactive States

This book probed into the dynamics of paradigmatic changes in states with low capacity to impose economic discipline. It particularly concentrated on economic crises as critical junctures to better explicate the underlying mechanisms that inform substantial divergence in terms of reform outcomes with reference to the Turkish and Greek cases. These two cases pose striking research puzzles. First, both of these states approximate to the ideal-typical configuration of reactive states. Second, both states have encountered a deep crisis that rocked the existing material and ideational balance to its foundations. Third, external actors, particularly the IMF-EU tandem, heavily intervened in the post-crisis restructuration.

The post-crisis reform performance, however, demonstrated a significant degree of divergence in these two countries. To address this puzzle, this book adopted a holistic three-stage framework based on the epistemological tradition of "analytic eclecticism" that aims to incorporate time and context-specific interactions between agents and institutional structures with particular reference to the interplay of external and domestic phenomena. The conceptual framework relies on state capacity, critical junctures, and policy entrepreneurship as organizing concepts. The framework is constructed with an explicit acknowledgement of the complex

M. Kutlay, *The Political Economies of Turkey and Greece*,
International Political Economy Series,
https://doi.org/10.1007/978-3-319-92789-3_7

multi-causal explanations and thick approaches in comparative politics,[1] which forsake the principle of parsimony to overcome the "mono-causal mania" in contemporary literature.[2] This chapter offers a comparative analysis of the Turkish and Greek cases and draws certain generalizable conclusions. It also discusses the potential contributions of this research to the broader literature. The final part concludes the chapter.

7.1 Revisiting the Three-Stage Framework

This section compares Turkish and Greek cases and discusses the main findings of the book. First, it concentrates on the first stage of the conceptual framework. Then, it offers a comparative analysis with respect to the second and third stages.

First Stage: Inertia and Procrastination of Reforms

The background chapters on Turkey (Chap. 3) and Greece (Chap. 5) dealt with the first phase of the three-stage framework. Accordingly, I strove to understand how the sub-optimal interaction of agents and institutional structures—that is, political context, state bureaucracy, and domestic policy coalitions—informed reactive state practices, which in turn exacerbated state's fiscal profligacy and economic vulnerabilities. The polarized political system in Greece that undermined consensus-based policy-making culture informed the political agents to deepen patronage networks in state bureaucracy and dominant policy communities—that is, state's relations with business and labor. In this institutional setting, state was conceived as an arena to be captured by rival political and economic actors for rent-seeking purposes rather than conceived as an autonomous player to govern the economy and steer sustainable reform activism. The procrastination of reforms, in turn, bloated the public sector and deteriorated financial discipline. The ultimate outcome, underpinned by the financialization of global economy, was the devastating turmoil Greece plunged into in 2009. Turkey also experienced similar ebb and flows during its troubled encounters with neoliberal globalization. Turkish

[1] Atul Kohli et al., "The Role of Theory in Comparative Politics: A Symposium," *World Politics* 48, no. 1 (1995): 1–49.

[2] This phrase belongs to John Gerard Ruggie, which is quoted in Jeffrey W. Legro and Andrew Moravcsik, "Is Anybody Still a Realist?" *International Security* 24, no. 2 (1999): 50.

policy-makers launched an entirely new economic paradigm after the 1980 military coup that relied on export-promotion and financial liberalization. The transformation, however, did take place within the context of immature institutional setting that paved the way for a strikingly perverse fisco-financial regime. As a result, Turkey entered a long-lasting turbulence during 1990s, which resulted in a severe economic turmoil in 2001.

The global factors also played adverse roles in the Turkish and Greek cases. It is a well-established fact that membership/candidacy to regional/multi-lateral organizations and integration to globalization trends condition the economic performance of national economies, as they tend to impose common standards, rules and disciplinary regulations. However, the impact of external anchors, whether disciplinary or reform instigating, are contingent upon how they are mediated, contested, and channeled by domestic intervening mechanisms. The state capacity, at this point, emerges as a key mechanism that informs the outcome of integration processes. Peripheral states with weak capacities tend to expose themselves to the side effects of global and regional transformations, which in turn amplify domestic economic fault-lines. Stated differently, in the absence of adequate state capacity, external anchors might exacerbate moral hazard problems through a set of perverse incentive mechanisms.

This is precisely what happened in Turkey and Greece. In the Turkish case, the EU did not play a significant anchor role until the turn of the century, though Turkey formed a customs union with the EU in 1996 that planted the seeds of a nascent regulatory state. Thus, it is plausible to argue that Turkey encountered the erratic flows of global finance earlier than Greece. Since Turkish economy was exposed to the vagaries of financial globalization in the absence of robust regulatory institutions, state's capacity to arrest fiscal profligacy and financial misbehavior quickly eroded. In this institutional setting, non-state economic players seized new borrowing opportunities to finance ever-expanding state sector at the behest of corrupt political elite. Not surprisingly, as a result, Turkey plunged into a devastating crisis in 2001 (see Chap. 3).

In the Greek case, the early membership to the European Economic Community in 1981 and the adhesion to the euro area in 2000 further informed rent-seeking agency behavior. Since Greece had a chance to exploit the lucrative EU funds and extremely favorable borrowing opportunities, ruling elites were encouraged to postpone urgently needed competitiveness-enhancing institutional reforms. The EU was unwilling and ill prepared to impose strict conditionality on the regulation of fiscal regime in Greece. The "undersupply of fiscal and financial stability,"[3] in turn, created demonstration effects for the Greek state agents and non-state economic players to maintain ample rent positions (see Chap. 5). The analysis of the first phase of three-stage framework reveals the limited, and even adverse, role of external actors to impose economic discipline when they hit reactive state structures. Thus, the findings of this book confirm the proposition that the impact of external actors is heavily dependent on how they are mediated by domestic institutions. If the conditionality principles are lax and porous, it is more likely that they lead to the procrastination of economic reforms in weak states.

Second and Third Stages: Uncertainty, Crisis Narratives, and Reform Outcomes

The preceding chapters maintained that institutional structures tend to encourage rent-seeking agency behavior in late-industrialized reactive states. The interests of domestic players are constructed in a way that the state in these political economies is entrapped in a vicious cycle, which brings about an inherent paradox: if political context, state bureaucracy, and domestic policy coalitions are inclined to inform massive rent seeking and if state autonomy vis-à-vis the non-state players tends to deteriorate in a gradual manner, how do paradigmatic transformations take place in these political economies?

The premise of this book is that critical junctures and policy entrepreneurship literatures offer fertile avenues to address these puzzles. Toward this end, the second stage of the conceptual framework quests for the favorable contexts that enable change agents to couple problems, policies, and politics. This book also strives to delineate the scope conditions under which critical junctures, particularly economic crises, invite paradigmatic changes.

It is said that, in Chinese language, the word "crisis" is composed of two characters: one represents "danger" and the other implies "opportunity." The analogy is perfectly applicable to weak states as well since critical junctures, triggered by an economic turmoil, open up interregnum episodes to reverse the existing patterns of power relations and ideational paradigms that guide reform resistant state-market relations. However, as Nehru once claimed in a rather different context, "every little thing counts

[3] Shawn Donnelly, "Power Politics and the Undersupply of Financial Stability in Europe," *Review of International Political Economy* 21, no. 4 (2014): 980–1005.

in a crisis."[4] Thus, in order to better understand under which conditions the opportunity windows are exploited in uncertain episodes, we need to turn the microscope on the timing, sequencing, and mode of interactions among a number of factors at critical junctures.

First, policy entrepreneurs could play their "change-agent role" if they emerge as key agents in the wake of a crisis. Second, crisis narratives of change agents must be coherent and compatible with those of most influential external anchors, which involve in post-crisis restructuration processes. The degree of narrative match at the domestic-external nexus informs the level of ownership of the crisis and reform measures to be implemented at the domestic scene. The degree of match and the bargaining scope of state agents are determined by the interests and ideas of the parties involved in the process. On the other hand, a possible mismatch—or a failure of narrative matching—might invite serious credibility and trust problems on the side of the domestic policy-makers, which in turn, put the entire reform program into jeopardy. Third, the responses of institutional players inform the ultimate reform performance. This book proposed in Chap. 2 that state agents must steer new winning coalitions at the domestic plane assembled around a dominant crisis narrative that explains the logic and direction of change. Based on the complex interactions along domestic-external nexus, either a dominant crisis narrative or fragmented narratives emerge in the third phase of the three-stage framework. If a dominant crisis narrative prevails, a new change-oriented paradigm is likely to replace the extant set of policies and policy coalitions; otherwise, multi-level blame games and muddling through dominate the policy-making agenda in the post-crisis context, which result in incomplete and shallow reforms at best. The empirical findings offer useful answers to reveal different aspects of the second and third-stages of the analytic framework proposed in this book. The four instances in two cases reveal different constellations of the key explanatory factors identified above. These cases altogether explicate the timing, direction, and political mechanisms of economic paradigm change.

7.2 Comparative Analysis of Turkey and Greece

The first—shadow—case is Turkey's 1994 economic crisis and the failed reform package adopted in the aftermath. As Chap. 3 offered an in-depth analysis, Turkey integrated into financial globalization before the rules of

[4] Jawaharlal Nehru, *Jawaharlal Nehru's Speeches 1949–1953* (New Delhi: The Publications Division, Ministry of Information and Broadcasting, Government of India, 1954), 144.

the game, namely fiscal and financial regulatory institutions, was set out properly. Furthermore, Turkey could not benefit from the EU cushion vis-à-vis predatory market sentiments as Greece enjoyed at the time. Thus, Turkish economy plunged into an early turbulence in the first quarter of 1994. The crisis, however, did not bring paradigmatic change in mainstream policies due to three main reasons.

First, Tansu Çiller, the prime minister and the architect of the post-crisis reform package, was not a transnational change agent in any sense of the term. Though Çiller was an economy professor, whose professional expertise concentrated on Turkish economy, she failed to ensure the credibility and trust of the market players because of the legacy of her pre-crisis populist policies. Also, the high level of non-coordination among the coalition government and the lack of a genuine political will further hindered the proper implementation of reform measures.

Second, the external context was quite unfavorable. In fact, the reform package, 5th of April Decisions, that was put into practice following the crisis was supplemented by a stand-by agreement signed with the IMF. Yet, the IMF failed to play a permanent anchor role to ensure a paradigm change in the Turkish economy. As a matter of fact, the design and policy mix of the reform package were flawed as it put exclusive emphasis on fiscal consolidation with very scant attention paid to the underlying causes of Turkey's economic woes. Crafted in line with the erroneous logic of the Washington Consensus, the reform package did not address accumulating moral hazard problems in a loosely regulated financial system. On the contrary, the government introduced blanket deposit guarantee to the savings held in commercial banks, which opened up ample room for extra moral hazard problems. Furthermore, the IMF could not act as a long-term stabilizing anchor because the stand-by agreement was canceled just one year after the crisis, following the collapse of the shaky coalition government. In the absence of a proper mix of financial incentives and reform conditionality, the credibility of the IMF-backed reform package quickly eroded in the eyes of market players.

Third reason as to why crisis did not invite any substantial change was related to the constraining role of domestic institutional players. A combination of weak external pressures and poor display of domestic leadership helped pro-status quo coalitions to weather the storm without any significant deterioration in their power positions. In the wake of the 1994 economic crisis, business associations and trade unions did not play enabling roles. The quick but obviously non-sustainable economic recovery just one year after the crisis led to complacency on the business side. Furthermore, the established finance capital took advantage of the reactive state practices by investing in government bills through affiliated banks and exploiting connected lending practices in a poorly regulated institutional environment. On the labor side, harsh austerity measures triggered the resistance of the trade unions. Having combined with poor coordination and communication of the reform package and extremely weak conditionality of external anchors, the 1994 economic crisis could not be seized as a turning point to launch a new path, backed by new winning coalitions that are assembled around a dominant crisis narrative.

The second—shadow—case is the reform attempts promoted by Kostas Simitis government in Greece. Simitis was a policy entrepreneur who dedicated himself to the modernization of the Greek economy. As a professor of economics and law, he had strong technocratic credentials and technical expertise on the functioning of the economic and political systems in Greece and across Europe. Simitis also developed strong networks in European epistemic communities as he served as a member of the European Commission for several years. He was known among the European circles as "a respected figure" and "safe pair of hands." Simitis also established trust-based relationship with domestic policy communities in Greece thanks to his transparent and compelling political career. The timing of his ascendance to power was also ripe since he assumed premiership at a turning point in the history of European integration—the final phase of the euro project. In this juncture, strongly backed by the EU, Simitis framed a change-oriented narrative to restructure the economy and compel the banks to finance growth-oriented sectors rather than swelling state deficits. Simitis was in a suitable position to couple the problems, policies (i.e., solutions), and the politics to address Greece's economic calamities. Simitis appointed reform-oriented bureaucrats as members of his team to set the governmental reform agenda with Lucas Papademos, the governor of the Greek Central Bank and Simitis' chief-advisor being the most popular one. Simitis, however, could achieve only limited success due to two main reasons.

First, despite the fact that Simitis assumed his post in a critical juncture, the EU-factor failed to play a genuine trigger role in instigating a virtuous cycle of reform activism because the criteria to be admitted to the euro membership were far from having long-lasting transformative impacts on candidate states. The criteria only concentrated on one-off budget discipline, nominal convergence of the fiscal debt targets, and some light-touch institutional reforms concerning the status of national central banks, without putting any attention to the competitiveness indicators, such as labor productivity, effective regulation of financial sector, and current account performance. Furthermore, even the declared technical performance criteria, that is, Stability and Growth Pact, were not implemented properly. The European Council, for instance, dismissed the warnings of the European Commission highlighting the ineligibility of Greece to adopt euro due to the geopolitical significance of the country and political symbolism attached to being in/out of the euro area. As a result, Greece became a member with a very high public debt figures, loosely regulated financial system, and burning competitiveness problems.

The second reason that explains Simitis' failure to accomplish his agenda is related to the adverse role played by domestic institutional players. Simitis was aware of the deep-seated problems associated with the Greek economy at the time, thus proposed comprehensive reform measures. Accordingly, he pushed for labor market regulations, pension system reform, budgetary discipline, and massive privatizations. These measures, however, could not be implemented in a coherent and decisive fashion because Simitis failed to receive a genuine support from the political parties, trade unions, and business associations to steer pro-chance coalitions. Despite the emergence of a consensus on Greece's membership in the euro area, the scope of necessary reforms to achieve this goal was limited to the nominal convergence criteria. In retrospect, it would be fair to argue that, in the absence of a strong exogenous shock that would exhaust dominant policy paradigms and redistribute domestic power balances, pro-status quo forces triumphed over tenuous pro-change coalitions. Simitis could not have enough political space to implement comprehensive policies because the privileged status of the incumbent rent-seeking coalitions was not fundamentally questioned in the absence of a paradigm-exhausting shock. Thus, Simitis could not succeed in penetrating into dominant policy communities to generate ownership of his political agenda. Greece, as a result, joined the euro area with short-lived stabilization measures, which further eroded state capacity in the post-2000 period.

In addition to the shadow cases, this book also focused on Turkey's 2001 turmoil and Greece's 2009 crisis (in Chaps. 4 and 6, respectively) as the main cases. The 2001 economic crisis constituted by far the deepest economic shock in the contemporary history of Turkey. The long-term collateral damage of the crisis on social fabric notwithstanding, 2001 represented a real turning point in Turkish political economy. Following the abysmal shock, the government launched a bold reform program to discipline the public finance and overhaul the financial system, underwritten by the IMF and the EU. The Turkish case poses interesting puzzles, especially compared to Greece, as it demonstrates the diverging reform outcomes in post-crisis contexts. As Chap. 6 discussed at length, *Turkey's Transition Program* was carefully planned and reforms were well sequenced. The interview data also revealed that the emergence of pro-change coalitions in the aftermath of the crisis was the outcome of complex interplay between domestic and external factors. The crisis exhausted the rent-seeking development paradigm and weakened the material and ideational superiority of the status quo-oriented incumbent coalitions. The crisis was exceptionally devastating so that it opened up a rare opportunity window to introduce paradigmatic changes.

Kemal Derviş, a policy entrepreneur in the strict sense of the term, exploited the crisis-induced opportunity to link problems, policies, and politics toward introducing a new reform program. The coalition government led by Bülent Ecevit also demonstrated strong ownership of the crisis. As a result, Derviş was provided a large political room to maneuver and to implement his ideas effectively, which was strikingly absent in the Greek case. Thanks to his professional background as a prominent scholar and transnational technocrat, Derviş adopted a coherent narrative from the early phases of the crisis. Derviş also positioned as a credible mediator linking transnational and domestic policy communities that ensured the trust of the external anchors. Derviş narrated the crisis as an outcome of the reactive state practices that informed pervasive rent-seeking and widespread corruption, which reached its zenith in the ill-functioning financial sector. The crisis narrative put forth by Derviş and Turkish economic team significantly overlapped with the IMF's approach. Given that Derviş had worked for the World Bank for more than two-decades, it is not surprising that he internalized the mainstream policy paradigms prevalent in the Bretton Woods institutions. However, the IMF-sponsored reform program was a more sophisticated and tailor-made package in comparison to the previous ones. In addition, the program was backed by a large amount of financial assistance unmatched in the history of the Fund.

Apart from the functional role that Derviş played, a set of other crucial factors along the lines of interests-ideas nexus expanded Turkey's bargaining space toward a more domesticized reform package. First, the IMF suffered from credibility and reputation problems at the time due to the spectacular failure of the previous stand-by agreements implemented in Turkey. The top members of the Turkish economic team at the time highlighted that this situation strengthened the hands of the Turkish economic bureaucracy vis-à-vis the IMF staff.[5] Also, the preparedness of the Turkish economic bureaucracy proved a crucial factor for effective formulation of the post-crisis reform package. In a rather stark contrast to the Greek case, Turkish bureaucracy, spearheaded by Derviş, actively contributed to the content and implementation of the economic reforms, which in turn, improved domestic ownership. Second, Turkey's geopolitical importance for the US foreign policy interests became increasingly important at the time as the neoconservative US administration was in the midst of reformulating its policies toward the Middle East. The spearhead role attributed to Turkey in the Middle East also partially explains the large amount of the IMF support. Third, the rise of the Post-Washington Consensus at the turn of the century as a new economic paradigm informed the policy mix of the post-crisis program. The emphasis on the efficient regulation of the banking sector, rather than single-minded insistence on orthodox fiscal austerity measures, turned out to be a crucial element in the policy agenda of the IMF as well, which increased the legitimacy of the reform program in the eyes of relevant stakeholders (see Fig. 7.1).

The combined effects of these mechanisms at work altogether led the external actors to provide more space to the Turkish state agents. The degree of flexibility, in turn, facilitated crafting an applicable and attainable reform program. The dominant crisis narrative emerged along domestic-external nexus set the tone of the post-crisis governance agenda.

In a stark contrast to the Greek case, domestic institutional players also displayed enabling role in the Turkish context. On the business side, the crisis was not only instrumental in discrediting the inherent fragilities of rent-seeking practices but also functional in eliminating the inward-looking policy communities since many conglomerates and their affiliated banks declared bankruptcy during the crisis. Stated differently, the crisis crystallized the intra-capital bifurcation in Turkish political economy in the sense that relatively more integrationist and growth-oriented segments of the business class, which were in favor of change, gained the upper hand. TÜSİAD, as the main institutional representative of the integrationist segments of Turkish finance capital, threw full support behind the reform program. The IMF-backed crisis narrative communicated by

[5] For interview data, see Chap. 4.

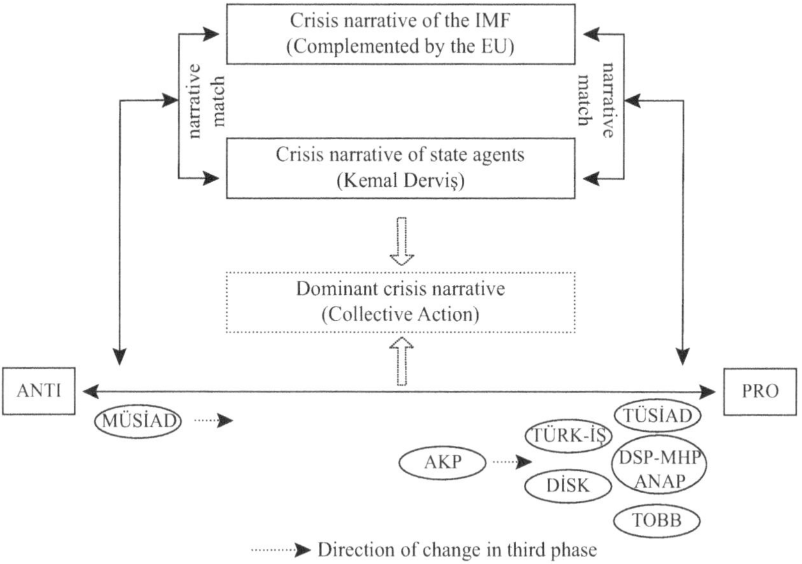

Fig. 7.1 The logic of pro-reform equilibrium in Turkey

Derviş coincided with the changing interests of TÜSİAD. TOBB, the main representative of the small- and medium-sized enterprises, also backed *Turkey's Transition Program* starting from mid-2001 because TOBB representatives perceived the existing mode of state-market relations unsustainable. On the labor side, the major trade unions (DİSK and TÜRK-İŞ) did not categorically reject the reform program as their counterparts did in the Greek context. Though labor unions were not sympathetic to the IMF policies for understandable reasons, their critical stance did not turn into well-organized street demonstrations not only because the labor movement was in a weak position in terms of domestic power constellations but also since the leaders of the labor movement deliberately avoided this happening. The field research revealed that Derviş and the coalition government regularly informed the leaders of the labor unions and business representatives, which in turn, improved the legitimacy and ownership of the reform program in the eyes of domestic stakeholders.[6]

[6] Interview with senior official of TÜRK-İŞ, September 10, 2014; interview with senior official of DİSK, September 9, 2014; interview with senior advisor to President, TÜSİAD, September 24, 2014; interview with senior advisor to Kemal DerviŞ September 26, 2014.

The Turkish case, therefore, confirms the proposition that it is more likely that the economic reforms emanate from reformist state agents' capacity to steer new policy communities. It also demonstrates, however, that the enabling roles played by institutional stakeholders are equally crucial.

Finally, one should add the complementary function of the EU-anchor that underpinned the consolidation of a dominant crisis narrative. The European Council Helsinki Summit in 1999 was a turning point that invited profound changes in the EU's transformative role over Turkey, since "Turkey's long association with the EU has finally produced a certain level of certainty."[7] The reform program is framed as an integral and inseparable aspect of Turkey's EU bid. Thus, the double IMF-EU anchor unprecedentedly tilted the material and ideational power equilibrium in favor of a pro-change narrative that promoted a new paradigm.

In the final phase of the three-stage conceptual framework, the new economic regime entered into a consolidation phase, which dispersed the fears about a possible return to the pre-crisis populist and short-sided equilibrium. As Ünay suggested, "the government promptly declared its unequivocal commitment to the on-going economic restructuring program under the aegis of the IMF, while declaring its willingness to discover new ways of financing economic recovery and cease dependence on IMF funds at the earliest possible opportunity."[8] The AKP government's tenacious commitment to the reform program led to the enhancement of regulatory state capacity during 2002–2007 that led to the eye-catching improvements in the main fiscal and financial indicators. That being said, the stark policy-reversals of the AKP government during its third term in office is also worth noting to account for dynamics of persistence and change in reactive states (see Chap. 4). The conclusion (Chap. 8) shall revisit the drivers of the U-turn in Turkish political economy.

Greece also plunged into the worst economic turmoil that the country had ever experienced throughout its peacetime history starting from late 2009. The unexpectedly devastating crisis was the product of structural economic problems accumulated over the years (see Chap. 5). Moreover, the asymmetric architecture of the euro area, which paved the way for

[7] E. Fuat Keyman and Ahmet İçduygu, "Introduction: Citizenship, Identity, and the Question of Democracy in Turkey," in E. Fuat Keyman and Ahmet İçduygu, *Citizenship in a Global World: European Questions and Turkish Experiences* (London: Routledge), 11.

[8] Ünay, *Neoliberal Globalization and Institutional Reform*, 170.

further "peripheralization of southern countries" within the European single market, amplified the magnitude of the financialization and speculation-led growth in southern European economies.[9] On the other side of the coin, the crisis turned into a potential tipping point to introduce paradigmatic transformations by way of a virtuous cycle of reform activism. In fact, the Memorandum of Economic and Financial Policies, underwritten by the "troika's super sovereign status,"[10] constituted the most coercive phase of conditionality that Greece had confronted since its candidacy to the then European Economic Community. In retrospect, however, even the most optimistic accounts acknowledge the existence of notable reform failures and shallow implementation of the troika program. Based on the conceptual framework, this book argued that fragmented crisis narratives dominated the agenda, which in turn, enfeebled pro-change coalitions and empowered anti-memorandum forces in the post-crisis Greece.

At the domestic agency level, at the beginning, Papandreou could not assume the role of a change agent, capable of developing a coherent crisis narrative and generating domestic ownership toward reformist rhetoric. In fact, Papandreou sent hazy messages and contradictory signals due to the very low level of preparedness and intense fear of domestic audience costs. Later on, Papandreou strove to frame the Greek crisis as a "test case" for European integration, particularly asking for more generous EU support attached to more favorable lending conditions to protect his country against the ruthless zeal of international speculators, who, in the words of Papandreou, were "trying to make fortunes on the misfortune of Greece." The crisis narrative of Germany, the hegemonic actor that shaped the parameters of the troika program, however, spectacularly diverged from Papandreou's perspective. German chancellor Angela Merkel narrated the Greek crisis as "exceptional case," stemming from the profligate behavior of Greek political elite and people alike. According to the German leadership, Greeks were recklessly living high off the hog, accustomed to retire too early, borrow too irresponsibly, and pay too little taxes.[11] German finance minister, Wolfgang Schäuble, even lamented Greece as "a bottom-

[9] Francesca Gambarotto and Stefano Solari, "The Peripheralization of Southern European Capitalism Within the EMU," *Review of International Political Economy* 22 (4): 788–812. Also see Fouskas and Dimoulas, *Greece, Financialization, and the EU.*

[10] Susan Watkins, "Another Turn of the Screw," *New Left Review*, no. 75 (2012): 12.

[11] Valentina Pop, "Merkel Under Fire for 'Lazy Greeks' Comment," *EUobserver*, May 19, 2011.

less pit."[12] Germany's overly moralistic crisis narrative led to over-estimating the domestic causes of the Greek problem and under-estimating the failures arising from the flawed design of the euro area. Thus, this approach overlooked the crucial point that the havoc was also the outcome of the coexistence of incompatible political economy systems in the euro area, thereby deserving a determined European-level response beyond savage fiscal cuts and self-defeating austerity measures.[13]

A set of factors along interest-ideas nexus conditioned the character of Germany's narrative toward the Greek crisis. From an interest-based perspective, keeping Greece in the euro area served the interests of the core European states, first and foremost Germany, due to high volume of financial exposure and increasing risks of a potential domino effect triggered by Greece's eventual default. This approach resonated with the interests of Greek policy-makers since they also considered remaining in the euro area as the least of all possible evils. In terms of ideas, however, Germany's narrative radically diverged from the perspective of Papandreou government. Having been informed by uncompromising ordoliberal paradigm, Germany imposed an extremely austere reform package implicitly dressed up in an antagonizing moralistic rhetoric. As a result, the troika program asked for harsh front-loaded fiscal measures rather than structural reforms congruent with the priorities of the Greek economy. Social democrat and Keynesian Papandreou, consequently, felt squeezed between a rock and a hard place since he considered the austerity measures as nothing but a set of unjust measures to punish ordinary Greek citizens.

Field research also revealed that Greek political and economic elites had grave doubts about the logic of the reform packages.[14] In fact, they were not mistaken, given that more than two-thirds of the bailout funds were immediately transferred to service-existing debts, which meant that core members, Germany in particular, bailed out their own banks.[15] The narrative mismatch at the agency level, therefore, created a sub-optimal equilibrium in the first place and forced Papandreou to implement a reform

[12] Quoted in Nick Malkoutzis, "Is Greece a Failed State?" *Foreign Policy*, March 1, 2012.

[13] Peter A. Hall, "The Economics and Politics of the Euro Crisis," *German Politics* 21, no. 4 (2012): 365.

[14] For the analysis of the interview data, see Chap. 6.

[15] For the full list of my interviews with the representatives of Greek political parties, trade unions, business associations, and third-party observers see appendix. Also see, Liz Alderman and Jack Ewing, "Most Aid to Athens Circles Back to Europe," *New York Times*, May 29, 2012.

program while denouncing it simultaneously. As a result, this narrative mismatch intensified ownership problems of the reform program at the domestic plane (see Fig. 7.2).

The ownership problems further exacerbated as domestic institutional players bitterly contested the troika memoranda, which in turn, adversely informed Greece's post-crisis reform performance. The opposition parties (mainly ND and SYRIZA), the well-entrenched cliques within Papandreou government (PASOK), trade unions (ADEDY, GSEE), and the major institutional representative of small- and medium-sized enterprises (GSVEE) categorically rejected the policy mix of the reform program. The only institutional player that supported the troika memorandum in the early phases was SEV, Greece's most influential business association (see Fig. 7.2). Even SEV changed its initial position in the later months, as the chairman and senior advisors of SEV raised harsh criticisms to the memoranda.[16] The fragmented crisis narratives and pervasive collective action

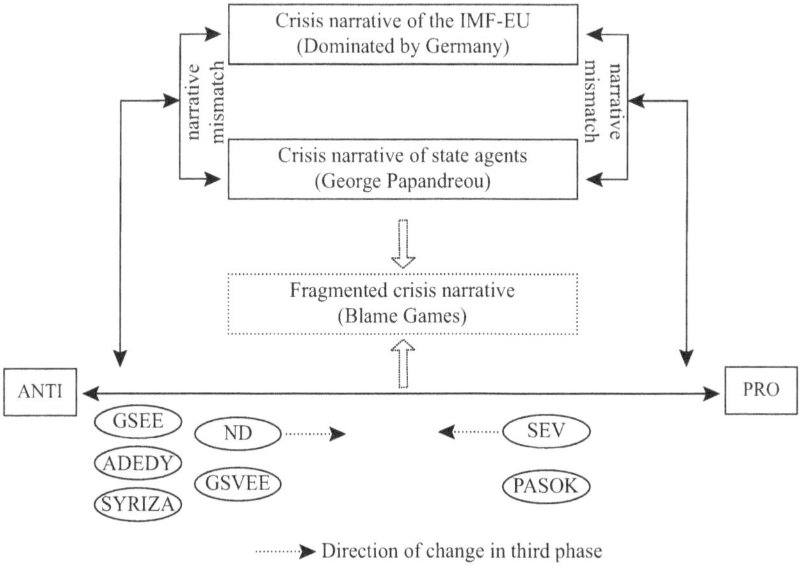

Fig. 7.2 The logic of anti-reform equilibrium in Greece

[16] Interview with senior official, SEV, June 24, 2014; interview with senior advisor to the President of SEV, June 23, 2014; interview with former senior official, SEV, June 25, 2014.

problems led to the never-ending blame games and muddling through in the third phase of the three-stage framework.

The appointment of Lucas Papademos as the leader of "national unity government" in November 2011 also could not alter this negative policy environment. In theory, Papademos was a competent policy entrepreneur capable of coupling the problems and policies to initiate a consensus-based credible change agenda. He was a well-respected transnational technocrat mastering the theory and practice of economic crises and subsequent reform processes. In addition to a stupendous academic background, his experience as the governor of the Central Bank of Greece and the vice-president of the European Central Bank catapulted Papademos into a position to play a meditating role between the transnational and domestic policy communities. The troika, in particular German leadership, also threw full support behind Papademos to assume premiership. However, Papademos government failed to reverse the vicious policy path that Greece plunged in the post-2009 period due to the adverse "politics" stream. Papademos could not soften the stance of the Germany-led IMF-EU anchor and create new supportive coalitions in favor of the troika memoranda. The Papademos case clearly demonstrates that the degree of flexibility provided by external anchors and the enabling role of domestic institutional players are crucially important for policy entrepreneurs to succeed. All in all, the complex mutual interactions that informed narrative mismatch and blame games laid the groundwork for the deepening of the Greek economic debacle; an almost total collapse of Greece's socio-political fabric epitomized by violent mass demonstrations; and a spectacular rise of anti-memorandum parties, championed by radical-left SYRIZA coalition and far-right Golden Dawn party. SYRIZA's rise to power was a strong response of the disappointed and disenfranchised masses in Greece that shouldered the onus of the crisis since the inception of the Greek turmoil.

Having compared and contrasted the four cases, it is now time to put the parts of the jigsaw together. It seems that paradigmatic reforms in reactive states are informed by time and context-specific interactions along the domestic-external nexus. Table 7.1 presents the fragile joining up of these factors in four episodes in two cases.

In summary, a set of time and context-specific factors are in order for successful and sustainable economic transformations in reactive states: (a) crises constitute critical junctures to introduce a non-trivial change in extant policy paradigms, (b) existence of political will and policy entrepre-

Table 7.1 Reform dynamics in reactive states: putting the jigsaw together

	Crisis	*Policy entrepreneur*	*Enabling impact of institutional structures*	*Reform outcomes*
1994-Turkey	Yes	No	Weak	No substantial reforms
1996-Greece	No	Yes	Weak	No substantial reforms
2001-Turkey	Yes	Yes	Strong	Consensus-led substantial reforms
2009-Greece	Yes	Yes[a]	Mixed[b]	Conflict-led fragmented reforms

[a]A policy entrepreneur, Lucas Papademos, emerged in the later phases, not at earlier stages of the crisis

[b]The EU-IMF played a strong external anchor role that imposes strict conditionality along with ample financial resources. Yet, diverging crisis narratives at the agency level adversely informed domestic stakeholders, which in turn, played a constraining role in terms of creating new winning coalitions

neurs capable of communicating a coherent crisis narrative poses an asset in times of crisis-induced uncertainty. However, the crisis narratives of state agents must be matched with external actors or the narratives of external actors need to be internalized at the domestic level, and (c) institutional structures, that is, political context, state bureaucracy, and domestic policy coalitions, should play enabling roles toward creating change-oriented coalitions assembled around a dominant narrative.

7.3 Beyond Turkey and Greece

This section discusses the broader implications of the findings in this book. This study extends the debate on the literature on three strands. First, this book applies the "state capacity" concept to the late-industrialized reactive states in a comparative perspective. Following the trailblazing research program advanced by Weiss and other institutionalist political economists,[17] this book started from the main assumption and argument that state capacity appears as the single most important intervening variable that calibrates reform performance of national economies operating in international political economy system. The state capacity, however, is a much

[17]Linda Weiss, "The State in the Economy: Neoliberal or Neoactivist?" in Glenn Morgan et al., eds., *The Oxford Handbook of Comparative Institutional Analysis* (Oxford: Oxford University Press, 2010), 183–209.

used, and to a certain extent, an abused concept in political science. Having taken this challenge into consideration, this book reclassified the relevant literature around two central concepts: "stateness" and "state capacity." The first term refers to the extent to which a state is capable of providing core functions such as control over territory, internal/external legitimacy, and basic collective goods—for example, security, education, and healthcare. This definition of the concept is associated with the research agenda on "failed states." The second term, on the other hand, takes certain level of stateness for granted. Accordingly, state capacity literature ponders the sources and implications of diverging capacities of modern states to govern economic restructuration processes in coordination with domestic policy communities. In this sense of the term, this study applied the term to the late-industrialized cases, which remains a relatively neglected aspect of state capacity debates.[18] The term "reactive state" needs to be reconceptualized and placed in a broader political economy setting since the dynamics of paradigmatic changes are qualitatively different in these political economies due to two main qualifications. First, institutional arrangement of domestic political context in late developers paints a distinct pattern. The ideal-typical configuration of state capacity relies on three pillars: political context, state bureaucracy, and domestic policy communities. In late-industrialized cases, the idiosyncratic historical set-up of political systems tends to be subjugated by an under-developed culture of consensus-based policy-making. State economic bureaucracy also suffers from polarizing patronage politics and high degree of politicization, which put bureaucratic autonomy and embeddedness into serious jeopardy. Furthermore, state-business and state-labor relations reflect a non-institutionalized and fragmented pattern of interest intermediation so that coordinated reform activism turns into an arduous task in the normal course of politics.[19] Therefore, the polities in question tend to suffer from pervasive rent-seeking, patronage politics, and clientelistic exchange relationship.

The external anchors also play a much more pronounced role in the sub-set of states investigated in this book, either enabling or constraining,

[18] Also see Öniş and Şenses, "Global Dynamics, Domestic Coalitions and Reactive State," *METU Studies in Development*.

[19] That being said, I should underline that the long-term causes of political polarization, political patronage, clientelism, and lopsided state-business and state-labor relations are beyond the scope of this study.

in comparison to the advanced capitalist economies. The late-industrialized reactive states do not only suffer from "state capture" at the domestic scene but also tend to enjoy a low degree of autonomy vis-à-vis the hegemonic power centers as a result of which they are inclined to pursue undifferentiated implementation of the mainstream economic paradigms. Also, in crisis episodes, external actors play crucial roles by intervening in the restructuration processes via a set of conditionality measures attached to bailout packages. This necessitates a thorough analysis of the role of external actors in relation to the positions of domestic change agents.

That being said, reactive states also depict significant divergence in terms of their post-crisis reform performance. In this sense, a comparative analysis of Turkey and Greece with reference to the three-stage framework enables us to offer certain "bounded generalizations" regarding the dynamics of persistence and change. The approach adopted here also has ramifications for the literature on southern European studies in general and Turkey-Greece comparisons, which is a neglected aspect in the relevant strand of literature. Even though these two countries depict significant similarities in terms of the organization of state-market relations, scant attention is paid to this dimension of the debate.[20] More often than not "high politics" dominated Turkey-Greece comparisons in the literature thanks to the fragile security environment in which these two states socialize and interact with each other including the Cyprus question and border problems. Furthermore, it is quite interesting that Turkey is often neglected in the discussions clustered around "varieties of capitalism" approach. Despite the acknowledgement of a kind of "southern varieties of capitalism," Turkey is excluded from these debates. The empirical findings of this book suggest that Turkey and Greece are similar cases in terms of the organization of domestic markets. Thus, a comparative analysis of these two countries through the lens of state capacity offers new avenues to advance research programs on the comparative political economy of southern Europe. Moreover, to the best knowledge of the author, this research is the first attempt that compares Turkey and Greece within the context of crises and dynamics of post-crisis change.

Second, in a broader context, this book seeks to join the debate and add on the literature that deals with the intricate and intriguing relation-

[20] For a discussion on comparative political economy of labor markets in Greece and Turkey, see Özgün Sarımehmet Duman, *The Political Economy of Labour Market Reforms: Greece, Turkey and the Global Economic Crisis* (Basingstoke: Palgrave Macmillan, 2014).

ship between economic crisis and major paradigm changes. The idea that crisis-triggers-change turns out to be a conventional wisdom in the mainstream accounts.[21] If one considers that a crisis is in fact an obvious case of a paradigm failure, "that reform should follow crisis, then, is no more surprising than smoke following fire."[22] However, the relationship between crisis and paradigm change is not as straightforward as it appears.[23] In the midst of post-crisis politicking, non-trivial transformative agendas are initiated when the rhetoric of pro-change coalitions crowd out pro-status quo forces. Therefore, a careful process tracing proves beneficial to open the black box of the complex crisis-change relationship and *endogenize* the critical junctures approach. In fact, as indicated previously, in crisis episodes, the leverage of external anchors tends to increase precipitously vis-à-vis the domestic stakeholders in reactive states. This does not, however, automatically bring about major transformations. In order to account for inner workings of crisis-change relationship, this book offered a crisis narratives approach, which integrates external and domestic-level phenomena. Accordingly, it precipitates that external anchors could assume change-instigating role only if their policy paradigms are coupled with the narratives at the domestic level.

The empirical chapters on Turkey and Greece bring new evidence to substantiate this argument. The recent crisis in Greece catapulted the IMF-EU anchor into an unmatched status that, in the words of Lavdas, even the sovereignty of the Greek state was put into question.[24] The political might of Germany in particular magnified in imposing its crisis narrative over Greece since, as Beck pointed out, the entire "Europe has become German."[25] This privileged position, however, did not translate into a sustainable reform activism in Greece. On the contrary, the domestic audi-

[21] For an early review, see Tommasia and Velascoa, "Where Are We in the Political Economy of Reform," *The Journal of Policy Reform*. Also see, Allan Drazen and William Easterly, "Do Crises Induce Reform? Simple Empirical Tests of Conventional Wisdom," *Economics and Politics* 13, no. 2 (2001): 129–157.

[22] Rodrik, "Understanding Economic Policy Reform," *Journal of Economic Literature*, 27.

[23] Boin, McConnell and 't Hart, eds., *Governing After Crisis.*

[24] Kostas A. Lavdas, Spyridon N. Litsas, and Dimitrios V. Skiadas, *Stateness and Sovereign Debt: Greece in the European Conundrum* (New York: Lexington Books, 2013).

[25] Ulrich Beck, *German Europe* (Cambridge: Polity Press, 2013). For the structure of economic exchange mechanisms between Germany and southern Europe that underpin unbearable power asymmetries, see Annamaria Simonazzi, Andrea Ginzburg, and Gianluigi Nocella, "Economic Relations Between Germany and the Southern Europe," *Cambridge Journal of Economics* 37, no. 3 (2013): 653–675.

ence bitterly disputed the IMF-EU conditionality, which led to muddling through and deleterious blame games. The reform package, right from the very beginning, lacked popular legitimacy in the eyes of domestic constituency since social justice dimension perceived lacking. In the Turkish case, however, a dominant crisis narrative emerged from the early phases of the crisis and the IMF-EU anchor turned into a strong pressurizing machinery toward economic transformation. The EU created bias for hope and informed the legitimacy of the reform packages that the pro-change agents skillfully capitalized on. The contrasting performance of the IMF-EU anchor with regard to the Greek and Turkish cases demonstrates that external anchors' transformative capacity is conditioned by domestic institutional mechanisms. Thus, the same anchors appear to have totally divergent impacts in different settings.

The EU's changing role in this context is also quite illuminating. In the Greek case, the EU-anchor played an adverse role in terms of reform activism. The domestic constituency perceived the demands of the EU as "unilateral imposition" and breach of the sovereignty of the Greek state. Despite the fact that the EU imposed strict conditionality, these measures backfired. Rather than empowering the pro-change coalitions, the EU's extravagant demands delegitimized the reform packages. It is ironic that the anti-systemic political actors, such as SYRIZA leader Tsipras, strongly legitimized their positions in the eyes of domestic beholders. On the other hand, the EU anchor positively informed the reform dynamics in the post-2001 crisis. Turkish policy entrepreneur, Kemal Derviş, meticulously linked the reform packages to Turkey's candidacy process at the time. The delegitimized political parties, particularly the members of the coalition government, also supported Turkey's EU bid in order to repair their deteriorated legitimacy. Stated differently, the EU turned into a source of legitimacy for Turkish political elite in order to relegitimize their positions. Therefore, paradigmatic changes were not only perceived as the most secure way to ensure quick economic recovery but also conceived as the only way to clear Turkey's EU membership path. The divergence of the EU's impact on domestic politics suggests that external anchors play context-specific roles at critical junctures. The present book, therefore, argues that enduring economic reforms are the products of dialectical processes, which requires interactive narrative matching between external actors and domestic policy communities mediated by capable change agents, presumably by policy entrepreneurs.

Third, as a follow-up to the previous point, this book adds on the stream of research enquiring policy entrepreneurship. Kingdon offers "multiple-streams approach" to place reformist change agents within the context of three kinds of processes: problems, policies (i.e., solutions), and politics.[26] Accordingly, policy entrepreneurs are defined as actors who are capable of attaching "problems to their solutions and find politicians receptive to their ideas."[27] The basic parameters of multiple-streams research, however, are set in a way that the policy entrepreneurship concept is utilized mainly within the context of "governmental agenda-setting." As Zahariadis points out, "Kingdon used the framework to explain agenda-setting in the United States… and because most analysts do research at the sub-national level, the lens' [the framework] utility remained limited."[28] Bakır went beyond the narrow governmental agenda-setting by adapting policy entrepreneurship framework in a broader context.[29] In this direction, this book investigated both successful and unsuccessful cases in crisis and non-crisis contexts to explore more on the scope conditions that inform the performance of policy entrepreneurs in reactive states.

In a non-crisis context, Simitis emerged as a dedicated change agent in Greece. When Simitis assumed premiership, a critical juncture opened in Greek politics thanks to the final stage of the EMU membership. Simitis, in a momentous turning point of the European integration project, launched a series of policies that aimed to redress the calamities of the Greek economy and ensure Greece's competitiveness in the euro area. However, Simitis mostly failed in his reform attempts. It seems that despite the EU emerged as reformist-anchor at a critical juncture, the flawed conditionality criteria targeting one-off Potemkin reforms and the constraining role played by domestic institutional structures impeded significant changes. Thus, Simitis case confirms that policy windows are more likely to open when an acute crisis hits political agenda. In addition, it also demonstrates that the role of external actors and domestic institutional structures should also be taken into consideration in order to fully reveal the conditions under which change agents succeed in their attempts.

[26] Kingdon, *Agendas, Alternatives, and Public Policies*, 16.

[27] Zahariadis, "The Multiple Streams Framework: Structure, Limitations, Prospects," 74.

[28] Ibid., 80.

[29] Bakır, "Policy Entrepreneurship and Institutional Change," *Governance: An International Journal of Policy, Administration and Institutions*, 593.

A comparative analysis of the Derviş and Papademos cases is quite illuminating in this regard. Both Derviş and Papademos were competent technocratic figures capable of identifying economic problems and crafting attainable policies. They also had strong linkages with international and domestic epistemic communities. Moreover, both of them were appointed to their posts as non-partisan figures, unequivocally supported by transnational actors. Their policy legacy, however, diverged sharply, which enables us make two inferences.

First one is related to the timing. As stated above, the current literature suggests that crisis-induced opportunity window is a facilitating factor that conditions the success of change agents. This research also revealed that at a critical juncture as well, the timing matters significantly. Papademos was appointed in the later phases of the Greek economic crisis in a very hostile environment toward the troika program. In this political context, Papademos was considered as one of the crystal clear reflections of the deepening "democratic deficits" in European politics. The appointment of technocratic Monti government in Italy also reinforced this perception not only in Greece but also across Europe.[30] Therefore, the political parties and trade unions bitterly contested his position on the ground that the appointment of Papademos was an outright attack at the sovereignty of the Greek state. In the Turkish case, Derviş was appointed in the immediate aftermath of the crisis with wide-ranging policy and political autonomy, which positively informed the handling of the post-crisis economic governance. Furthermore, domestic interest groups adopted an accommodative stance and played relatively facilitating roles from the initial phases.

The second inference is related to the context. In the Turkish case, the IMF-EU actor played a reform-steering role thanks to an appropriate combination of carrots and sticks. Stated differently, for certain reasons explored in preceding chapters, the IMF-EU anchor provided enough policy and political space for domestic state agents to contribute to the design and implementation of the reform package. However, in the Greek case, the IMF-EU anchor imposed a very strict ordoliberal paradigm, which suffocated all possibilities to craft an exercisable reform program from the very beginning. The domestic state agents and pro-reform coalitions had no virtual space to contribute to the policy mix of the memoranda, which not surprisingly amplified ownership problems. It therefore

[30] Matthias Matthijs, "Mediterranean Blues: The Crisis in Southern Europe," *Journal of Democracy* 25, no. 1 (2014): 102.

seems that in late-developed reactive states, domestic policy entrepreneurs are more likely to couple problems, policies, and politics when external actors provide enough flexibility to operate.

7.4 Conclusion

This chapter laid out the main findings of the present book. Accordingly, an in-depth analysis of four cases in two reactive states put the parts of the three-stage framework together. Main findings intend to advance the debate on three possible strands. First, this book applied the revised version of "reactive state" concept to late-industrialized political economies, which has more explanatory capacity in grasping the dynamics of continuity and change in these sub-set of states. Second, the role and function of external actors need to be contextualized especially in crisis episodes. The main point is that external actors play a true reform-triggering role when a dominant crisis narrative emerges along the domestic-external nexus. Third, the chapter compared the performance of policy entrepreneurs in three different cases. The findings suggest that in late-developed reactive states transnational policy entrepreneurs are more likely to instigate paradigmatic changes when external actors provide enough room to operate and domestic institutional structures play an enabling role.

References

Alderman, Liz and Jack Ewing. "Most Aid to Athens Circles Back to Europe." *New York Times*, May 29, 2012.

Bakır, Caner. "Policy Entrepreneurship and Institutional Change: Multilevel Governance of Central Banking Reform." *Governance: An International Journal of Policy, Administration and Institutions* 22, no. 4 (2009): 571–598.

Beck, Ulrich. *German Europe*. Cambridge: Polity Press, 2013.

Boin, Arjen, Allan McConnell, and Paul 't Hart. *Governing After Crisis: The Politics of Investigation, Accountability and Learning*. Cambridge: Cambridge University Press, 2008.

Donnelly, Shawn. "Power Politics and the Undersupply of Financial Stability in Europe." *Review of International Political Economy* 21, no. 4 (2014): 980–1005.

Drazen, Allan, and William Easterly. "Do Crises Induce Reform? Simple Empirical Tests of Conventional Wisdom." *Economics and Politics* 13, no. 2 (2001): 129–157.

Duman, Özgün Sarımehmet. *The Political Economy of Labour Market Reforms: Greece, Turkey and the Global Economic Crisis.* Basingstoke: Palgrave Macmillan, 2014.

Fouskas, Vassilis K., and Constantine Dimoulas. *Greece, Financialization, and the EU.* Basingstoke: Palgrave Macmillan, 2013.

Gambarotto, Francesca, and Stefano Solari. "The Peripheralization of Southern European Capitalism within the EMU." *Review of International Political Economy*, ifirst version (2014): 1–25.

Hall, Peter A. "The Economics and Politics of the Euro Crisis." *German Politics* 21, no. 4 (2012): 355–371.

Keyman, E. Fuat, and Ahmet İçduygu. "Introduction: Citizenship, Identity, and the Question of Democracy in Turkey." In *Citizenship in a Global World: European Questions and Turkish Experiences*, edited by E. Fuat Keyman, and Ahmet İçduygu, 1–28. London: Routledge, 2005.

Kingdon, John W. *Agendas, Alternatives, and Public Policies.* New York: Longman, 1995.

Kohli, Atul, Peter Evans, Peter J. Katzenstein, Adam Przeworski, Susanne Hoeber Rudolph, James C. Scott, and Theda Skocpol. "The Role of Theory in Comparative Politics: A Symposium." *World Politics* 48, no. 1 (1995): 1–49.

Lavdas, Kostas A., Spyridon N. Litsas, and Dimitrios V. Skiadas. *Stateness and Sovereign Debt: Greece in the European Conundrum.* New York: Lexington Books, 2013.

Legro, Jeffrey W., and Andrew Moravcsik. "Is Anybody Still a Realist?" *International Security* 24, no. 2 (1999): 5–55.

Matthijs, Matthias. "Mediterranean Blues: The Crisis in Southern Europe." *Journal of Democracy* 25, no. 1 (2014): 101–115.

Nehru, Jawaharlal. *Jawaharlal Nehru's Speeches 1949–1953.* New Delhi: The Publications Division, Ministry of Information and Broadcasting, Government of India, 1954.

Öniş, Ziya, and Fikret Şenses. "Global Dynamics, Domestic Coalitions and Reactive State: Major Policy Shifts in Post-War Turkish Economic Development." *METU Studies in Development*, no. 34 (2007): 251–286.

Pop, Valentina. "Merkel Under Fire for 'Lazy Greeks' Comment." *EUobserver*, May 19, 2011.

Rodrik, Dani. "Understanding Economic Policy Reform." *Journal of Economic Literature* XXXIV (1996): 9–41.

Simonazzi, Annamaria, Andrea Ginzburg, and Gianluigi Nocella. "Economic Relations between Germany and the Southern Europe." *Cambridge Journal of Economics* 37, no. 3 (2013): 653–675.

Tommasia, Mariano, and Andrés Velascoa. "Where are we in the Political Economy of Reform." *The Journal of Policy Reform* 1, no. 2 (1996): 187–238.

Ünay, Sadık. *Neoliberal Globalization and Institutional Reform: The Political Economy of Development Planning in Turkey.* New York: Nova Science Publishers, 2006.

Watkins, Susan. "Another Turn of the Screw." *New Left Review*, no. 75 (2012): 5–13.

Weiss, Linda. "The State in the Economy: Neoliberal or Neoactivist?" In *The Oxford Handbook of Comparative Institutional Analysis*, edited by Glenn Morgan, John Campbell, Colin Crouch, Ove Kai Pedersen, and Richard Whitley, 183–209. Oxford: Oxford University Press, 2010.

Zahariadis, Nikolaos. "The Multiple Streams Framework: Structures, Limitations, Prospects." In *Theories of the Policy Process*, edited by Paul A. Sabatier, 65–92. Boulder, Co: Westview Press, 2007.

CHAPTER 8

Conclusion

This book offered a three-stage framework that explains political dynamics of economic change in a sub-set of states. The present study, in particular, strove to understand the complex relationship between crisis and reform processes. Accordingly, Turkey and Greece are compared as similar cases. These two countries pose striking research puzzles. Both states are late developers with weak capacities to discipline their economic regimes. They were hit by severe economic shocks that not only led to serious humanitarian costs but also opened up opportunity windows to reform the sticky institutions favoring status quo. Furthermore, external actors, particularly the IMF-EU tandem, imposed strict conditionality measures during the post-crisis restructuration process. However, their adjustment capacity showed remarkable divergence. It appears that Turkey introduced a consensus-based reformist agenda to adopt a new fisco-financial regime. Greece, on the other hand, plunged into a virtual deadlock that precipitated endless blame games among domestic distributional coalitions and international creditors. For these reasons, a comparative analysis of Turkey and Greece enables us to offer some useful answers to the main research questions posed in this book.

The main argument of the present book is that paradigmatic reforms are the outcomes of complex interactions of a set of factors. A fragile joining up of several agency-level and institutional factors makes reform processes intricate, contingent, and context-dependent. This short concluding

M. Kutlay, *The Political Economies of Turkey and Greece*,
International Political Economy Series,
https://doi.org/10.1007/978-3-319-92789-3_8

chapter compares conceptual framework of this book with some major explanations and offer three main propositions. Finally, avenues for future research are mapped out.

8.1 Three Propositions on Crisis and Change

The literature offers various explanations on how successful economic reforms are initiated and consolidated. For the sake of categorization, it is apt to claim that three sets of arguments dominate the debate: timing-based explanations, structure/anchor-based explanations, and actor-based explanations. The first, and plausibly the most cited, triggering factor for paradigmatic reforms is the "crisis hypothesis." It is assumed that adverse external shocks enfeeble the resistance of pro-status quo groups, which in turn, are expected to speed up the introduction of paradigmatic changes. The crisis hypothesis, however, needs to be substantiated with context-specific analysis, as it remains too crude to suggest that reforms would follow crisis straightforwardly. Chapter 5, for instance, demonstrated that the 1994 economic crisis in Turkey did not invite substantial reforms due to a number of factors, which were also revisited in Chap. 7.

The recent economic crisis in Greece explored in Chap. 6 also paints a mixed picture because the resistance of domestic policy communities was not substantially weakened. In fact, a careless handling of the economic turmoil plunged the Greek economy into a deeper chaos, which entirely turned into an enigma when SYRIZA assumed power to rule the country. The field research findings hint that the crisis could not be exploited as an opportunity window to strengthen pro-change coalitions vis-à-vis the pro-status quo forces, despite the fact that certain changes did take place in the economic regime and political system of the country. In spite of the achievement that Greece being successfully kept in the euro area, this should be considered as a "Pyrrhic victory," since, after seven tortuous years of depression, the gross domestic product contracted as never seen before with rampant structural unemployment. It turned out to be conventional wisdom in Greece that "Greek society has lost a great deal and gained little in return."[1] The Turkish economic crisis of 2001, on the other hand, led to the introduction of a better-crafted fisco-financial regime, backed by new winning coalitions. It becomes apparent in

[1] Nicos Konstandaras, "Greece's Economic and Political Traps," *New York Times*, October 26, 2014.

retrospect that the Turkish state's fiscal house was put in order and the out-dated financial system was overhauled. Partially thanks to the reforms that the Turkish economy weathered the global financial storm that broke out in 2008. The intra- and intercase analyses of the Greek and Turkish cases suggest that crises per se fall short of explaining the magnitude, direction, and durability of change, despite the fact that they render the existing institutional arrangements fluid and potentially weaken the incumbent pro-status quo coalitions. The diverging reform performance of Greece, Portugal, and Ireland in the recent euro area crisis might also shed light on the intricate relationship between crisis and post-crisis reform performance in this regard. Despite these three countries went through similar bailout packages, their adjustment capacity seems to differ considerably.

A second set of explanations on how successful economic reforms are initiated and consolidated concentrate on structure/anchor-based explanations. The structural adjustment programs under-written by the international organizations such as the IMF and the EU are pointed out as constraining factors to adopt disciplined economic regimes (see Chap. 2). For obvious reasons, the anchor-based explanations also prove to be time and context sensitive that is mediated by a set of domestic intervening mechanisms since external actors are more likely to enjoy a high level of transformative impact over national economies, especially when a state seeks to join an international institution or to apply for external funding in hard times. The functions of external anchors can be subsumed into two categories: the supply of resources and the supply of credibility. Accordingly, from an interest-based perspective external anchors provide material support to facilitate post-crisis transformations, as the availability of financial resources is crucially important to initiate substantial reforms since it alleviates the distributional pressures emanating from adjustment measures. The resources in question might be fiscal transfers, generally attached to conditionality programs. Furthermore, external anchors are supposed to supply information and technical support as part of conditionality programs. Their role, however, needs to be contextualized as they perform a transformative role only if a set of facilitating factors is at work on the domestic plane.

The divergent role of the IMF-EU tandem in the Turkish and Greek cases (see Chaps. 4 and 6) is an illustrative case in point. While the IMF program and the EU-anchor were not severely challenged in the Turkish case, an opposite trend turned to be the case in Greece. Thus, what matters most is how their role is interpreted and translated into the domestic scene by state agents, which inextricably brings us to the agent-based explanations. Alesina, Ardagna, and Trebbi, inter alia, estimated in their empirical model that enduring reforms are instigated when a strong executive, either in the form of single-party governments or presidential systems, is in charge of the management.[2] Chapter 2 discussed in detail that emergence of reform-oriented agents and political will turn out to be a crucial factor in explaining the outcomes. Accordingly, the "change agents or norm entrepreneurs,"[3] "transnational policy actors,"[4] or "policy entrepreneurs," as referred to in this book, are listed as mediators between external and domestic policy communities toward the creation of new winning coalitions. This book demonstrated, however, that in late-developed reactive states transnational actors are more likely to conjugate problems, policies, and politics when external anchors provide enough flexibility to maneuver and domestic institutional structures play enabling roles in terms of ownership of the crisis and subsequent reform measures.

This very broad review suggests that existing literature sheds light on different dimensions of persistence and change in domestic political economy structures. This book also aimed at building on these major accounts by trying to link timing-based, anchor-based, and actor-based explanations in order to offer a synthetic framework applicable to a specific sub-set of states. Having compared the four cases, it is claimed that reform outcomes are informed by the interactions of agency-level and institutional dynamics along domestic-external lines. In conclusion, the discussion so far leads to three propositions that can be tested in future studies to better understand economic transformations in weak states:

Proposition 1 State capacity emerges as a crucial variable that determines the long-term adjustment capacity of domestic economies. The policy changes undermining state capacity, whether they are statist or neoliberal, tend to inform subsequent reform failures.

[2] Alesina, Ardagna, and Trebbi, "Who Adjusts and When?," *IMF Staff Paper*.

[3] Tanja Börzel and Thomas Risse, "When Europe Hits Home: Europeanization and Domestic Change," *EIoP Online Papers* 4, no. 15 (2000): 2.

[4] Öniş and Şenses, "Global Dynamics, Domestic Coalitions and Reactive State," *METU Studies in Development*, 258.

Proposition 2 The "crisis hypothesis" postulating the reform-instigating functions of exogenous shocks tends to be valid if a narrative match emerges between state agents and external anchors in the wake of the crisis and if a dominant crisis narrative penetrates into domestic institutional structures.

Proposition 3 Policy entrepreneurs are instrumental in linking external dynamics with domestic policy coalitions toward generating a dominant crisis narrative. However, their potential to link problems, policies, and politics are conditioned by the degree of flexibility provided by external actors.

This book offered a holistic framework that applies to reactive states. It does not deal with developed political economies, developmental states, or predatory states. The findings, however, enable us to offer certain bounded generalizations in a sub-set of states as it compared Turkey and Greece: Two states with lackluster performance in the economic realms faced severe exogenous shocks but showed divergent reform performance in the post-crisis period. The comparative analysis of Turkey and Greece, therefore, provide insights for other states.

8.2 Avenues for Further Research

Comparative analysis of different dimensions of state capacity in southern European economies appears to be a promising avenue for further research. For instance, Spain, Portugal, Greece, and Turkey can be compared and contrasted in terms of their regulatory, transformative, and distributive capacities. It is the case that the southern European economies concerned would diverge in these three different dimensions. Therefore, a stylized comparison is likely to shed fresh light on the sources, dynamics, and mechanisms of transformations from "reactive" to "proactive," or vice versa, in these polities. This can also extend the boundaries of our understanding by enabling researchers to concentrate on the dialectical relationships between different capacities within the same state.

The resilience of reforms initiated in the wake of the crises and drivers of sharp policy reversals in the aftermath is another related area that deserves further scrutiny. Turkish case depicts striking puzzles in this regard. Despite substantial improvements achieved in the economic indicators (see Chap. 4), Turkey suffers from structural deficiencies. Despite some initiatives put into practice over the last decade, such as budgetary improvements in research and development expenditures, introduction of new investment incentive systems, and the restructuration of the state economic bureaucracy dealing with industrial policies, the transformation degree of the domestic production structures is far from being a success story. According to the World Bank data, for instance, the share of high-value-added goods as percentage of total manufactured exports is still below 2 percent. Furthermore, there are also strong signs indicating institutional regression in the third term of the AKP in office. The mounting evidence suggests that the government's commitment to the regulatory state paradigm waned.[5] The intensifying critique of the independent status of the Central Bank over the interest rate policies, the frequent interventions into the functioning of the banking sector regulatory agencies mainly because of the political concerns, and the increasing politicization of other independent agencies should be interpreted as important signs of this institutional erosion.

The Turkish government's increasingly lukewarm approach to rule-based economic governance is closely related to the changing political context of the country. The AKP succeeded in winning four general elections in addition to a series of clear-cut victory in local elections and presidential contest. The extraordinary success catapulted the AKP into hegemonic position in Turkish politics. The dominant party politics, in turn, informed the political landscape in a way that political polarization eradicated all possibilities of compromise and consensus-based policy-making. The weakening of the Turkey-EU relations due to the Cyprus question and stalemate in the negotiation process further undermined the rule of law and transparent management of the economy. The global economic crisis erupted in 2008 and the subsequent retreat in liberal international order also informed state-market dynamics in a way that Turkey gradually drifted away from the rule-based liberal market economy model. It is fair to argue that the increasing polarization of the domestic political setting tends to inform state capacity adversely, as it reinvigorated a vicious cycle in economic bureaucracy and state's relations with non-state economic actors. The extraordinary political developments in the aftermath of the thwarted coup attempt in July 2016 also demonstrate how fragile the

[5] Işık Özel, "The politics of De-delegation: Regulatory (In)dependence in Turkey," *Regulation and Governance* 6, no. 1 (2012): 119–129.

equilibrium remains in reactive states. Therefore, Turkey poses interesting puzzles regarding the political origins and long-term sustainability of reform-activism in weak states. Both the depth of reforms in the first two terms of the government and the massive reversals during its third term in office are equally striking that deserves further comparative research.

References

Alesina, lberto, Silvia Ardagna, and Francesco Trebbi. "Who Adjusts and When? On the Political Economy of Reforms." *IMF Staff Papers* 53 (2006): 1–29.

Börzel, Tanja, and Thomas Risse. "When Europe Hits Home: Europeanization and Domestic Change." *EIoP Online Papers* 4, no. 15 (2000).

Konstandaras, Nicos. "Greece's Economic and Political Traps." *New York Times*. October 26, 2014.

Öniş, Ziya, and Fikret Şenses. "Global Dynamics, Domestic Coalitions and Reactive State: Major Policy Shifts in Post-War Turkish Economic Development." *METU Studies in Development*, no. 34 (2007): 251–286.

Özel, Işık. "The Politics of De-delegation: Regulatory (In)dependence in Turkey." *Regulation and Governance* 6, no. 1 (2012): 119–129.

Appendix: List of Interviews

The interviews were conducted in Greece and Turkey. Purposive sampling was utilized to reflect the views of the main state actors and major interest groups that inform the post-crisis reform outcomes. Interviews with third-party observers and opinion leaders were also conducted to gain more information about the inner workings of the Greek and Turkish political economy systems. The affiliations in the Turkish case reflect the positions of interviewees who were in active duty during 2001–2002.

Greece

Advisor to GSEE/ADEDY, June 26, 2014
Advisor to Lucas Papademos, June 24, 2014
Former senior official, SEV, June 25, 2014
Senior policy analyst, ELIAMEP, June 24, 2014
Senior official, Organization for Mediation and Arbitration in Greece, June 26, 2014
Senior member, Hellenic Observatory, LSE, June 11, 2014
Member of Parliament, New Democracy, June 25, 2014
Member of Parliament, PASOK, June 19, 2014
Senior advisor to Lucas Papademos, June 24, 2014
Senior advisor to the President of SEV, June 23, 2014
Senior official, European Studies Centre, Oxford University, June 13, 2014
Senior official, GSEE, June 26, 2014

M. Kutlay, *The Political Economies of Turkey and Greece*,
International Political Economy Series,
https://doi.org/10.1007/978-3-319-92789-3

Senior official, Labour Institute (INE)/GSEE-ADEDY, June 24, 2014
Senior official, SEV, June 24, 2014
SYRIZA London representative, June 16, 2014
SYRIZA representative, June 7, 2014

Turkey

Senior advisor to Kemal Derviş, September 26, 2014
Senior official, Yapı Kredi Bank, September 28, 2014
Senior official, MHP, September 4, 2014
Former Minister of Industry and Trade, September 12, 2014
Senior advisor to President, TÜSİAD, September 24, 2014
Senior official, Capital Markets Board of Turkey, September 11, 2014
Senior official, Central Bank of the Republic of Turkey, September 15, 2014
Senior official, Undersecretary of Treasury, September 10, 2014
Senior official, Ministry of Economic Affairs, September 11, 2014
Member of the Economic Advisors Committee to Bülent Ecevit, September 10, 2014
Senior official, DİSK, September 9, 2014
Senior official, MÜSİAD, September 16, 2014
Senior official, TÜRK-İŞ, September 10, 2014

Index[1]

[1]Note: Page numbers followed by 'n' refer to notes.

M. Kutlay, *The Political Economies of Turkey and Greece*,
International Political Economy Series,
https://doi.org/10.1007/978-3-319-92789-3

L

M

N

O

P

The manufacturer's authorised representative in the EU is Springer Nature Customer Service Centre GmbH, Europaplatz 3, 69115 Heidelberg, Germany. If you have any concerns regarding our products, please contact ProductSafety@springernature.com

Printed and bound by CPI Group (UK) Ltd, Croydon, CR0 4YY
30/09/2026
02225653-0005